Advance Praise

"*Your Suicide Didn't Kill Me* is an important resource for readers trying to navigate the unique grief and mourning that follows the suicide of a loved one. Cathie Godfrey weaves her personal story about losing her husband Brian together with wise words and advice that will help all of us who have been touched by suicide. Her honesty, courage, and warmth are reflected on every page."
— Carla Fine, author of *No Time to Say Goodbye: Surviving the Suicide of a Loved One* and *Touched by Suicide: Hope and Healing After Loss*

"If death is taboo, suicide is a hundred times more so. Cathie bravely pulls back the curtain on the suicide of her husband Brian to reveal the intimate and personal details of dealing with the suicide of a loved one. She provides insights, information, and a lived experienced that will help the reader understand what surviving a successful suicide is truly like."
— Reverend Stephen Garrett, MA, Death Educator and End of Life Coach, author of *When Cancer Came Knocking: How One Family Answered* and *When Death Speaks*

"Courageous vulnerability. Honest. Inspiring and empowering to those who are survivors of loss. Would love to see *Your Suicide Didn't Kill Me* in every library. Have tissue handy!"
— Barbara Mays, author of *The Healing Seasons: Conversations in the Soul Garden*

"Cathie does what is necessary. She does not sugarcoat suicide. She describes a detailed, raw glimpse into the painful experience of a survivor. Cathie's story provides comfort and understanding. Her book is a powerful read for any survivor of suicide grappling with grief and unanswered questions."
— Dr. Peggy Doherty DeLong, Psychologist, Speaker, and author of *I Can See Clearly Now: A Memoir about Love, Grief, and Gratitude* and *Feeling Good: Thirty-Five Proven Ways to Happiness, Even During Tough Times*

"The author has shared her personal, emotional grief very honestly in such a way that I couldn't put the book down. Every page she shares her poignant journey to forgiveness with deep sincerity and a hint of humor to help the reader understand how her life has moved forward in a very positive direction. Awesome read!"
— Sherry Pysyk, RN, BScN

"Cathie Godfrey's book is a survival guide for those who have lost a loved one to suicide. Her powerful story will inspire and give strength to others afflicted by this unique grief, helping them find strength and carry on through the darkest of days. Loaded with resources, grief coping strategies, and wisdom, Cathie tells a vulnerable story so raw, personal, and real that one can't help but admire her tenacity, resilience, and grit. As a fellow survivor, I could relate to many of Cathie's emotions, struggles, and fears. She also raises awareness and shines a light on mental health. I highly recommend this book to everyone.
— Aida Šibić, author of *Luck Follows the Brave: From Refugee Camps, Abuse, and Suicide Loss to Living the Dream*

"I started reading *Your Suicide Didn't Kill Me* cautiously because of the gloomy topic. My doubts were quickly dispelled as I got to know Cathie, who has the gift of balancing her sadness with an inherent sense of humor. This is a 'dare to enter if you would' book, yet surprisingly easy to read. A courageous, inspiring story that I believe would benefit anyone, not only those who have had personal encounters with suicide."
— Marie Duddle, Reader's Favorite – 5 stars ★★★★★

"*Your Suicide Didn't Kill Me* is a thoughtful, honest, and sometimes humorous recounting of the aftermath of a loved one's suicide. I finished the book with a greater understanding, and hopefully a kinder and softer approach to the topic.
— Wendy Beller, Business Consultant

"I, too, am a survivor of loss by suicide and one who has also struggled and healed from the grief associated with this type of loss. They say we all grieve differently, but reading Cathie's story reminded me of all the struggles I, too, overcame. I strongly recommend this book."
— Jay Deutsch, Self Love and Mindset Coach

"Heartfelt, thought-provoking, honest, candid, and witty, Cathie takes you through a myriad of emotions as she invites you to walk with her on her journey choosing to live and love again. Written with compassion, Cathie offers valuable insights into mental health, suicide, and choice."

— Bonnie Hunka, MA Education, Concordia University of Edmonton

"Cathie Godfrey has shared her intimate journey of finding true love and the unimaginable ending of her 'Happily-Ever-After' life by her husband's death by suicide. I experienced the profound roller coaster of emotions and unimaginable challenges Godfrey faced prior to and following her husband's death. *Your Suicide Didn't Kill Me* is relevant, real, and educational. Cathie has gifted her readers with new terminology and a deeper understanding of how to find support and be supportive when death is a result of suicide."

— Meina J. Dubetz, RN, Certified Death Educator, author of *When Death Comes Knocking for Your Patients*

"For those directly affected by suicide, this book is a beacon of hope. The personal recollections and thoughtful reflections can support anyone living with profound loss. Godfrey's introductory analogy about losing sandcastles and choosing to re-build is a lasting image to reinforce her message of choosing life and love after loss.

— Val Hunt, Retired Teacher

"What a read! Powerful and moving. I could not put the book down. I kept stopping and thinking, this book is going to make such a profound difference for anyone experiencing the death of someone they love by suicide. I was moved to tears often, and at the same time, I felt such hope for what can be possible, even when you don't think you can live after such a loss."

— Wendy Bowman, Retired RN, Massage Therapist

"Cathie intricately weaves her personal story with the perfect amount of research to engage the readers' curiosity and help them make meaning of their own experiences. This book sheds light on what is often perceived as a dark or taboo topic. Once I started reading, I could not put it down. It's a must read for those impacted by suicide and those who are simply curious."

— Lucie Honey-Ray, BA Ad. Ed., MA Comm. Dev., People and Community Builder, contributing author to *Women of Worth*

"A riveting, can't-put-down story of love, vulnerability, and acceptance about living fully after suicide loss. Cathie Godfrey offers an intimate look into her life and relationships before, during, and after her husband died by suicide. She offers definitive quotes, resources, and practices for personal development and growth beyond the experience of grief."
— Tiara M. Crouse, MSW, VP of Grant Development, Terros Health Services, Arizona

"A masterful, engaging, informative book that leaves the reader with hope. Godfrey shares the devastation she and her school aged children worked through to rebuild their lives following her husband's suicide. She openly recounts the role mental health care played in helping her family process the shock and trauma as they grieved. Godfrey corrects faulty suicide narratives circulating in society. A must-read book for anyone working with the public clergy, social workers, educators, law enforcement, and healthcare providers."
— Kathleen Shrader, Executive Director, Changing Lives India, Inc., Former Children's Ministry Director, High Point Church, Madison, Wisconsin

"Cathie Godfrey's clear and powerful voice joins others who refuse to allow death by suicide shameful and secretive. She chooses to name it not hide it immediately after her husband dies by suicide. This brave act helps remove the ignorant and long-held assumptions that death by suicide is weak or cowardly. Godfrey's book validates those whose loved one has died by suicide, but also those who have felt suicidal, survived suicide, or are grieving the loss of a loved one. I wept with sorrow and joy as I read her candid story of learning to live and love again."
—Janet Peterson, PhD, Director of Professional Development, San Juan College, Farmington, New Mexico

your suicide didn't kill me

Choosing to Live & Love Again After Loss

cathie godfrey

your suicide didn't kill me

Choosing to Live & Love Again After Loss

cathie godfrey

PEACOCK PROUD PRESS
Phoenix, Arizona

Your Suicide Didn't Kill Me: Choosing to Live and Love Again After Loss

First Published in the USA in 2022 by Peacock Proud Press, Phoenix, Arizona

ISBN 978-1-957232-07-2 Paperback
ISBN 978-1-957232-08-9 eBook
Library of Congress Control Number: 2022914690

Editors
Laura L. Bush, PhD, peacockproud.com
Wendy Ledger, votype.com
M. Lisa Forner

Cover and Interior Layout
Jana Linnell
Melinda Tipton Martin

Portrait Photographer
Stephanie Cragg, stephaniecraggcorporate.com

Table of Contents

For David and Jennifer

If you are experiencing mental health-related distress
or are worried about a loved one
who may need crisis support in Canada or the United States:

In CANADA

Call Talk Suicide available 24/7/365
to speak with a crisis responder.

Confidential and Toll-Free

Call 1-833-456-4566

Text 45645 (Currently available 4:00 p.m. to midnight EST)
Website talksuicide.ca

In THE UNITED STATES

Call the 988 Suicide and Crisis Lifeline
to connect with a trained crisis counselor 24/7/365.

Calls are confidential and free.

Call or Text 988

Chat at 988lifeline.org

In either country,
if this is an emergency, dial 911.

Foreword

I am a Survivor of Suicide Loss, having lost my husband in September 2010. I'm also a Board Member with the Greater Kansas Chapter of the American Foundation for Suicide Prevention, which covers Kansas and eleven counties in Western Missouri.

To help survivors like me, I serve as the admin for "Solos Survivors of Spouse/Partner Loss," with over 2,000 members, and "Solos Support Group for Friends and other Family Members" with almost 500 members. In addition, before COVID, I facilitated a face-to-face support group of up to fifteen people that now meets via Zoom on the second and fourth Tuesday of each month with members from coast to coast.

I highly recommend Cathie Godfrey's book, *Your Suicide Didn't Kill Me*, to all Suicide Loss Survivors, especially those who have lost a spouse or partner. Suicide loss is like no other loss an individual will go through. When someone who is not a survivor tells you they "get it," they don't. No one understands the pain of losing a loved one in this way unless it happens to them. Cathie puts into plain English what it's like to lose someone to suicide. Her story illustrates how the loss isn't a loss for just a few weeks, but goes on throughout our lifetime.

When I took facilitator training through the American Society for Suicide Prevention, we learned, and pass along to other survivors, that we are not to blame. Our family member's or friend's suicide was not our fault. In most suicides, an underlying mental illness has gone undetected or untreated. As a society, we need to educate ourselves about the warning signs. My husband showed many signs, but at the time, I wasn't educated about what to look for. I know now, though, which is why I reach out to other survivors, wanting to help them through their journey with grief.

As with any book about suicide loss, I try to find hope. Cathie's book lets readers know there is hope. While reading, I laughed at some parts and cried through others. A suicide survivor goes though shock and trauma, so they need hope. I laughed for the first time about thirty days after my husband's death. I thought there was something wrong with me. But my laughter let me know I was a human being and that I was going to survive this awful situation. I could move forward with life after a suicide loss.

In so many places, Cathie's writing enabled me to put myself exactly where she was because I related to what she was going through. I wish I'd had this book to read when I lost my husband. Maybe then I would have understood the feelings I experienced and had access to possible answers about some of the unanswered questions that remain for me today. For example, I still wonder why? After reading Cathie's book, I now know I will never have that answer, but her book helps me and other survivors know there is HOPE after the loss of a loved one to suicide.

Caroline Allen

Introduction

Every time a wave knocks down your sandcastle, you build it again.
— *Anonymous*

Have you ever built a sandcastle? How about a snow fort? Living in Canada where it's often cold, I've built more snow forts than sandcastles in my life, but given a choice, I would choose a sandcastle. Probably because that meant it was hot outside, and my family was on a summer trip to the lake. Armed with pails and shovels, my brothers and I would spend hours creating entire villages, often with moats surrounding the castle and bridges carved out of the wet sand.

Building a sandcastle takes technique, work, and a little creativity. Building a sandcastle with my brothers also required collaboration. As the younger sister, I didn't often have a voice in how my brothers built the sandcastle. To play with them, they expected me to help haul pails of water to moisten the sand.

The secret to a good sandcastle is to start with a solid foundation. It's important to pack down the sand and be willing to rebuild when structures collapse. Having good sand to work with is always a bonus. Having fun—necessary. If you've built a sandcastle or watched others involved in a build, you may remember screams of laughter or a frustrated word or two when things don't work as planned.

When building a sandcastle, there's a sweet spot on which to build. Not too close to the water, or the castle may meet an early demise. Not too far away from the water, or it becomes laborious to fetch more water. The sandcastle is art; it is your creation. It is yours to design.

No matter how close or how far from the shoreline, one thing we all know about sandcastles. They don't last. Often, they wash away with the tide; sometimes older brothers destroy them. When we finish our castles, we take pictures of them, trying to keep them past their expiration date. My friend Meina asked me one day, "Many of the sandcastles of life that you've given your time and your creativity to don't last. When the sandcastle's gone, will you rebuild it? Why or why not?"

"I'm not sure," I told her. "It depends."

When Meina asked me that question, the "sandcastle" of my marriage to Brian popped in my head. We were married for fifteen years, had two children, and shared many hopes and dreams for the future. Brian and I built a solid foundation. We packed our relationship with love, respect, and laughter, and then one day, the sandcastle was gone. Brian died by suicide.

His death changed my world. To say I was devastated would be an understatement. Over time, I became sure of one thing. I had a choice. I could choose to merely exist or choose to live. I chose to live, for my children and especially for myself. When I say "live," I mean live fully, not just go through the motions of life and become a walking zombie. I mean living a life I loved, making a difference in the world, experiencing joy. I believed that death and grief could be the ultimate dream stealers. I wouldn't allow that to happen.

By writing this book, I intend to share my journey following Brian's suicide. To my family and friends, I acknowledge your version of the events may be different from mine. I can only discuss my journey, my experiences, my truth. I trust you will accept me sharing my story. I do so not to suggest I've done anything heroic, because I have not. I have strived every day to put my own oxygen mask on and work toward becoming the best person I can be. My intention for sharing my story is to touch, move, and inspire others who may find themselves on a similar journey.

If you have lost someone you love to suicide, you are not alone. It has been over twenty-one years since Brian's death in December 2000. Time has been a great healer. It has taken work, determination, and an abundance of love from friends and family to get me where I am today. For me, the secret was making the conscious decision to live. To get up every day and face my fears; to live large and boldly. I desperately wanted to set an example for my children and guide them to make life-affirming choices, even when I knew life would kick them where it hurts.

It hasn't been an easy journey, but I'm tremendously grateful that I took this path. I have become a different person. I sometimes hid behind Brian. But now I've come out of the shadows and stepped into my own strength and power. I have done things I never dreamed I would be capable of doing. I share stories in this book with the hope that you will be inspired to live a life you love.

My purpose in life is to raise the vibration of love in the world. My desire is to continue to contribute and make this world a better place to live in. I love the words of Henry Wadsworth:

> *Lives of great men all remind us*
> *We can make our lives sublime*
> *And, departing, leave behind us,*
> *Footprints in the sands of time.*[1]

I love the analogy of the sandcastles we build in life. I want to continue living my life from a place of building, exploring, and creating. I have lost sandcastles throughout my life. Losing Brian was the biggest loss for me. Now my greatest joy and my greatest learning comes in seeing and acknowledging the results of my efforts to build and rebuild.

My wish for you, gentle reader, is that you will choose to continue building sandcastles, too.

CHAPTER 1

A Non-Negotiable Marriage

A woman knows the face of the man she loves as a sailor knows the open sea.
— Honoré de Balzac

Suicides can feel like mysteries. Survivors can spend a great deal of time trying to figure out what happened and wonder about all the clues. I want to begin by telling you what our life was like before Brian's suicide, giving you a greater understanding of us and how this tragic loss could have occurred.

Two years before I met Brian, in the summer of 1982, I became engaged to Mark, a man I'd been dating for several months. He was extremely good looking, with premature salt and pepper hair, the bluest eyes, and a lithe but muscular body. After accepting Mark's proposal, we went to my parents' home with a bottle of champagne to tell them the good news. They were excited and happy for me. I thought I was living out my dream of getting married and being happy, especially since my previous three-year relationship had failed.

The next morning, I sat straight up in bed and had a panic attack. I instinctively knew this wasn't the person I was meant to marry. *How can I tell Mark? How can I disappoint my parents?* I had always been the "good girl" who never wanted to hurt anyone. I didn't have the guts to tell Mark about my fears. *Feeling nervous is normal, I told myself. Give it more time. I'm sure I'll realize he is the man for me.*

In retrospect, I wish I'd had the courage to speak my truth right then; it took me another nine months to call off the wedding. Until that moment, I kept postponing wedding plans using numerous excuses. I told him things like, "I just can't decide if it should be an indoor or outdoor wedding," or "We need to save money for the wedding because my parents can't afford to help us." In my heart, I knew

I couldn't make a lifelong commitment to Mark. Our definitions of success were not a match. He owned and operated his own taxi. I thought he was underemployed. He loved driving his taxi, talking to people he didn't know, and sharing his ideas on world politics and quantum physics; this made him happy. I told him he would make an amazing university professor because he was so smart and loved teaching. I thought I knew what was best for him. I was wrong. You don't marry someone to change them. In retrospect, I'm ashamed I was such a jerk.

Mark was hurt but handled the situation with dignity and grace. After I broke off our engagement, we continued to be friends, dating casually on and off for two years. We made better friends than lovers, but I felt comfortable being with someone I knew well. He moved to a basement rental suite and sometimes told me stories about the man who lived on the main floor of the house. "He's a nice guy," Mark said. "But he's also a slob." I pictured Pigpen from the Charlie Brown comics with a constant cloud of dirt surrounding him.

One afternoon, Mark and I were having a picnic in his backyard; the upstairs neighbour came out to say hello. I was stunned by his looks. Tall, dark, and handsome may be a bit cliché, but it described this man completely. He took my breath away. Mark introduced me to Brian. The three of us chatted for a few minutes and the conversation drifted to Mark teasing Brian about being messy. With a cocky smile Brian said, "Well, I guess I'll have to find a wife to clean for me."

I could feel the feminist anger start to boil up from my toes. Although I had just met the guy, I blurted out, "I cannot believe what you just said. You're a chauvinist pig! In this day and age, you've got a lot of nerve thinking there'd be a woman who'd be willing to marry you to be your maid." Brian just smiled. He knew he'd goaded me and pushed my buttons. What shocked me to the core, though, was the little voice inside my head: *I will be the one that marries you.*

A few weeks later, I went out for dinner with my dear friends Michael and Dawn. Michael and I shared an office at a not-for-profit organization supporting teenagers to live independently. Michael was slightly younger than me, over six feet tall with dark, curly hair and freckles. He was like a brother to me. If I ever had a problem, I knew I could turn to Michael. Dawn was about my height, five foot eight, with dark blonde spiky hair. She and I got along, but I found her more reserved. It took me a while to get to know her and call her my friend.

Michael and Dawn had been married about five years. Dawn was older than him by about eight years. "He's an old soul," Dawn told me, "So I don't really notice the difference in our ages." Michael and Dawn always held hands, constantly making each other laugh. I loved watching them intimately whisper into each other's ear. I never heard Michael say a bad word about his wife. *That's the kind of relationship I want. I want someone who loves me just the way I am, and just the way I am not. Someone who speaks highly of me. Also, someone who makes me laugh.*

Absently scanning the restaurant, I noticed Brian sitting at another table with a mutual friend. Small world. We invited Brian and her to join us. Before I knew it, Brian was sitting beside me making a point of saying his dinner companion was just a friend. I started doing an inner happy dance. Apparently, I really liked this guy.

I don't recall how the conversation started, but eventually we talked about relationships and what each of us was looking for in a partner. Brian told me he was looking for three things: she must love airplanes, love football, and most of all, bake brownies.

I told him I liked airplanes, which was true. I loved to travel and had flown many times. "I love football," I added, which was mostly true. I enjoyed going to a live game but rarely watched football on television. And finally, I told him confidently, "I make great brownies." Well, I've made them before and no one died, so I think I told the truth about that as well. As dinner came to an end, and it became time to leave, Brian and I exchanged phone numbers and talked about getting together for coffee. As we walked to the car, Michael teased me about having a new man in my life. I downplayed it, but inwardly, I was giddy with excitement.

Brian and I met for breakfast the following week. I was already smitten with this guy and so drawn to his intelligence and mischievous smile. I couldn't stop thinking about him. Did I mention how good-looking he was? He was wearing white jeans and a royal blue sweatshirt that looked like it just came out of the dryer, full of wrinkles with an overstretched neck . My first thought was, *He didn't care enough to wear something nicer.* My second thought was, *No worries. He just needs some help with his wardrobe. I'm up for the task.*

Obviously, I had not yet learned from past experiences about the futility of trying to change a man.

Brian was very smart and well-read. He was not put off by my insatiable curiosity. I naturally ask questions and revel in learning new things. He relished sharing information and teaching others about things he's studied.

"Tell me why you chose to leave Quebec and come to Alberta?" I asked.

He explained the Front de libération du Québec (FLQ) crisis in 1970, along with the rising popularity of the Separatist movement, which prompted him to move west. "I knew I would need to get out of the province because I didn't agree with the politics. There's been a mass exodus of English-speaking people leaving Quebec over the past few years," he said. "So, when my girlfriend moved to Alberta, I decided to follow her. It became an easy decision."

"What happened to your girlfriend?" I asked cautiously, hoping she was no longer in the picture.

"We broke up about a year ago. We were together for five years and finally both agreed we were better as friends. She has a new partner now," he explained, as I quietly sighed a breath of relief.

Brian knew a great deal about world history, politics, women's issues, movies, and books. We were both vegetarians, liked to meditate, and wanted to make a difference in the world. He talked about his passion for airplanes and proceeded to explain commercial versus military aircraft. There was never a lull in the conversation. I loved listening and had the advantage of looking into his deep brown eyes while he talked. *What a great match,* I thought!

As our brunch date ended, Brian asked if I would like to go with him to an air show the following week. The show took place outside of Red Deer, about an hour and a half from Calgary. It wouldn't normally be my idea of fun, but given Brian's love for airplanes, I was willing to make an exception. Fortunately, Mark would be out of town for a wedding. Even though we were not technically together, I didn't plan to tell Mark I had a date with his upstairs neighbour.

Brian picked me up in his 1970 brown Dodge Charger. I was nervous to get into the car: it was well used and the type of car we would call a beater. I took a deep breath and told myself; *I have ridden in worse vehicles.* I said a silent prayer the car would drive the distance. A male friend of his I'd never met was in the backseat—so much for it being a date. I was immediately deflated. Maybe he was seeing me as a friend, or maybe a new airplane-loving recruit?

There was flirtation though. As we neared the gate for the event, Brian asked me what is in the small cooler I brought. I told him I brought beer, oblivious to the fact it was illegal.

"I will give you my first born for a beer," he said with a wink.

"That won't be necessary," I replied with a side glance.

"So, you don't want to have my children?"

I was hooked.

The rest of the day Brian taught me about airplanes: what company made each one, specifics of their design, and the countries that fly them. He knew volumes of detail about their origins and history. We visited each airplane and helicopter on display, both military and civilian. This was followed by the aerial performances, we watched in awe as planes looped through the sky, demonstrating the skill and bravery of each pilot. The highlight of the day was watching the majesty of The Canadian Forces Snowbirds (Air Demonstration Squadron) perform amazing formations. Throughout, Brian was a walking encyclopedia about airplanes and military history. With each airplane, each performance, he taught me something about their story. I had never met anyone so passionate about airplanes, or anything else for that matter.

We had a fabulous time at the air show. He dropped off his friend first and then took me home. "Can I see you again?" he asked. Without hesitating, I said, "Yes."

A few days later, I picked up Mark at the airport and suggested we stop for a drink at a local pub on the way home. I was nervous when I told him why I couldn't continue to see him casually. He immediately said, "It's Brian, isn't it?" How the heck did he know about Brian? I didn't realize how transparent I was being. Maybe he saw something in my eyes when I met Brian in their shared backyard. It was difficult to tell Mark the truth, but I felt I owed him that much. "Yes, it's Brian." I felt bad this could be awkward since they lived in the same house, even though they have separate suites. But I didn't feel bad enough to stop seeing Brian.

After dating Brian for a few weeks, I found out he'd already made plans to move to the Kootenays in British Columbia for a year. He was reluctant to tell me at first. Brian agreed to housesit while his friend moved to Vancouver to further his studies. Although Brian was tempted to tell his friend he has changed his mind, he decided he must keep his word and go. Having integrity like this is one of the things I admired about him. We decided we would continue to date, regardless of the six-hour drive.

Brian packed his belongings into his crappy old car and made the move to Sirdar, British Columbia, in August 1984. A month later, I drove my yellow Honda Civic, "Rhonda the Honda," to visit him. He was living in a huge log home on the side of a hill that his friend built himself. It was two stories with a very open concept. There were no doors, not even for the bathroom. This was way out of my comfort zone, and I got Brian to nail a blanket over the opening to the bathroom door so I would have a bit of privacy. There was a large deck outside with two Adirondack chairs facing west. In the evenings we'd sit and watch the beautiful British Columbia sunsets.

"I want to take you canoeing," Brian said.

I loved canoeing. I learned how when I was seventeen and went on a five-day canoe trip through Wasaga Lakes in Ontario. I loved being on the water—portaging not so much. The sixteen-foot fiberglass canoe we were about to use rested on sawhorses behind the house. Brian and I lifted the canoe and carried it down the hill to a small pathway leading to the shore of Duck Lake, one hundred meters from the house. Brian sat in the back of the canoe, the stern, as he was the more experienced canoer. When he saw that I knew how to paddle, he laughed. "I think I could add one more thing to my list of what to look for in a partner. She must know how to paddle a canoe."

It was mid-afternoon, the sun was shining brightly and white, puffy clouds floated in the sky. Except for the sound of the paddles dipping into the water, there was very little sound. Occasionally we could hear a loon calling its mate. In the middle of the lake, Brian slowly stood up and started taking one step at a time toward the front of the boat where I was sitting. I turned around and looked at him. "What the hell are you doing?" I screamed, thinking he was going to tip us over. His steps were measured. He made sure to maintain balance as he moved. *Maybe he was going to throw me overboard as a joke?* Instead, he crouched beside me, got me to swing my legs around so I was facing him, took my hands, and looked me in the eye. "I love you," he said softly. I looked into those dark brown eyes searching mine to see if his declaration would be well received. I was stunned at how quickly Brian had decided to reveal his love for me. My heart was racing, and I hesitated for a moment to answer. Memories of Mark flashed before me. I didn't want to rush into anything, so I search my heart and realized I was already in love with this man.

"I love you, too," I whispered, as Brian leaned in to kiss me.

In the movie, *The Princess Bride* (screenplay by William Goldman), the storyteller described the kiss I'd always dreamed of: "Since the invention of the kiss, there have been five kisses that have been rated the most passionate, the most pure. This one left them all behind." In the middle of Duck Lake, north of Creston, British Columbia, I experienced the most passionate, the most pure, perfect kiss. That was the single most romantic moment of my life.

For five months after Brian moved away, we took turns visiting each other once or twice a month. It was his turn to visit me in Calgary, and we were out for dessert at one of our favourite restaurants, Decadent Desserts. After Brian scraped the plate and put the last bite of chocolate brownie and ice cream in his mouth, he said, "Once this one-year housesitting commitment to my friend is over, I'm considering moving farther west to the coast." I sat silently. Choosing my words carefully, I said, "If you choose to move in the opposite direction of where I live, then our relationship must end. I'm not prepared to continue a long-distance relationship for an indefinite period." Brian was silent. I don't think he expected that response. He stared at the empty plate and then looked at me. "I don't want to lose you. I love you." Another minute of silence. Then he leaned forward across the small table for two, reached for my hand, and looked into my eyes for a moment before saying, "Well then, will you marry me?"

Maybe it was his cocked eyebrow, but I found it hard to determine if he was serious. "Are you really sure?" A minute ago, he talked about moving further away from me. Now he was talking about creating a future together. "Yes, 100%," he said.

For a moment I sat in silence, replaying the previous six months and especially the last fifteen minutes. Then I took a breath and said, "Yes! Yes, I will marry you, but I have one condition. Please don't tell anyone for three days that we're engaged. That way, if either of us changes our mind, we can do so without losing face. I don't want to repeat what I went through with Mark when he proposed." I finally offered, "I want you to ask me to marry you again in three days. By then, both of us will know for sure." Brian agreed.

The next three days included lots of conversation about the future. Where would we live? How soon would we get married? How big should the wedding be? I already knew by the morning after the proposal that I wanted to say yes when he asked me again. We didn't tell anyone. It was our little secret. On the third day, in my apartment, Brian checked the clock to be sure seventy-two hours had passed. At 8:15 p.m. on January 26, 1985, Brian got down on bended knee and asked, "Will you marry me?" This time I didn't panic. This time I didn't hesitate. Instead, I confidently said, "Yes."

We set the wedding date for Saturday, July 13, 1985, less than six months after getting engaged. Six weeks before our wedding date, my good friend and colleague Michael sat in the chair beside my desk. "I've asked Dawn for a divorce" he told me. "I've found the love of my life," My mouth dropped; I was speechless. I was grateful to be sitting at my desk because I doubted my legs would hold me up when I heard his declaration. *This cannot be happening. If this can happen to a man I perceive to be in love with his wife, what guarantees did I have that I was making the right decision about marrying Brian?* Later that night, I called Brian long distance to tell him the news. "Now I'm scared," I admitted. "I'm having second thoughts about getting married." Brian was kind and supportive, but wrapped up in my own doubts, I failed to realize he was silent for most of the conversation. I was the one doing all the talking, the one expressing my fears.

The next day I phoned him repeatedly to tell him I was overreacting. Brian didn't answer any of my calls or return any of my messages. Finally, after about thirty-six hours, he called me back. By then, I was almost certifiable.

"I decided to unplug my phone and meditate on what you told me the other night about not wanting to get married. I didn't want to worry you. I just needed some space to figure out what I wanted to do," he explained.

"I'm getting on a Greyhound bus first thing tomorrow morning to come see you so we can talk face-to-face," I declared. I didn't trust myself to make the drive safely.

I had over six hours to think about what I was going to say when I saw Brian. As I got off the bus, he was waiting for me. One look at his face, and I knew he was the right one for me. Without a doubt, I was going to marry this man. Everything was going to be all right.

We married on a hot summer day. We were able to get the church and the reception hall with only six months' notice as most people did not want to marry on the 13th. Perhaps they saw it as a bad omen. I saw it as a good sign as my Uncle Archie and his wife Sybil were married on July 13th, and they were married for forty-five years before her death.

I wore my mother's pearl-coloured wedding dress, altered at the neckline as it had been wrapped in a box for thirty-eight years, leaving the collar somewhat yellowed. I loved the covered buttons that ran up the sleeves and down the back of the dress. The men wore morning suits; my bridesmaid Barb wore royal blue. During the ceremony, it started to pour, just like it did on my parents' wedding day. "It's a good sign to have rain on your wedding day," my mom insisted.

My father passed away seven months before my wedding, in November of 1984. When he died, Brian was unsure if he could get time off work to make the trip to Calgary. "I need you here," I said. "If you can't be here for me when I need you most, maybe this isn't the right relationship." With that, Brian begged another staff member to take his shifts at the group home where he worked, hopped in his car, and drove to Calgary. One of the reasons I was willing to say yes when Brian asked me to marry him came as a result of him being there for me during this most traumatic time.

I am grateful my dad had the chance to meet Brian before his death. My mom, dad, Brian and I went for dinner one night when Brian was in Calgary, about three weeks after our perfect kiss in the canoe. That night, my dad showed up wearing a bright red shirt, red pants, and white shoes. At first, I thought he intended to wave a red cape in Brian's direction, like a matador. I was mortified by his choice of clothing. I had never seen him wear this combination before.

Brian seemed nervous and asked my dad what his drink of choice was. "Rye and Coke," my dad responded. "Perfect, mine too," said Brian. With that, Brian ordered wine for me and my mom and R & Cs for the two of them. My dad liked Brian. It was the first time he ever liked one of my boyfriends. I knew Brian preferred beer, but he made a point of connecting with my dad. One more reason I fell deeply and madly in love with this man.

"This is the first time I'm going to marry you," Brian whispered in my ear, holding me close as we moved slowly across the wooden floor during our first dance as husband and wife. "We will have to renew our vows in fifty to sixty years," he added, followed by a soft kiss. Until then, he told me I was stuck with him. Our marriage was not negotiable. In fact, our non-negotiable relationship became an ongoing joke throughout our marriage.

Brian promised me endless years together.

He only gave me fifteen.

CHAPTER 2
Why Suicide?

I'm like an onion. You can peel away my layers,
but the further you go, the more it'll make you cry.
— Laura Carstairs-Waters

Suicide is not typically the result of just one thing going wrong in someone's life. Instead, it's usually driven by complex or compounded issues that become overwhelming. Each issue layers upon the one before it. As the layers build, a person's ability to manage them simultaneously diminishes and stress increases.

Stress is a normal human reaction to changes or challenges in our lives. Although each person responds to stress differently, stress can be caused by positive or negative life events. Whereas the death of a spouse or divorce are high on the list of stressors, getting married or having a baby also create change and thus create stress.

In some cases, stress can be a motivator to get things done or to keep you safe. Walking alone at night might bring on a stress response but may help you become more aware of your surroundings. It's the amount of stress in one's life (real or perceived) that can make the difference. According to Hedy Marks of *Web*Md, "Our bodies are designed to handle small doses of stress. But, we are not equipped to handle long-term, chronic stress without ill consequences."[2]

Stress is also about a person's reaction to a situation—not the actual situation. People who die by suicide might have the ability to problem-solve or work through one or even a few issues at a time. However, when more and more problems arise together, their stress increases and their resiliency decreases, and they can find themselves unable to deal with their problems. These crises can be compounded by existing or emerging mental health issues.

I used to believe Brian chose suicide. As I read articles by psychologists and psychiatrists on the subject, I started to change my mind. I previously thought Brian had the capacity to make a rational decision. He did not. John M. Grohol, Psy.D., says, "People who die by suicide aren't making a choice — they're losing a fight against intolerable pain, emotional turmoil, and loss of hope."[3]

Brian suffered from depression, exacerbated by a prescribed narcotic. I now know Brian's suicide was not a choice. At that moment, Brian experienced so much pain that he no longer had the ability to tap into his resources or "toolbox" to find another solution. He was experiencing many layers of stress; he lost his ability to cope. Financial, emotional, physical, and mental challenges pushed him beyond the brink of his typical coping ability. From my vantage point, it initially seemed like he made a choice, a terrible choice. From Brian's point of view, suicide became his only option.

In our marriage, Brian and I were blessed to have a house, a vehicle, and employment. Two years into our marriage, we took jobs as Teaching Parents, living and working in a group home with six dual-diagnosed teenagers. "Dual-diagnosed" means the teens had two or more presenting problems, often mental health issues and behavioural problems. We had a separate suite upstairs, and a few assistants worked shifts so Brian and I could have some private family time. When we took on the position, our son, David, was only one year old.

Brian and I both felt this job allowed us to truly look after David while still working full time. As Teaching Parents, we used behaviourally-based education skills to correct the teens' problem behaviours and teach them life skills. In fact, we became the first Canadian couple certified twice using the Teaching-Family Model of America (TFA). Brian and I often said that it was the most challenging job we ever had, but it became less of a job and more of a lifestyle over time.

I loved working with my husband, especially watching him teach these very hard-to-reach young people with patience and compassion. The kids could be considered the most difficult in the child-care system. They often had a hard time establishing relationships. In addition to their cognitive delays, these teenagers tended to be very self-centered. Brian often used humour to engage the kids, and in return they easily gravitated to him. He earned their respect by encouraging them to keep trying when they faltered during a task or hesitated while learning a new skill. When they did accomplish their goals, Brian showered them with praise and recognition.

Obviously, it wasn't a nine-to-five job. It was more like parenting—twenty-four/seven. Anytime day or night, If the kids needed us, we were available. Friends and family thought we were crazy to take on such a difficult position. When we loaded up a fifteen-passenger van and drove with those teenagers from Calgary, Alberta, to Disneyland, some told us we were nuts. But we wanted those kids to have extraordinary experiences.

Brian and I taught these teenagers how to follow instructions, accept no for an answer, and develop good friendship skills. They developed basic life skills such as cooking and cleaning with our guidance. We parented these kids and helped them learn enough to move into a more independent living situation. I found the experience rewarding yet challenging. Without Brian, I would not have wanted to do this job.

When I became pregnant in 1990 with our second child, Brian accepted a promotion as the manager of the Teaching Home along with additional semi-independent living programs. Consequently, we moved out of the Teaching Home and back into the bungalow we purchased shortly after getting married, so I could become a stay-at-home mom. Unfortunately, if there was an emergency, Brian was now more than half an hour away. It soon became clear that we needed to live closer to the group home and to Brian's office at the treatment centre. In 1992, we sold our bungalow and moved across the city into our dream home, just five minutes away from the treatment centre.

Two years later, in 1994, six years before he took his own life, Brian came home at the same time he normally did after work. I was making supper and when I looked at him, I could tell something was wrong.

"I was fired three weeks ago, and I was hoping to find another job before telling you," he said with tears in his eyes.

I was shocked by the news and by finding out he hadn't had the courage to tell me. I stood by the kitchen sink in silence. No words came. I stared at him in anger and disbelief. Lowering his head, Brian apologized. His revelation felt like I'd been stabbed in the heart. Thoughts rapidly fired through my brain.

Sorry? Are you fucking kidding me?

Sorry you lost your job, or sorry you didn't have the balls to tell me?

Why are you only telling me now?

Fired? What the hell happened?

How are we going to pay the bills?

What do we tell our friends?

Are we going to lose our home?

Am I such a bitch you can't tell me what's going on in your life?

Instead of saying any of these thoughts out loud, I said only two words, laced with confusion and anger, "What happened?"

Standing in front of me, struggling to make eye contact, Brian explained how an ongoing issue with his supervisor, Kim, had escalated.

"I had a fight with Kim. He was being an ass, and I said some things I shouldn't have said," Brian responded sheepishly. "I feel awful, and there's evidence. He secretly taped what I thought was a private conversation. I think years of my frustration working under him came out badly. I feel bad for getting fired, but I don't regret saying what I did."

Brian was one of the most patient, forgiving men I've ever known, an easygoing guy who got along with everyone. However, he always had a hard time getting along with Kim. When we ran the group home, we had both struggled in our interactions with Kim. Brian and I spent hours talking about how we could create a better working relationship with him. One time, one of our clients became enraged and started punching holes through the drywall and ripped the telephone off the wall. Brian worked diligently with this seventeen-year-old boy to calm him down. We could not restrain this kid; he was six-foot-six with the mind of a seven-year-old. After the situation was under control, Kim came over to the group home. In our debriefing session, Brian and I insisted that this young man be moved out of the group home. We felt he was dangerous, and we were afraid for everyone's safety.

Kim's response was, "We don't give up on kids."

Two weeks later, Brian, David, and I traveled to Montreal to visit family and get away from the group home for a while. When we returned, we found out that this young man no longer lived in the home. He had been sent off on a Greyhound bus to his relatives in northern Alberta. Apparently, this young man smashed the kitchen windows with a shovel from the shed. Kim happened to be working that day, and as he stood in the kitchen, glass flew toward him. After that incident, Kim decided it was okay to give up on a kid.

Unfortunately, when Brian had to deal with Kim on his own, he reached a point where he could no longer contain his frustration. They never liked each other, and words were spoken that could not be unsaid. Brian loved his job supervising five programs, supporting children and youth in care. He loved making a difference for these kids. He loved seeing them learn new things and celebrated their milestones. As they moved to less-structured environments, Brian continued to be a mentor for them. No matter how difficult these kids were, Brian could handle them. He just couldn't deal with Kim.

This was not the first time Brian had lied or withheld information. Throughout our marriage, I had caught him in a few deceptions. None of them were heinous, but they led me to question his integrity. For example, Brian had lied to me about having two university degrees when he only had one. I only discovered the truth when his university buddy, Bill, talked about an alumni party for the school of business.

"Hey, that sounds like fun. When is it?" I asked him.

"You have to be a graduate to go to the party," Bill told me.

I looked questioningly at Brian as he whispered in my ear, "I'll talk to you at home."

We sat at a wooden table at Chuck-E Cheese along with Bill and Judy and their two kids. Meanwhile, our four kids played in the ball area right next to our table. Bill's words shocked me. I opened my mouth to say something, and Brian kicked me—hard—under the table. I stared white-hot daggers at him. *Did you just kick me?* I was furious but said nothing, continuing the silent treatment until after we got home. I put the kids to bed, and after a couple of hours of no talking, Brian probably felt it was safe to apologize.

"I am so sorry for kicking you," he said, knowing full well why I was so angry.

After much groveling, I accepted his apology, warning him to never do anything like that again. He never did.

Brian did have a degree in military history but had told me he also completed his degree in business. When I asked why he lied, he was embarrassed to admit he was threatened by one of my previous boyfriends who had two degrees. *I couldn't care less;* I didn't measure success by how many letters there were behind your name.

"If you're lying about this," I'd always tell him, "what else are you lying about?"

Whenever I thought about it, I was most concerned about infidelity. If Brian was ever unfaithful to me, I did not think I could forgive him. To complicate matters further, even though I wanted Brian to always be honest with me, I was not always honest with him. I spent money without telling him, so I lied as well. It was easier to point the finger of blame. I never told Brian about my lies.

Brian was devastated. He had never been fired before. He was also furious that Kim had secretly taped their conversation. We discussed hiring a lawyer to fight the dismissal. However, we didn't have the money to hire a lawyer, and we didn't even consider that a lawyer may have taken on the case pro bono. Honestly, I don't think we had it in us to sue a not-for-profit organization. In the end, Brian decided he did not want to work for anyone else and instead set up a business for himself in financial management.

Brian always swore he never wanted a desk job, but it's amazing what a person will do when he has a family to support. At first, he was very excited about his new career. We both dreamed of the life we would have with all the money he was going to make. Brian was an amazing teacher, so he could explain investments in a way people really understood. His clients made money. The trick in being a financial consultant, though, is you must be good at sales and bring on new clients. That wasn't Brian's strength. Month after month, he sought out clients, taught them how to position their portfolio, then created financial plans for them—only to have the deals fall through. Hearing "no" over and over again wore on his self-confidence.

Even though Brian had been fired from the treatment centre, I took a job there as a night counsellor to keep us going while Brian built his business. I knew that I wouldn't be working directly with Kim, and I had lots of positive connections with the other staff members. With this job, I could work full time, and my children wouldn't have to go to daycare. I worked the night shift from 11:00 p.m. to 7:00 a.m. while most of the teenagers were sleeping, so I didn't have to expend much energy interacting with them. However, for those five years I did not sleep very much. I'd have a couple of naps during the day, but never a full eight hours, even on my days off. My body clock struggled to adjust, and the lack of quality sleep negatively impacted my health.

Nine months before Brian's death, my immune system crashed. I started having severe allergic reactions to a multitude of irritants, including foods, scents, and chemicals. During a reaction, the area around my eyes swelled and turned bright red as if I had a sunburn. Within a day or two, the skin from my eyebrows to my cheekbones cracked and bled. My stomach hurt, and I was in constant pain. I was allergic to so many things and was often at a loss as to what caused the reaction. Sometimes the reaction was a combination of two or more items. It was frustrating and debilitating. I spent money we really didn't have, getting treatments to rid myself of this affliction. Brian never questioned the money or time I spent trying to get better. He didn't live long enough to see me recover, which took several years. But he was supportive. I became depressed and even thought death would be preferable to the extreme pain. But when I thought of how my death would impact my children, I stopped thinking about creating a plan.

I stuck close to home. I didn't want others to see me with swollen, bloodshot eyes. Aside from going to work (luckily it was at night and my co-workers were awesome) and seeing a few close friends and family, I spent a lot of time in bed. Brian was seriously impacted by my illness. He felt helpless seeing me so sick. I had been his biggest cheerleader, but when I became ill, I didn't have the energy to support him.

I also didn't realize that Brian was already in a steep, downward slide. I didn't see his pain because I was in my own. To make matters worse, Brian sometimes lied about paying bills during this time. I only found out about the unpaid household bills when collection agencies started to call. I also didn't know Brian was in arrears paying his personal taxes. The Canada Revenue Agency (CRA) had been regularly contacting him, demanding payment. I didn't learn until after his death that he drove the car for nine months without renewing his license. I also discovered that he had not paid the insurance premium on our car, which we drove daily.

Two weeks before he died, Brian suffered an injury while I was at work. He had a knack for fixing things. That day he was trying to figure out why our car kept making weird noises. When I returned home, I found Brian lying on the couch with ice on his neck.

"I heard a pop in my neck when I was trying to tighten a bolt under the hood," he told me.

Then he took some Tylenol and thought it would be better the next day. After a fitful night, where Brian woke up in even more pain, I called our doctor who recommended an X-ray.

We spent the entire next day in the emergency ward. Doctors poked and prodded and ran test after test. The conclusion was a herniated disc in his neck, but he would need an MRI to be sure. One catch: there would be a three-month waiting list for a provincially funded MRI. He could, however, get one done at a private clinic for $750.

Money had been very tight lately. Brian's business was not doing well. I had tucked a little money aside for the children's Christmas presents. Our choice between Christmas presents or the MRI was a no-brainer. We would figure out how to pay for presents later.

We made a quick call to the clinic and Brian was in the next day, where the test confirmed it was in fact a herniated disc. The treatment was surgery but that meant a wait list of up to eight weeks. *Holy crap. How could he go on in extreme pain for that long?* To ease his pain, the doctor prescribed Demerol. Since it was close to Christmas, the prescription was for enough pills to get him through the holidays, sixty in total.

When a friend learned about Brian's situation, she told us her chiropractor used inversion therapy to help ease pain. The next morning, I called to make an appointment. After hearing about Brian's pain level, the receptionist agreed to fit him in that day. I don't think Brian had ever been to a chiropractor before, but he was willing to try anything. Inversion therapy involves strapping a patient by the ankles to a large gurney. Then a hydraulic lift tilts the entire frame upside down. The theory is that removing the gravitational pull from a person's spine helps to create space between the vertebrae, which "stretches" the spine. This alternative therapy isn't intended to provide lasting relief from pain, but we welcomed even momentary respite for Brian.

As Brian hung upside down, I saw his face relax. Smiling, I called him Batman and got a smile in return. I cherished that moment we had together. It seemed like a long time since I had seen Brian smile. The thought occurred to me that he hadn't smiled, I mean really smiled, for months—not just since he hurt his neck. *When did he stop smiling? Was it when I got sick? Was it when he lost a promotion because he didn't close that big contract?* The realization that I couldn't pinpoint the moment bothered me, but I pushed aside the thought.

As soon as the chiropractor rotated him into an upright position and the treatment was over, the contortion in Brian's face returned. We returned daily for three more treatments that week. I looked forward to the sessions. I savoured seeing the muscles in Brian's face relax. I liked Batman.

A week before his death, Brian came into the bedroom and said he was sorry he could not *take care of my needs* because of the herniated disc in his back.

"We need to find someone else to take care of your needs" were his exact words.

What a weird thing to say. Who says something like that to their wife? Even though he didn't say it directly, I knew he was talking about my sexual needs. I had absolutely no interest or intention of finding a lover outside of marriage. If I had taken a moment to reflect on what he was saying, I might have clued into his intent. It was a sign. He was leaving. He was giving me permission to find someone new. At the time, all I could think was, *this is awkward. It must be the drugs he's taking to make him talk like that.*

When Brian herniated the disc in his back, he could not work at all. Being self-employed meant no paid sick leave. This added another layer of stress about money. If Brian faced only the financial issues without the pain from the herniated disc, he might have been able to figure a way out. But everything layered together, including the side effects of his Demerol prescription, which was more than Brian could bear.

A few days before Brian took his life, he gave me another clue.

I didn't know what to say when he apologized for being a burden to us, adding, "You all would be better off without me."

I was chopping onions at the counter. I froze, holding the knife in my right hand. *What the hell is he saying? Where is this coming from? How am I supposed to respond to such an asinine statement?*

I took a deep breath, put the knife on the cutting board, and said, "Honey, you are not a burden. You are going through a tough time, and I am here to help you through it. Somehow, we are going to get through this."

Brian's statement shocked me. I wasn't convinced we would get through these tough times, but I knew I could never say that to him when he was in such physical pain. Instead, I justified his words, telling myself they were a result of his pain and medication. At that moment, I didn't realize this seemingly offhand, but unsettling comment was my husband's attempt to reach out and express the depth of his emotional pain. I didn't realize he might already have a plan to leave us. Despite my training in suicide prevention, I would not allow my mind to go there.

In retrospect, I lived in denial. I couldn't imagine that he might be thinking of leaving us. I pretended everything would be okay, even though my gut told me we were living a lie. We weren't okay. Brian was not okay. I certainly was not okay. During this time, I fell back into my way of thinking as a young girl, a Pollyanna view of situations that I probably inherited from my mom's positive outlook on life. I kept focused on my hopes and prayers, imagining sunnier days. *Life is sometimes just too painful.* My inability to face reality prevented me from really hearing Brian.

My closest friends later told me they saw Brian "behaving oddly" in the last year of his life. I asked them why they never said anything. They all told me they didn't want to interfere, assuming I had noticed it too. I had not. I had been too wrapped up in my own challenges. I could see he was in severe pain. But I never thought to ask if he had thoughts of hurting himself because I never thought he would. I falsely believed he was still in his "right" mind. Brian and I had previously talked about suicide, and we had both agreed that suicide would never be an option because at the time, that's what we believed it was an option. I trusted him to keep his word. He did that, until he could not.

A narcotic such as Demerol should never be taken lightly. I now know anyone taking a narcotic, regardless of whether a doctor prescribes it, should be monitored closely. This realization became one of those "would have, should have, could have" moments. Hopefully, my story will encourage someone else to pay closer attention to their loved one who is on medication, especially a narcotic.

It took several years after Brian's death before I could put all the puzzle pieces together and stop blaming myself for not seeing the signs and not recognizing the layers of stress he was experiencing. Even though Brian gave verbal cues, I could not imagine he would ever take his own life. I know now that I did the best I could with what I knew and what I was willing to accept.

And as much as I wish I could have stopped Brian; I could not.

CHAPTER 3

Missing

Sometimes when one person is missing, the whole world seems depopulated.
— *Alphonse de Lamartine, French writer, poet, politician (1790-1869)*

There are days in my life I always remember. The day I got married, the day each of my two children were born. And then there is Tuesday, December 19th, 2000, the day my life changed forever. I picked up my daughter Jennifer after school promptly at 3:35 p.m. She was ten years old and in grade five. She hopped into the backseat of the van, her blonde hair peeking out from under her winter hat. She quickly removed her scarf once she was buckled into the vehicle. It was extremely cold outside, and even the short walk from the school to the van was worth covering her face. My son, David, who was fourteen and in grade eight, arrived home by school bus about an hour later. He had stayed after school for basketball practice. He was already over six feet tall, with light brown hair and beautiful brown eyes, like his dad.

"Where's Dad?" David asked when he got home.

"I don't know," I replied, trying to take the panic out of my voice.

David was old enough to know something was wrong. He had watched his dad wince in pain over the past couple of weeks, and he knew his dad should be there.

But Brian was not there. Strange, I thought. And stranger yet, there was no note, nothing to tell me where he was. This was so unlike him. Where could he be? I searched the house room by room, calling his name and looking for clues to his whereabouts. A little voice in my head said, *Look in the kitchen cupboard. See if his Demerol is still there.* The bottle was gone. My body started to shake. My intuition told me *something was wrong, very wrong.* I dismissed those thoughts and told myself

You're being too dramatic. There must be a good explanation. I called two of my neighbours to see if Brian was at their house. No luck.

"I'm going to ask a few neighbours if they have seen your dad. Maybe he's visiting one of them. David, can you make up some macaroni and cheese for you and your sister while I take a walk?"

"Sure Mom," David said as we exchanged worried glances.

I put on my coat and went outside. Trudging through two feet of snow, I walked around the perimeter of the house. I even looked at the roof, as if, for some ungodly reason, he might have been up there. Nothing. No sign of him. I knocked on other neighbours' doors.

"Have you seen Brian?" I asked.

I was sure they could hear the panic in my voice. Tears welled up in my eyes. No, they hadn't seen him. As much as I tried to remain calm, I could see in their faces they were at a loss for what else to say. *Where could he have gone? Why would he make me worry?*

As I returned home, a voice in my head kept telling me, *Do not panic in front of the kids.* They already knew something was wrong. David was playing video games to distract himself. Jennifer sat on the couch behind him, reading. I took the phone downstairs to the laundry room where I thought I would have the most privacy and called the police.

"What is the reason for your call?" the authoritative male voice asked.

"My husband is missing," I said, trying to keep my voice from quivering. "He's in a lot of pain, and his prescription of Demerol is gone."

"When was the last time you saw him?"

"This morning."

"I'm sorry, ma'am," he said, his voice slightly softening but still in professional mode. "We don't accept missing person's reports until twenty-four hours has passed."

"Are you kidding me? Is there nothing that you can do?"

"Sorry, ma'am," he said with compassion in his voice. "Those are our procedures."

I thanked him for his help and hung up the phone. *Shit, shit, shit! What do I do now?* Tears flowed down my face, and my chest tightened even more as the panic rose.

I looked around the very small laundry room that doubled as Brian's office. The floor was covered with piles of documents and file folders. A cabinet drawer was open, and it looked like he had pulled out every file and thrown all the contents on the floor. Clean clothes were heaped on top of the dryer, waiting to be folded. The picture on the wall was crooked, as if it had been hit. The room was in chaos. *What the hell happened here?*

My kids came into the laundry room. David ducked to avoid hitting his head on the bulkhead. Slowly, they looked around the room at the mess on the floor and saw the tears running down my face. I could see the panic on their faces. The moment of truth was here.

Trying to comfort them, I said, "I don't know where Dad is, and I hope he'll come home soon."

But my voice was shaky, and the tears kept leaking. David pulled me into his arms and held me. Too old to be a child and not quite yet a man, he was old enough to recognize his mother was having a meltdown. Jennifer came to my side and wrapped her arms around the both of us, connecting all three of us in our most horrible moment of fear and the unknown. *How can I protect my kids from what I fear could be happening?*

Earlier that morning, Brian walked into the kitchen with his head crooked. It had been over two weeks since he severely injured his back, and I could see his pain was still agonizing. His face was contorted, and his skin was pale. He looked like he hadn't slept well, which made sense because he spent the night trying to sleep on the borrowed La-Z-Boy recliner, dominating the middle of our living room. A neighbour loaned it to us to ease Brian's pain. The chair provided him only temporary relief and not that much better sleep.

It was six days before Christmas, and our decorated tree sat in the family room downstairs. Despite its festive appearance, there was a pervasive heaviness in our home because of Brian's health. We all seemed to be walking on eggshells. I watched Brian move slowly to the kitchen table. He was slightly hunched as his neck leaned to the right. His left arm was crooked, and he held it close to his chest. This position seemed to provide a little relief from the pain. It devastated me to see him like this.

This was the man who stole my heart fifteen years earlier. His thick brown hair had streaks of grey, and I often told him how lucky he was. I absolutely love salt and pepper-coloured hair on a man because it's so damn sexy. He was approaching his fifties. His greying mustache and five o'clock shadow attested to that fact. Once a runner, he had a dad bod, with an extra twenty-five pounds he was trying to lose. Through his glasses, I could see his deep brown eyes, with wrinkles emerging at the corners.

"How are you this morning?" I asked.

"Fine," he mumbled, sliding gently into a chair at the table.

"You don't look fine to me," I said quietly.

I was met with silence. He stared at the morning paper, refusing to look at me. There was nothing I wanted more than to take away his pain, but I had no idea how. Brian and I committed to the standard marriage vow, "in sickness and in health." I thought that meant bringing my normally cheerful partner chicken soup to get over the flu or expressing empathy if his hearing started to deteriorate. I didn't realize it would mean watching him wince, moan, and sometimes cry in extreme pain because his neck and back hurt so much.

I poured Brian a cup of hot coffee as he read the morning paper.

"Can I get you anything else before I go to work?" I asked.

"No," he replied curtly, still not looking at me.

I noted his one-word answers. In that moment, I thought I should call in sick and stay home with him. Then I remembered that I'd already rescheduled the training I was about to lead that day twice because I'd taken so much time to go with Brian to medical appointments. My children followed their morning routine. They had breakfast, got dressed, brushed their teeth and dressed warmly for the day. David was the first to leave as he had to walk a block to catch the school bus.

"Bye, Dad. Hope you feel better soon," said David, standing in the doorway to the kitchen, looking directly at his father before he went downstairs to put on his winter boots and coat.

Brian turned to look at him, "Good luck with basketball practice today."

"Thanks, Dad."

I gave Brian a reluctant goodbye kiss on his forehead before I headed out the door. Jennifer was already in the backseat of the van. I dropped her off at school before heading to work. Throughout the day, I was distracted by thoughts of Brian and his pain. I called once around noon to see how he was, but Brian didn't answer the phone. *He's probably napping.* At the end of the day, I closed my laptop and thought, *I only have a couple more days of work before the Christmas break. Somehow, we'll get through this.*

Shortly after my call to the police, I sent the kids upstairs. Then I phoned my sister-in-law, Gloria.

"Hi there," I managed to say before I started crying.

"What's wrong?' I heard Gloria ask.

"Brian is missing. And so is his medication," I said between heaving sobs. "I don't know where he is, and I'm so scared." I could feel the phone shaking in my hand. She promised to be right over and told me everything was going to be okay.

I was not convinced, but I was grateful she and my brother Wayne would come and help me; Wayne was the second oldest of our four siblings. He and Gloria were high school sweethearts and married almost immediately after graduating. Wayne was the quiet brother. He didn't say much, but when he did, he was thoughtful and had a brilliant sense of humour. Most often he'd let Gloria do the talking. Gloria and I were like sisters, finishing each other's sentences and using our intuition to know when the other was going through a rough time.

Gloria didn't tell me she was rallying the troops. In less than an hour, they arrived along with my mother and Gloria's daughter, Shannon, who was a nurse. The oldest of Wayne and Gloria's two daughters, Shannon had training and experience dealing with people going through trauma. Of all the children and grandchildren in our family, Shannon got the beautiful red hair from my mother's side of the family. She had always been feisty, assertive, and outspoken, something our family attributed to her red hair. I think these traits helped her to be an excellent nurse. I appreciated her ability to take charge. Although I was surprised to see Shannon, having her there brought me great comfort. Given her profession and her take-charge personality, I relaxed a bit, knowing she could help me navigate these murky waters.

I didn't want to worry my mom. I chose not to call her, but I am forever grateful Gloria did and arranged to bring her along. Osteoporosis may have shrunken her body from five-foot six to barely five foot tall, but there is no doubt she remained the matriarch of the family. Despite her white hair, my mom's crystal blue eyes and winning smile fooled people into thinking she was younger than her eighty-two years. She was forever the eternal optimist. Even though my mom had gone through a war, taken care of my sick father, and dealt with a son who had addiction issues, she always chose to focus on the positive. How she did it has always been a bit of a mystery to me. When I saw her that night, I fell into my mother's arms. The tears wouldn't stop. My body shook. Whatever happened now, I knew I was not alone. My family was there.

We settled into the living room while Shannon supervised my kids' bedtime. "Let's have some tea," my mother said.

It didn't matter if we were celebrating an event or facing the worst trauma imaginable, tea was always the answer. As part of our British heritage, I was raised to believe there is something calming in hot tea. Maybe it's the ritual involved that calms me down. Pouring boiling hot water into the teapot to warm the pot, then dumping it out, adding teabags and then adding more boiling hot water. Finally, covering the teapot with a cozy to ensure the tea stayed hot. In the past, we sat in the living room to chat and sip. Today we sat there in silence. We waited. *Maybe he'll walk in the door and offer a good explanation about why he wasn't home and why all his Demerol was gone. Perhaps he will call and say he went to a movie.* I made up stories like this in my head to keep myself from worrying. But it didn't alleviate the terror I felt.

I hadn't eaten anything since lunch. My stomach felt empty, but I didn't care. I couldn't even think of putting food in my mouth. The pain in my stomach was different than one of my allergic reactions, when I would feel my stomach twisting and knotting. This felt like I had been punched in the stomach; I wanted to double over in pain.

Finally, around ten thirty, I rushed to the bathroom and vomited. I threw up until there were only dry heaves left. Afterward, I lay on my bed and cried. Not the tears trickling down my face kind of cry, but the ugly tears with great big sobs, snot running down my chin, can't catch my breath, intermittent screaming kind of cry. I sensed Mom sitting on the bed with me. When my crying started to subside, another wave came, and I couldn't stop.

My mom soothed, "Let it out. Let it go."

After several cycles of crying and calming down, my body started to relax. I noticed a sense of numbness in my arms and legs. My mom rubbed my back and handed me a Kleenex.

"I am going to be okay," I shakily told her.

My mom quietly left me lying on the bed, staring at the ceiling. I didn't remember ever feeling this exhausted. I didn't even trust my legs to hold me if I tried to stand up. The pain around my heart was intense; it radiated throughout my body. As sick as I had been over the previous nine months, nothing could compare to the agony I felt in that moment. *Brian loves me; he would never do anything to hurt me. Why would he disappear? Where could he be? This must be a bad dream.*

I was unaware of how much time passed. Eventually, I pulled myself to my feet. I decided to look around the bedroom one more time for any clue that he may have left. I loved our bedroom. One of the reasons I wanted to buy this house was its spaciousness. The bedroom was large enough to include our pine queen-size sleigh bed, three matching dressers, a comfy chair, and space to exercise. Double doors opened to the hallway. The walls were cream, and the bedspread and pillows were gold. We had talked about painting and redecorating once we had a little more money. Other than the messy bedspread where I cried, nothing looked out of place.

Just to be sure, I walked from corner to corner and scanned the room, trying not to miss anything. Finally, I noticed on the high-boy dresser on his side of the bed, lying flat in the far corner near the wall and obstructed by the lamp, a manila envelope with my name written in ink. The colour of the envelope blended in with the colour of the dresser. I saw a thick gold band with a solitary diamond in the centre sitting on top of the envelope. Brian had never taken his wedding ring off in our fifteen years of marriage.

I ran back to the bathroom and dry heaved again.

CHAPTER 4
The Search

If I cease searching, then, woe is me, I am lost.
That is how I look at it; keep going—keep going come what may.
— Vincent van Gogh

Trembling, I held Brian's wedding ring in my right hand, cautiously picking up the manila envelope with my left. Taking a few deep breaths, I opened the yellow flap and pulled out two pieces of paper. The first was a note written to me in Brian's shaky handwriting; the second, a copy of our life insurance policy. In his final letter to me, he wrote: "I have always loved you, and I have always been faithful. Have someone help you file the insurance claim."

My hands were shaking so violently that I could barely hold the papers.

Just two brief sentences. Did he include our insurance policy to make things easier for me and save me searching for paperwork? Maybe that was what he was looking for when he tore his office apart. Just two brief sentences but so many questions unanswered.

Am I to blame? Will others blame me? Was there something I could have said or done that would have changed this outcome? As a social worker, I had worked with several suicidal youths. I was trained and certified in suicide prevention to recognize the signs of suicidal behaviour, for God's sake. *Why didn't I see the signs? Why did I not leave work early and come home that day? Would it have made a difference?*

However, I know that even if I had come home the day he left, even if I could have potentially stopped him, if he were genuinely intent on dying, he would have found another time, another day. I didn't see the signs because I was too close and did not believe Brian would ever take his own life. Over the years, Brian and I had talked about suicide. We discussed it after a family friend had hung herself in her garage and another time more recently with the suicide of one of the kids I worked with. Both of us promised we would never choose to die by suicide. What neither of us understood at the time was that suicidal people don't have the capacity to make rational choices.

Death is final, and I could not get the answers I so desperately needed. I wanted Brian to tell me why. Why did his life seem so bleak that ending it became a possibility and then a certainty? Why could Brian not tell me what he was going through? I wanted to know when he began contemplating suicide. When did he come up with a plan? I wanted Brian to tell me what could have made a difference for him. What could I have done differently? What was the tipping point? What made him choose his method of suicide? This is where I believe choice does play a part. Was it accessibility? He didn't die in our house. He didn't own a gun; but he did have a lot of Demerol available to him. I wanted Brian to tell me how he could leave his children. How did he think his death would impact us? I was so hurt, and it seemed personal. I wanted to know exactly how Brian, my husband of fifteen years, could do this to me and to our family.

How? How? How?

Much later, I learned that victims rarely leave a suicide note. Only 15 to 38 percent of victims will create a last message in the form of a written note, video, audio file, or text for their loved ones.[4]

Many famous people have left suicide notes: Virginia Woolf, English feminist and author; Kurt Cobain, leader of the band Nirvana; and in 2018, Kate Spade, a well-known designer, left a much-discussed note to her daughter. She wrote, "I have always loved you. This is not your fault. Ask Daddy!"

So, why leave a note? For some, it may be a way to say a final goodbye and express their final wishes, such as who should get their favorite belongings or instructions on what to feed the cat. Or it may be to tell their loved ones not to blame themselves. For others, it may be an opportunity to project blame and guilt onto those left behind. Regardless of the message, those who died evidently felt the need to say some final words. Although Brian's note did not provide closure, I counted myself one of the fortunate ones to have received anything at all.

Writing a suicide note doesn't seem like it would be an easy thing to do. I imagine it would feel like yet another overwhelming task. Perhaps it seems pointless for those who choose not to leave a note. A few lines could barely capture the extent of what they were going through.

A survivor of suicide loss once shared with me his son's note. His son scrawled one word in thick, black felt pen and hid this message on the back of a painting hanging on a living room wall. "Sorry." This young man stepped in front of a train, and his father was devastated, not knowing why. While cleaning out his son's apartment, the father fell to his knees when he discovered what his son had written. He still could not understand why his son took his own life. The hidden note only added to the unanswered questions. Only the son would know if this was a note of closure or one of revenge.

In researching this chapter, I was shocked to learn there are online instructions on how to write a suicide note. Regardless of the author's intention, as I read through the instructions, it felt like a punch to the gut. *What kind of a person would offer this guidance? Why?* I just don't get it. It's hard for me to see this information as helpful, and yet, it probably has helped someone who didn't know what to say. Reading the website left me furious and disgusted, probably because it was one more person I could blame.

Over the years, people have asked me if Brian left a note, as if that message could provide some insight or answers to why he killed himself. When asked, I tell them I still feel conflicted about the meaning and the value of his note. Yes, Brian left a message to let me know he loved me and was always faithful to me. I imagine he thought he answered a question I had wondered for some time: *Was he faithful?* Perhaps in his mind, his statement would answer my question of his fidelity. I am happy to say it did. I finally felt he had no more reason to lie.

In his note, Brian probably mentioned the life insurance because he wanted to take care of us after he was gone. Was it enough to ensure financial stability for our family in years to come? No, it wasn't. It was only enough to pay off our mortgage and a little bit more.

Did his note answer any of the myriad of questions I had for him? No, it didn't.

With the note still in my hands, I took a few deep breaths. Once I gained some composure, I made a second call to the police at approximately eleven-thirty that night. This time I told them I found a suicide note and my husband's wedding ring. The officer on the other end of the line said he would send a police car to my house as soon as possible. My mother, brother, sister-in-law, niece, and I sat in the living room and made small talk, anxiously waiting for the next step. The police arrived in under thirty minutes, although it seemed much longer. The more mature of the two was in his mid-forties, about Brian's age, with dirty blond hair starting to thin on top. The younger officer looked like he was in his twenties, with thick dark hair and brown eyes. He seemed a bit nervous, as if he might be a new graduate on the force. They sat with us in the living room and pulled out their notepads.

The older officer looked at me with warm but searching eyes. "Tell me exactly what has happened."

"My husband Brian has not come home. He is taking Demerol for back pain, and over fifty-five pills are missing. I found a suicide note in our bedroom," I said shakily. It seemed the words were coming out of someone else's mouth, not mine.

"When did you last see him?"

"This morning, at breakfast."

"Can you describe him?"

"He is about 6'1" and weighs about 235 lbs. He has a muscular build with extra padding." Both officers smiled. "His hair was brown, and now it is more salt and pepper."

"What was he wearing when you last saw him?"

I mentally pulled the image of the last time I saw Brian, "A sweatshirt and pajama bottoms." *Is this how I will remember him? Wearing his favourite sweatshirt, his hair uncombed, a two-week growth of hair on his chin because he had not bothered to shave?*

"Does he wear glasses?"

"Yes, metal aviator frames."

"What was his overall disposition when you last saw him?"

I replayed our conversation of this morning in my head.

"He seemed sullen and quiet." Then I quickly added, "He's usually a very happy guy. Over the past couple of weeks, his attitude changed a lot when he got hurt, and he had intense back pain."

"Where do you think he might have gone?" the younger cop interjected.

"I don't know. If I knew, I would go there." I realized this officer was only doing his job, but I probably came off a little annoyed at his question and thought, Rookie Cop.

I knew the police officers were asking standard questions, and yet, I wanted to scream. I was doing my best to be cordial and appear composed. What I wanted to do was demand that the entire city police force stop everything they were doing RIGHT NOW and find my husband. Send out the Bat Signal for fuck's sake. I handed them the suicide note. They explained they needed to take it for evidence.

I panicked.

This suicide note was the last thing Brian left for me. I didn't want to hand it over, despite their explanations about why they needed it for the investigation. I worried if I didn't comply, they wouldn't think this was legitimate, and nothing would be done to search for Brian.

The older officer explained that they would take it to the station, make a copy, and I could pick up the original in a few days.

"You'll need to be the one to retrieve the letter," he told me, with compassion in his eyes and his voice.

It seemed he had done this before, and the younger officer was closely watching his lead. *A teaching opportunity,* I thought to myself. *What if they lose the note?* I worked briefly in correctional services when I went through college. I saw things go "missing" all the time. I wanted to rip the note out of the officer's hand and run upstairs. The thought of letting it out of my sight scared me. I felt five years old, longing for the comfort of my mother's arms and my pink stuffed animal. Reluctantly, I handed over the piece of paper.

After gathering the necessary information and completing their notes, the police explained an "all call" would be sent out to all police officers so every car would have Brian's description. They asked if I would like two members of the Victim Services Team to visit.

"They're volunteers who have been providing support to victims for years. We work closely with them, and I assure you they can provide you the emotional support we just can't give right now."

I readily agreed, wanting all the support I could get. After a quick phone call, the officers were gone.

Within thirty minutes, a man and woman in their mid-fifties were at my door. By now, it was nearly one o'clock in the morning. I invited them into the foyer and offered to hang up their coats. I invited them to sit on the love seat in the living room.

The volunteers introduced themselves as Sharon and Bill (not their real names). Initially I thought they were a couple, but they were not.

"We have worked together over ten years as volunteers, but we're sometimes matched up with different partners," Sharon explained. "Our job is to be the intermediaries between you and the police. The service is not exclusive to Calgary. It's a worldwide service, providing support to victims of crime and tragedy, allowing the police to do what they do best. The police don't have the time needed to guide victims through the system. Our job is to provide information to both sides. If the volunteers don't know the answer, they have multiple resources to access it."

Unlike the police, these two were not in uniform. Sharon wore yoga pants and a knee-length flowing top. Her bouncy red curls were accentuated by thick silver hoop earrings. *She has a very artistic flair,* I thought to myself. Bill wore khakis and a beige sweater. They reminded me of an aunt and uncle coming over for tea.

"Tell us what has happened," Sharon said. "Take your time; we're not in a rush."

Her green eyes softened as she looked at me. Her ability to look me in the eye helped me trust her. She sat on the edge of the love seat, leaning forward as if she was interested in hearing every word I said. Both listened intently as I took them through the last heart-wrenching hours. As I repeated the same story that I'd told the officers, their ability to listen without interruption helped put me at ease. They nodded their heads as I shared how difficult it was to release the suicide note to the officers.

"You'll get the note back," Bill assured me. "I give you my word."

I started to relax a bit. The knot in my stomach started to release. The tension in my muscles began to subside. I felt like they were truly there to help me.

Sharon said the police took suicides very seriously. She explained what the police could and couldn't do. Although the resources weren't there to create a search team, all units would be briefed on the information given to the officers tonight, just as the officers had explained. My heart sank when I realized it was true the police couldn't actively do anything to find him. It was up to us, Brian's family and friends. We needed a plan. Until we found Brian, Sharon and Bill would be my go-to people. They told me I could call Victim's Services twenty-four hours a day, seven days a week, and a message would go directly to both.

Sharon and Bill, with their years of experience, metaphorically brought an oxygen mask to my door. They were masterful in building connection by listening to every word I said, answering all my questions, using compassion in their voices, and assuring me I was not alone. They provided a human touch in contrast to the authority of the officers. Their help and support made me feel like I could breathe a little easier. They offered words of encouragement and hope. They promised to be with me throughout this trauma.

The clock said it was almost two thirty in the morning by the time Sharon and Bill left. My niece Shannon poured me four fingers of scotch, which I threw back in three gulps. Shannon told me she wanted to stay the night. My mother headed to the guest room. I grabbed some blankets for Shannon to curl up on the couch. Wayne and Gloria decided to head home and get some rest. I collapsed into bed.

In the darkness of my bedroom, my body felt exhausted, but my mind was still active. I stared at the ceiling and talked to God, asking for this to be a dream. A bad dream. I prayed angels would be sent to talk to Brian and convince him to come home safely. *We are not bad people. Why is this happening to our family? Why did I not see the signs? Did I see them and consciously ignore them?* I didn't think so. I didn't know. I felt like I knew nothing.

I rolled over to Brian's side of the bed and smelled his pillow, taking deep, lung-filling breaths. I recognized the scent of his underarm deodorant. In the months of my illness, Brian often slept on the couch, sometimes until four or five o'clock in the morning. I told myself it was to let me sleep in peace, without his snoring. For the first time, I wondered if he slept downstairs because he was deeply depressed. The thought shocked me. *How did I not see it before? Was I so caught up in my own illness, I couldn't see what my husband was going through?*

Even though I had often slept alone in recent months, I was acutely aware of an emptiness in my bed. If Brian followed through on killing himself, he would never lie next to me again. I would never feel the strength of his arms around me.

We would never make love again. The thought brought me to tears once again. Between the tears and the scotch, I finally fell asleep.

Morning came much too quickly. I slept on and off for several hours, each time waking up with a start and getting lost in my thoughts again. My body screamed for rest, but my brain wouldn't shut off. I ran through possible scenarios in my mind. *Who will help me look for him? Who should I tell? Should I take this to the media?*

My head hurt but my bladder called, so I dragged myself out of bed. I rummaged through the medicine cabinet to find some Tylenol. Due to allergic reactions, I typically avoided taking chemicals. That morning I couldn't give a shit. I still felt sick to my stomach. I decided my kids wouldn't be going back to school. There were only two more days before their Christmas holidays began. They were already awake, each snuggled in a blanket in front of the fireplace in the family room watching television.

"Good morning," my mother said in her typical singsong manner. "Can I make you some tea?'

"Yes, tea would be lovely," I replied.

I still didn't want to eat, but she convinced me to try some toast. It was pointless to argue with my mother.

Our house happened to be located just minutes from a sprawling provincial park. The officers had recommended calling on the expertise of forest rangers stationed in the park to be on the lookout. I called them and explained the situation. The ranger I spoke with said one of their staff would come to my house to discuss strategies for a missing-person search.

A woman ranger showed up an hour later. I expected a man. Mentally, I chastised myself. *I guess I'm not a real feminist. Why do I care about that shit now? Who cares!* I thought of Ranger Smith trying to stop Yogi Bear from stealing picnic baskets. Maybe it was her uniform: matching beige shirt and pants with a thick brown belt. No hat. Straight brown hair pulled back into a ponytail. No makeup. Somewhat plain-looking, though I was drawn to her beautiful brown eyes. She had a firm handshake and excellent eye contact, two things I looked for when trying to get a read on someone. I liked her.

She introduced herself, and I immediately forgot her name but was too embarrassed to ask her again. Mentally, I called her Ranger Smith. Smith was so kind, so professional, and so knowledgeable.

"I am so sorry you are going through this," she said, "I have never had some-one in my life go missing or be suicidal. I cannot imagine what you are going through. Let me share with you what we are taught as rangers about suicidal be-haviour."

My mom, Shannon, Ranger Smith, and I all sat at the dining room table. Smith pulled out a map of the park and spread it across the table. We huddled at one end of the dining room table as the ranger selected a red Sharpie pen to highlight the areas where we needed to concentrate our search.

"I think your best bet is to focus on these four areas. It's out of scope for our department to coordinate a search in the park," she said, "but I assure you that all our rangers will be alerted and on the lookout while they do their daily patrols."

Ranger Smith provided us with a profile of a suicidal person: they tend to go to an isolated place where they can monitor the area around them. Quite often, they choose a higher vantage point so they can see who's coming. They typically stay within a three-kilometer radius of their home. They might sit under a tree for shelter or protection from the cold.

"These are things I never learned when I took Suicide Prevention training," I offered.

Her knowledge felt like it would help us focus our search. I left the map on the table so we could study it further. Ranger Smith gave me her card.

"Call me if you have any more questions," she said as she opened her arms for a hug.

I stepped into her arms and hugged her tightly.

"Thank you," I said softly.

After the ranger left, I had a thought to call the local chapter of Search and Rescue to ask for their help. A woman answered.

"Hello, my name is Cathie, and my husband is missing. He left a suicide note yesterday and left the house. Can your organization help me find him?" I asked.

"I'm very sorry, but we don't search for adults, only children," she replied.

"What do you mean you only help if it's a child?" I said angrily, my voice ris-ing. "I have children, and their father is missing! Doesn't that count for anything?"

"I am so sorry," she said. "Those are our rules."

"Trust me. I will never donate money to your organization . . . EVER! I will spread the word to everyone I know not to support you!"

I screamed my fury into the phone before I slammed down the receiver. At that moment, my outburst felt completely justified. Hot, angry tears rolled down my cheeks. *How can they be so cruel? It's just days before Christmas. Where's your Christmas spirit? Why don't you want to help someone in need?* Once I calmed down, I realized how crazy I must have sounded. My crazy thoughts matched how crazy I was feeling. Typically, I was a calm, kind person. This situation was anything but typical.

I thought of calling the media to get the word out that Brian was missing. (It was the year 2000, and social media was still years away.) I imagined the story would be snapped up. Calgary, a city of more than one million people known for its volunteer spirit (think 1988 Olympics), would respond to the call for help. Tens of thousands of people would join my quest to look for him. This was the kind of story I felt sure would solicit a tsunami of sympathy, especially days before Christmas.

On the flip side, contacting the media might push my family into an unwelcome spotlight. I stopped myself to rethink taking this action. I envisioned Brian's picture being splashed on the front page of both newspapers, his face filling the screen as the top story on the six o'clock news. I could see the headline, "Suicidal Father of Two Missing Days before Christmas." I imagined reporters knocking on our door, searching for the inside story.

Of course, I have since learned media typically do not report on suicides, except for high-profile victims. Experts have long been concerned with the possibility of a "contagion" effect—people who read details of a suicide may then consider taking their own lives. They may start to see it as a viable alternative to their pain. At the time though, the thought of unwanted media attention was enough to dissuade me from reaching out for coverage.

By Wednesday afternoon, about fourteen hours after finding the suicide note, my living room was full of people wanting to help. My niece, Shannon's friends, all in their mid-twenties, gathered there, ready to search for Brian. They were dressed in layers, prepared for the brutal temperature of minus thirty degrees Celsius. Each of these young people dropped whatever they were doing to answer the call for help. My heart swelled with gratitude for their kindness and willingness to support our family. I would never forget what they were willing to do for me and my children. We broke into teams, and I shared the information from Ranger Smith.

Meanwhile, my children played video games. For the most part they got along, except when they didn't, as with most siblings. That day they agreed to put aside their differences—and I knew I didn't need to worry about refereeing their arguments. My mother remained with them. She could answer the phone if someone called. I was torn between staying home to comfort my children and being part of the search team. David assured me he would help watch over Jennifer and my mother. He was what I called an old soul, nurturing, very loving, and beyond devastated by his father's disappearance. He looked like he was constantly on the verge of tears.

"Why would he do this? Was it something we said, something we did?" David repeated over and over as I held him.

He was confused. How could the father he admired so deeply leave him? Jennifer kept her emotions closer to herself. My heart ached every time I looked at them. A myriad of thoughts raced through my head. *How could he do this to our beautiful children? How could he inflict such pain? If only he could see their faces, their torment. Did he even think about the impact of his actions? Will he have second thoughts? Will he come home alive?*

We checked that everyone was warmly dressed and had a watch and phone. We agreed to meet back at the house in three hours, when winter darkness would be setting in. Shannon and I decided to go to the golf course five minutes from my house. Brian loved to golf, and his dad was an avid golfer. It was one of the first places I thought of when I imagined where he would go. We drove to the clubhouse and met the maintenance man, Hank, in the bar.

"Hi, I know this may sound very weird, but we live really close by and my husband, Brian, went missing last night. He left a suicide note, and we are looking for him," I said nervously.

"Wow, I'm so sorry to hear that.," Hank replied, sincere concern on his face.

I took a deep breath. "His dad was an avid golfer, and I thought my husband might have come to the golf course to feel connected to his dad who passed away six years ago. I know this is asking a lot, but could we walk through the course and look for him?"

This is a high-end golf course, so I expected Hank to say no.

Hank's reply startled me. "Let me get my truck, and we can drive through the course together. I know this course really well, and it would take you hours to cover the entire area."

"Seriously, you would do that?" I replied in awe.

"Of course, I will. I cannot imagine what you're going through. It's the least I can do to help."

My faith in the kindness of strangers was restored. After the call to Search and Rescue, I thought we would have to do everything ourselves. Hank showed me that was not true.

We drove slowly through the snow, the three of us scanning the surrounding area for any sign of Brian. I was amazed this man was willing to drive his truck all over the grounds, leaving tire tracks, and in some cases, ruts, in our wake. Surely this couldn't be good for the grounds. I was afraid if I mentioned how the tires may tear up the greens, Hank would stop driving through the course. I chose not to say anything. After more than an hour, we covered the area with no luck. We returned to the clubhouse, and I impulsively gave Hank a hug along with my deepest thanks.

"I'm overwhelmed by your kindness. Thank you from the bottom of my heart," I said, my eyes flooding with tears.

"I only pray you find your husband, and he's okay," said Hank, wiping a tear from his right eye.

For weeks to come, when I drove past the golf course, I could see the tire tracks in the snow and silently blessed this man for his willingness to help.

The rest of our makeshift search team went to the provincial park, splitting up to cover more ground. When we all reconvened, there was a sense of lightness, thanks to our shared camaraderie, despite the fact we'd found no leads on my husband. At least we are doing something. We agreed to meet again the next day and resume our search.

Early Thursday morning, my brother Barry and sister-in-law Sandra arrived from their home three hundred kilometers away. Their adult daughter Krista was working and would arrive two days later. Barry is ten years older than me. We've remained close through the years. Sandra was always my champion. I was comforted having them with me.

For the next two days, we focused entirely on searching the provincial park, more than thirteen square kilometers in area. Searching such isolated areas takes time. Sandra and I teamed up. At one point, we crossed over the creek on a wooden bridge about nine meters long and stopped in the middle for a moment.

"If there is a funeral," I told her, "I want someone to sing 'Bridge over Troubled Water.'"

Brian loved that song. I was already planning the funeral in my head.

Sandra held me by the shoulders, looked in my eyes, and said calmly, "That would be an excellent choice."

She had always believed in me and supported me in tough times. Now she was walking with me in the bitter cold as I mused what should happen at my husband's funeral. *Who will I get to speak? Should I get a pianist? A professional singer? It's near Christmas; who will come? How do I let everyone know? Who will do the eulogy?* Could I have pictured myself at the front of the church talking about the love of my life? Not a hope in hell. I was struck by the absurdity of calmly making funeral plans while searching for my husband.

The sun lowered in the sky—time to return home. I wondered what I would do if we didn't find him. *But what if we do? What if Sandra and I are the ones that come across his body, tucked under a tree, frozen to death. Will I be able to handle the sight? Will I ever be able to erase the image of finding his body?*

Making decisions and acting helped me move forward. I could have chosen to crawl into bed and stay there. Instead, I was in frigid weather, taking one step at a time, most likely looking for my husband's body. It was, without a doubt, the most tortuous and difficult action I had ever taken in my life. Way worse than childbirth, and I was in labour for sixteen grueling hours with David. Just before his delivery, I experienced excruciating agony and prayed the baby would be ripped from my body so the pain would end. My reward was a beautiful baby boy. Now, with no warning, it seemed my heart was being ripped out of my chest, and there was no end in sight. No reward for the pain.

So, I walked, and I searched, not knowing whether Brian would ever be found.

CHAPTER 5

They Found a Body

No one loves the messenger who brings bad news.
— Sophocles, Antigone

On Friday night, three days after Brian's disappearance, I left for about ten minutes to get out of the house and pick up some milk. After I returned and parked the car in the garage, I opened the connecting door to enter the family room. Sandra was standing right there, waiting for me. Instantly I sensed her added level of tension.

"They found a body," she said, tears welling in her eyes.

I froze. My body went cold. *They found him.* Part of me felt relief that we no longer needed to search. Part of me was filled with horror, as my worst nightmare was about to come true. As much as I wanted to believe it might not be him, deep down I knew the truth. He was gone. He was dead. He followed through on his suicide note. At least when we were looking for his body, there was hope. Now that hope was gone.

Sandra led me upstairs to the couch in the living room where several more family members waited for me.

"I heard on the radio they found a body at the university," Sandra explained.

So no one called to tell us. She heard the news and thinks it might be Brian they're talking about. My gut tells me she's right.

The university was about twenty kilometers from our home, a more than a thirty-minute drive. It hadn't even crossed our radar as a possible location. It didn't fit the profile we were given regarding suicidal behaviour. Brian loved learning, and he loved the university. It must be him. My intuition told me, This is the truth.

Damn intuition. *Why the hell do you show up sometimes, but you're not there when I really need you? Where were you three days ago when you could have yelled at me to come home early from work, or just told me to stay at home that day? Why couldn't you have been louder then, so I could have stopped him?*

My body vibrated with panic. My mind continued to race. *How can I hear the words that my husband's body has been found? Will I die of a broken heart?* I remembered my mother telling me that their dog had died of heartbreak after my grandfather passed away. *Is that even possible? What will others say when they hear the word "suicide"? Will all my friends abandon me? Will I be a marked woman like Hester Prynne in The Scarlet Letter? Will others judge me based on Brian's actions?*

I felt ludicrous about my own thoughts, worried about how to do the "right thing" when nothing was right in my world. I felt like I was looking through the lens of a camera that had pulled back, and I was witnessing a panoramic view. I felt outside my body, watching myself move and speak in slow motion as if moving through quicksand.

I dialed the number for Victim's Services. After telling the operator who I was, I pleaded, "Please have Sharon or Bill call me right away. It's urgent!"

I was hoping they could confirm if the body was Brian's. Sharon and Bill came to the house every day since the first night. Sharon called and said she heard the news but didn't have any information about the identity of the body. She said she and Bill would come right over. It didn't seem very long before the doorbell rang.

Once inside, Sharon embraced me and held me in the hug longer than usual.

"I hope we have an answer soon," she said into my left ear.

Bill followed with a quick hug. They removed their coats, and we settled into the living room.

"Yes, we heard the news about the body being found at the university, but we don't have any more details right now," Sharon said. "I'll make a call to see if I can get more information."

She put back on her coat to go to her car to call the coroner's office. *Maybe she doesn't want me to see her reaction.* She came back inside, and we waited in uneasy anticipation for the coroner to call back. I imagined hearing a grandfather clock ticking quietly in the background: tick . . . tick . . . tick. I looked around the room and noticed the crease in the leather chair where Brian used to sit and read. I looked at the wall hanging we bought on our honeymoon in Mexico. His photo sat on the corner table. I felt his eyes watching us in our silence.

My heart started to beat faster. I felt like throwing up again. *Maybe it isn't him. Maybe this is all a mistake.* I didn't want to take the call, but I knew I needed to hear whatever the coroner had to say. The home phone rang in the kitchen. I held my breath. My brother Barry answered it.

"It's for you," he said, holding out the receiver.

I slowly rose from the couch and went to where the phone hung on the wall. He put a kitchen chair behind my legs, grabbed my shoulders, and forced me to sit.

The coroner's voice was female. She explained they found a body at the university near the bleachers on the soccer field. Soccer. That made sense. He was a soccer coach. He loved the university. *Why didn't I think of that combination?* It was like putting together the pieces of a puzzle. *Where on the soccer field? Under the goalpost? In the stands? Does he face up or face down? How did he decide where to die? Was this location random, or had he methodically planned this out?*

I found it difficult to focus on what she was saying. This all seemed too surreal. The coroner acknowledged this was a difficult phone call. *How many times has she had to do this? That's certainly not a job I would want.* There they went again, weird, random thoughts running through my head. *Why am I worried about how hard her job is?*

She explained a university student took a shortcut through the soccer field to get to the bus stop and noticed someone on the ground. He rushed over, thinking it was someone who needed help, only to find the body frozen solid. She described the clothing on the body: a grey and burgundy winter jacket, jeans, and white mukluk boots. We had purchased matching grey and burgundy jackets a couple of years ago. Mine still hung in the front hall closet. Hearing her describe his clothing was the last thing I remember before I fainted. My brother caught me as I slid out of the chair.

When I came to, the phone was back on the cradle. I saw Barry's tearful face in front of me. I was in shock. I was numb. I felt wetness down my face. *My world has just ended. How can I possibly go on?* I wanted to join my husband. The pain was so intense. All I wanted to do is stop the pain. Suddenly, I realized the same thought might have gone through Brian's head while he was waiting to die.

"I want to go to the morgue to see Brian. Will you drive me there?" I said with determination to my brother.

In a calm but stern voice, Barry responded, "No, you are not going to see him. His body will be frozen solid. His skin will be discoloured. Once you see him like that, you will never be able to erase the memory. He would not want you to see him this way. Remember him as he was alive."

I thought of all the television shows where someone from the family needed to go to the morgue to identify the body. Apparently, the coroner did not need any of us to come. I imagined what it would be like to walk into the morgue and have the coroner pull back the sheet. I imagined what my husband's frozen body would look like. I trembled at the thought. Several days later, we found out from the coroner that once his body thawed, Brian had his driver's license in his back pocket. Now there was no doubt.

Years ago, I saw my father's body shortly after he died peacefully of heart disease in a hospital. He had a massive heart attack when I was five years old. When I was fourteen, he had open-heart surgery. In 1984, when my father was sixty-seven years old, he was scheduled for another open-heart surgery. Sadly, he fell the night before. They placed him in intensive care, hooked up to life-saving machines. Ten days later, my mother signed the papers to remove the life support.

I was twenty-six at the time. I arrived at the hospital, oblivious to the fact my father had been lying dead in his room for about half an hour. I stood outside his door, waiting for the hospital personnel in the room to leave. A young nurse came from behind the desk at the central station and approached me to ask if I needed help. I explained I was waiting to visit my dad. I saw all the colour drain from her face, and she excused herself to get the head nurse. *This cannot be good.* The head nurse approached and asked me to join her in the visiting room.

There, she put her hand on top of mine, "I am so sorry. Your dad passed away about thirty minutes ago."

Time stood still. *Did she just tell me my dad had died? I just saw him yesterday. This can't be true.* My body went cold, and I started to shake uncontrollably.

She asked if I wanted to see him. I heard a voice say "yes" and then realized the word came from me. She held my elbow and guided me to his bedside. I had never seen a dead body before. There was my dad, no longer in pain, no longer moving. His skin already had a grey pallor. For some reason, I looked up at the ceiling to the corner opposite his bed. There I saw a white, translucent light without shape, hovering. After a minute or so, the light faded and disappeared. I believe it was my dad, waiting for me, waiting to say goodbye.

I was grateful for all the additional years I got to spend with my dad. His death, although traumatic, was somewhat expected. Brian's death was not. I thanked my brother Barry for his wisdom in keeping me from seeing the body. I would rather remember my husband full of life, laughing, watching airplanes fly by with a longing in his eyes. He loved airplanes. It's that memory I wanted etched into my brain.

The news about Brian was devastating enough. Now I had to find a way to tell my children their father was gone, really gone. Jennifer had been in my bedroom upstairs watching television. She was already in her pajamas when she came down the stairs. I was standing in front of the hall closet, holding the sleeve of the twin burgundy and grey jacket to the one Brian wore when he was found. My daughter and I looked at each other. I could tell she saw shock on my face and felt the energy in the room. I started to cry and rushed to her side, sweeping her into my arms.

"I'm so sorry, baby. I'm so sorry, baby," I repeated over and over.

Everyone was now crying, including Sharon and Bill.

I was finally able to get the words out. "They found your father. I'm so sorry, he is not alive."

She leaned into my body, sobbing and shaking. *You sonofabitch, how could you have done this to your little girl? How will she ever get over losing you? How could you leave me to tell her that her daddy will never be coming home? I hate you right now.* We held each other until our tears subsided. Sharon helped me to take Jennifer upstairs and get her into bed. Eventually, my little girl started to calm down. I told her how much I loved her and that we would get through this together.

David had been out for the evening with the youth minister from our church. They had gone to the city zoo to take in the Christmas light display. I am very grateful my son was not home when I heard the news. He didn't have to see his mother faint.

When David walked in the door, he studied our faces. I sat him down beside me on the couch and told him I had bad news.

"Someone has found your father's body."

David fell into my arms and screamed. Like a wounded animal, he wailed. We held each other and cried. As much as I was experiencing my own grief, nothing compares to the deep, guttural sounds of wrenching pain as David reacted to hearing his father had died. Other family members surrounded us, enfolding us in their embrace, connecting us all. In that moment of deep, deep pain, there was also much love. Love for each other, love for Brian. Their physical touch soothed me. We all wept together.

Soon, the doorbell rang, and someone answered it. Our minister was there, having heard the news through our youth minister. He sat and prayed with us in our living room, telling us a story about lost sheep that we all listened to while sobbing.

Sharon and Bill stayed with us to provide support and answer whatever questions we may have had. I was surprised to learn that when a body is found in the community, it is protocol for an autopsy to be performed to rule out foul play. The coroner's office needed to wait until Brian's body thawed. The temperature outside had stayed around minus thirty degrees for the previous few days. His body was frozen solid, so it would take three to four days before the autopsy could be performed. The date was December 22nd, so they wouldn't release Brian's body to us until after Christmas. In the days ahead, I would have to make many decisions. First, I needed to make sure my children were safely in bed before I had a stiff drink.

My heart was officially broken.

CHAPTER 6

Picking Up the Pieces

No matter what, we have to keep moving forward, even if we have to crawl.
Kellie Elmore

I 'm grateful Brian and I talked previously about our wishes regarding death. He wanted to be cremated. He didn't want a casket, and he certainly didn't want a viewing. He especially didn't want a funeral. He wanted a celebration of his life with singing and laughter. Whenever we had this discussion, we'd always say, "It will be a long time before this ever happens."

I called our minister to plan a celebration of Brian's life at our church. Alan offered December 29, 2000, seven days after Brian's official date of death. I was immediately struck by the irony of the number twenty-nine. My father and grandfather both died on November 29, forty-five years apart. My mother lost her father and husband on the same date. There are several birthdays in our family on the 29th, and my sister-in-law, Gloria, and I used to spend time looking at how many times the number twenty-nine showed up in our family. *Not a coincidence.* Of course, the service would be on the 29th.

I pulled together items that would sit on the altar during the service. With painstaking care, I leafed through our photo albums to decide which pictures to display. I finally chose two photos. One was a more recent picture of Brian taken in our living room. He was looking directly at the camera with a wide smile and that salt-and-pepper hair colour I loved. The other picture was my favourite; taken at an air show about fourteen years earlier, where Brian looked over his shoulder, wearing aviator glasses and a killer smile. This picture always made me swoon. *How was this guy single when I met him? He was really, really good looking. He was also a decent guy. Caring, funny, socially conscious. The kind of guy I always wanted but never thought would come my way.*

I also found an airplane model of an F-18, his favourite, to honour his love of airplanes, and I purchased two O'Henry chocolate bars, the candy he loved the most. I bought a condolence book for guests to write in because that was the right thing to do. I didn't really care about getting a book. I would probably look at the book once, maybe twice, if ever. I told myself that the signatures of those who attended would be important for my children, but I suspected they wouldn't ever look at the book. It would hold no meaning for them. Still, I bought the book. Following convention provided some structure when making even the smallest decision felt like a gargantuan task.

After spending hours writing Brian's obituary, I called the local newspaper and read each line slowly to the woman on the other end. She typed my words as I spoke, reading them back to me to ensure she had every word right. Frankly, since we'd scheduled this event between Christmas and New Year's, I didn't expect many people to attend Brian's funeral.

I was wrong. The church was packed. People from all facets of our lives came to honour him. In addition to the family already in town, Brian's brother flew in from Montreal, and our church family was in attendance, as well as many of Brian's work colleagues. Most notably, the community boys' basketball team, a group Brian coached, attended in their burgundy and grey jerseys. From our pew, David acknowledged his teammates with a nod.

"I never thought of wearing my jersey," he whispered to me.

He was wearing dress pants, along with a shirt and tie.

"You look amazing," I told him.

Jennifer and I both wore blue dresses. I refused to wear black, deliberately thumbing my nose at convention.

I looked over at this group of fourteen and fifteen-year-old boys sitting together, some crying, and I got choked up. *Did Brian think about how these boys who looked up to him might be affected? What if one of these impressionable boys copycats him and kill themselves? Will these boys fear their father or mother might kill themselves? What must be going through the minds of these boys?*

Our minister, Alan, recounted the story of the lost sheep in his sermon and how the shepherd would not rest until that sheep was found. The story suggested Brian was a lost sheep. I agreed. Brian was lost lost in his thoughts and his rational thinking, lost in his dreams and goals for himself, lost in his ability to find another way.

I hadn't talked with Alan beforehand about what he was going to say. In retrospect, I wish I had given him the green light to be open about how Brian died. *Maybe he thought I didn't want anyone to know?* He chose not to mention the word "suicide" in the service, but everyone knew. In retrospect, not saying the word "suicide" out loud, though, is a lost opportunity. I was grateful that as a minister, Alan did not suggest Brian had committed a sin. I was raised to believe suicide was a sin, but through my faith in God and his grace, I believed all sins were forgiven.

> "For I am convinced that neither death nor life, neither angels nor demons, neither the present nor the future, nor any powers, neither height nor depth, nor anything else in all creation, will be able to separate us from the love of God that is in Jesus Christ our Lord."
> **Romans 8:38-39**[5]

I had written most of Brian's eulogy with input from family, but I didn't trust myself to get up and speak. My sister-in-law Sandra delivered the eulogy. David, my brother Barry, and Brian's brother, Ralph, stood behind her. They didn't speak, but they provided her emotional support as she read the details of my husband's life. I was so proud of my son, bravely standing with the other men, honouring his father. He was not ashamed to wipe the tears that fell as his aunt read the eulogy.

"Brian was the son of Evans and Ruth, older brother to Dale and Ralph, and father to David and Jennifer. He was raised in Montreal and moved to Calgary in 1980. He was passionate about airplanes and had a degree in military history. He was fascinated by space travel and hitchhiked by himself to Florida in his late teens just so he could visit NASA. He wanted to be a pilot but could not pass the eye exam. He loved to read, and no one wanted to play against him in *Trivial Pursuit.* Brian was smart, funny, and had a huge capacity to love both people and animals. He was forty-six when he died."

My niece Krista read Brian's favorite poem, "High Flight" by John Magee, a Royal Canadian Air Force fighter pilot accidentally killed in a mid-air collision in 1941:

> Oh, I have slipped the surly bonds of earth,
> And danced the skies on laughter-silvered wings;
> Sunward I've climbed and joined the tumbling mirth
> Of sun-split clouds – and done a hundred things
> You have not dreamed of – wheeled and soared and swung
> High in the sunlit silence. Hov'ring there,
> I've chased the shouting wind along and flung
> My eager craft through footless halls of air.
>
> Up, up the long delirious burning blue
> I've topped the wind-swept heights with easy grace,
> Where never lark, or even eagle flew-
> And, while with silent, lifting mind I've trod
> The high untrespassed sanctity of space,
> Put out my hand and touched the face of God.[6]

Brian loved the picture he had of an airplane soaring in the clouds with the words "High Flight" superimposed over the image. He related to the way the pilot described the joy and freedom of flying—he "slipped the surly bonds of earth." Brian felt the poem captured the excitement he felt wheeling and soaring in the clouds.

Brian's friend once took him up in a turboprop plane and let him take the controls for a while, even though Brian did not have a pilot's license. Brian was enthralled by the experience. He thought flying was a spiritual experience, one where he could reach out and touch God. He said he felt flying was like meditating, to be out of one's body, to break the bonds of this earthly existence.

When Brian talked about this poem, his eyes grew brighter, his smile wider, and I felt his desire for the experience of more. More love, more freedom, more adventure. By choosing to have this poem read at his service, I was telling the congregation that Brian is with God now. He's left the confines of his body; he's no longer in pain. He's soaring in the clouds.

After the service, I took my place in the hall to shake hands with those who had come to say goodbye. It was a surreal experience. *This cannot be real life; this seems like a scene from a movie. Any moment now, Brian will come through the front door of the church and say "Gotcha!" All our friends will laugh and tell me they were part of the prank.*

Several of the boys from the basketball team, along with their parents, paid their respects to me. "We're going to win the City Championship this year for Coach Brian," one boy told me. The other boys chimed in: "Yeah! We're going to win!" as they high fived each other, determination in their eyes.

Some people took the time to tell me a story about how Brian made a difference in their life. A friend expressed her gratitude for how Brian really listened to her when she went through a bad breakup. Another said Brian was always someone he could count on if he needed help, whether it was moving furniture or letting friends borrow his tools. Several of the men told me to call them if I ever needed help doing minor repairs around the house. Others reminded me of funny stories. Once at a dinner theatre, Brian was chosen to act like one of the Village People. He wore a headdress and lip-synced "Y.M.C.A." with four other unsuspecting men. Another time, Brian signed up a colleague for amateur night at the local comedy club without her knowledge. Despite the difficulty of this time, I loved hearing all the stories and felt comforted by people's outpouring of love for me, Brian, and our family.

After the last guest left the hall, a few very close friends and family lingered behind with me. I invited everyone over to the house for a drink—a mini wake. As we arrived at the house, I used the remote to open the garage door and drive the vehicle inside. When I tried to open the door connecting to the house, it was locked. That door was never locked. I didn't have a key to open it. I didn't even have a key to the front or back door on my keychain. I always came in through the garage.

Apparently, as the last one out of the house, my brother Barry had locked the door out of a sense of security. He didn't realize what he had done because he didn't have an attached garage. We all laughed at the absurdity of the situation.

"I can climb up on the roof of the garage and get in the house through your bedroom window," said my friend Ron.

With great hilarity, we stood in the middle of the road to watch as Ron pulled himself onto the garage roof from my front steps. He shimmied his way to my bedroom window, trying not to slip on the icy shingles. So much for locking my doors at night. Someone could climb into my bedroom window. *Note to self: do something about making my window more secure.*

We sat around the kitchen table and raised a glass to Brian. He would have loved to hear the jokes, the laughter, the connection we shared as we told stories about him—how he made us laugh, made us think, and loved us all. There was the time, for example, when we had a dinner party to celebrate Robbie Burns Day in late January, and Brian embraced his Scottish heritage by wrapping blue plaid fabric around his waist, removing his shirt, applying blue face paint, and greeting our guests as Braveheart. Or when he first met my family at a barbecue. We played *Trivial Pursuit,* and he knew all the answers.

At that barbecue, after a few drinks, my sister-in-law Gloria stunned us all by asking, "You are pretty smart; are you as good in bed?"

Without missing a beat, Brian replied, "Half the women in Calgary aren't complaining."

He was witty, loved a good party, and would have laughed the hardest of all at the stories while making sure to replenish everyone's drink.

After New Year's, I returned to work. I told myself I must keep going. Keeping busy would be the best way I could get through this transition. I still worked at the treatment centre for kids, moving from nights to working in the Evaluation Department. On my second day back, as I entered data on my computer, I started to cry for what seemed like no reason. I couldn't stop. The tears kept coming, and I was a mess. My body was shaking. Once my crying subsided, a new burst of tears emerged.

I went to my boss, Kelly, and told him I couldn't do this; I couldn't function at work. He was kind and understanding and told me to go home. I applied for and was granted short-term disability from the organization's insurance provider with the support of upper management. I realized how blessed I was. Not everyone has an opportunity to step back from work to heal. I ended up being off work for five months.

Often, I didn't want to leave my house. I preferred to stay curled up in a ball or sip tea while watching television. *Oprah* became a daily lifeline. Seeing other people facing difficulties helped me feel less alone. I also watched comedies such as *Friends* and *Frasier* for laughter. I fell in love with reality television. *Survivor* and *Big Brother* became my favourite shows. Watching how people reacted to each other and made choices, some good, some not so good, helped me to get out of my head. I also loved the girls on *Sex and the City*. The clothes! The shoes! The sex! I thought I could be best friends with Carrie, and I fantasized about moving to New York. Retreating into fictional storylines helped me avoid dealing with my own reality.

I spent more time in bed, but my sleep was fitful. I felt tired most of the time. Insomnia plagued my nights. I had crying jags often triggered by a song on the radio, Enya's "Only Time" or "One More Day" by Diamond Rio, or by something I read or watched on TV. Beaches with Bette Midler and Barbara Hershey was my go-to movie when I was feeling sad and needed to cry, but it just wouldn't come out. It was a minimum six-Kleenex movie.

It was also an effort to get dressed each day. Finding clean clothes was a task unto itself. When I did get out of my pajamas, I lived in yoga pants and T-shirts, my hair tied up in a bun. I tried to remember to take a shower.

When David was born, my mother came to live with us for three weeks. I had no idea how to care for an infant. She patiently taught me how to bathe, swaddle, and rock him to sleep. After Brian's death, my mother moved in once again for about three weeks. Having her with me was such a gift. She created a safe space for me to talk, cry, and express my anger. My mom was especially there for my children when I was behaving like a walking zombie. I wasn't present in conversations. I didn't hear what others were saying, and I forgot my purpose for walking into a room. I was easily confused and felt numb emotionally. I'm not sure how I could have managed those weeks without her presence. She helped me retain my sanity when I thought I was losing my grip on reality.

My mother Florence was born in 1917. She gave birth to me, the only girl after three boys, at the age of forty. She was a stay-at-home mother, creating purpose in her life through taking care of her children, volunteering at church, and leading young girls through Girl Guides. Mom was loving, compassionate, and strict. My father travelled a lot, and my mother ran the house and made sure we all said please and thank you. Cheekiness was not allowed and resulted in a spanking with a wooden spoon. A common refrain was the threat: "Wait until your father gets home."

When my father died in 1984, my mom stayed holed up in their apartment for one whole year. She told me this was her time to mourn, and at the end of one year, she would get up and start living again. My dad had sold our family home one month after I moved out in 1980. I always thought he did this so I could not move back in. Since my mom lived in an apartment, she did not have the burden of selling the house when my father died. Maybe he intuitively knew he only had a few years left to live when he made the sale.

After her time of mourning, Mom started volunteering and making new friends. She started taking painting lessons and signed up for water fitness classes. She travelled internationally to many places she had always wanted to see. What I didn't realize at the time was she taught me how to grieve. She gave herself the time to feel all the emotions and then chose to do things that brought her joy.

She loved to laugh and had a fabulous sense of humour. She was also a bit mischievous, never telling me the full stories of her dating life before meeting my father. However, she did allude to sneaking out of her parents' home to meet boys.

Mom gave the best hugs. Wrapped in her arms, I could let all my worries disappear. She always had a positive word for everyone, and she hated gossip. If someone was in need, Mom was there. She told me how it bothered her when other people wouldn't step forward to help.

"It's always the same people who volunteer their time," she said. "Make sure you are one of those people who do."

I have often said if I could be half the woman my mother was, I would be satisfied with this life.

On the rare occasions I did venture from my home, it was either to get groceries or to attend therapy. Sometimes I found myself standing in the middle of a store, wondering why I was there. I was mostly confused. My mind was in a constant fog. I wrote everything down; I made lists because I couldn't trust my brain to remember. I never used to make lists, but it became the only way I could make it through each day.

The problem was, sometimes I forgot to take the list with me. Then I played a game with myself to see how many things I could remember from the list. I used to be very good at playing *Concentration,* the memory card game, when I was a kid. Experiencing grief, I found myself driving to the store multiple times because, inevitably, I forgot the key ingredient I went to purchase, such as milk or eggs. It was frustrating to lose the ability to remember. I tried to search through my brain's Rolodex, only to see blank pages. Over time, the brain fog lifted and my memory slowly returned.

Four months after Brian's death, the Fish Creek Celtics made it to the city basketball finals. The boys that vowed at Brian's funeral to win the city championship were on the threshold of realizing their dream. They were not in the top division, but they were kids with a passion for basketball, and they admired and respected their coach.

Brian played basketball in high school in Montreal and would often regale us with stories of his team and their successes. Coaching basketball was a way for Brian to give back what he had learned as well as to spend time with David. Brian was known as a tough but fun coach. He taught the boys the importance of never giving up, telling them the story of how his high school team beat their rivals in the last few seconds of the final game. It didn't matter how often he told the story. Brian always had people engrossed in the play-by-play of how his team was sure to lose, but one last three-point basket saved the game, and they became local heroes.

I thought of the impact Brian had on these boys. I thought of Ryan, shy and uncoordinated. Brian worked hard with him, teaching him how to do a better layup, resulting in him making more baskets. In addition, Brian encouraged Ryan to be more assertive and praised him whenever he would express an opinion to the team. With Brent, a boy who had issues talking with his single mom, Brian spent time after practice, giving him strategies to communicate more effectively. The boys knew Brian as more than just a basketball coach. He coached them to be better versions of themselves. Hopefully, the experience of having their beloved coach die by suicide will remind them to reach out for help whenever they face rough times in their lives.

Several of the team members told David how lucky he was to have such a great dad. David loved having his dad as a coach and struggled to stay on the team after his dad's death. Sometimes it was too much of a painful reminder of what life used to be like. David played whenever he could. Each game became another step toward the ultimate goal, the championship game. After placing in the finals, the big day finally arrived, and Jennifer, my mom, and I took our place in the stands at the gymnasium of a community recreation centre to watch the team battle for the gold medal. Parents and grandparents of the other boys surrounded us so we could cheer our boys on to victory together.

The team they were about to play had one player famous for three-point shots. Every time the Celtics scored, our cheering section went wild with abandon. The lead went back and forth between the two teams. The boys never gave up. As the clock ran down, the hotshot on the other team scored a three-point shot seconds before the buzzer rang. The scoreboard had some lights burnt out, and it looked like the other team had won. But the three points were not enough. The Celtics won by one point! The team and their families in the stands went wild. *I can't believe it! The boys did exactly what they said they would do. Brian would be so proud.*

After congratulating the opposing team, the Celtics lined up to greet me in the stands. Each one gave me a hug.

"This win is for the coach," many said to me.

There was not a dry eye in the stands. I became a blubbering mess. Parents around me were crying. I felt overwhelmed with pride—for the team, for Brian, and more importantly, for David.

Grief brought a rollercoaster of emotions. Brian was cremated, but I hadn't picked up his ashes from the crematorium. Even though we talked about cremation, Brian didn't give me any instructions about what to do with his ashes. I chose not to have them at the memorial service. Truth be told, I was angry. Very angry. I paid a monthly fee for his ashes to be stored at the crematorium until I could decide what I wanted to do with them.

More than fourteen months after his death, I finally decided to inter his ashes on what would have been his forty-eighth birthday. I went to a funeral home and chose what I thought would be a beautiful urn: a simple, gold-coloured box. I asked their artist to create a picture of an airplane on the front. I was happy with the drawing. I also chose roses shaped in metal to cascade down from the top of the urn. When I went to pick up the final product, I was sick to my stomach. The roses were ugly and gaudy. I asked if they could be removed, but they couldn't; they were welded to the urn. Unless I postponed the internment, there wasn't enough time to order a new urn.

Brian's ashes sat at the crematorium for 438 days. When I arrived to pick them up, I placed the heavy, ugly urn on the counter.

"Hi, I am here to pick up my husband," I said, before realizing how odd that sounded. I'm probably not the first person to say something odd to a cremationist.

"Hi, I'm Susan, and I'm happy to help you," said the woman behind the desk, smiling.

She was about my age, long dark hair pulled back into a braid that fell over her left shoulder.

"I've never been in a crematorium before. Where do you keep Brian?" I ventured.

"Would you like to come and see where his ashes are? I can bring you back there if you want," Susan offered.

I hesitated for a second, but my natural curiosity kicked in and I said, "Yes."

The room was spacious with two large metal doors on the right-side wall for the retorts. Until Susan told me, I didn't know these cremation chambers had a specific name. I always referred to them as ovens. The one that was currently in use was making the room rather warm. Huge ceiling fans blew overhead, so we raised our voices to hear one another.

"The cupboard is this way," Susan said, as she led me toward the back of the room to a simple metal shelving unit.

As she opened the double doors, I saw about ten clear, plastic bags with twist ties. Each bag had a tag on it with the person's name.

"When people asked me when I was going to inter my husband's ashes, I told them he could sit at the crematorium for a while and think about what he did."

Susan laughed.

I was nervous and a bit squeamish, so I asked her, "Could you please put Brian's ashes into the urn for me?"

I watched as she unscrewed the little circle on the bottom of the urn, then gently maneuvered the bag into the small opening. I was grateful I didn't need to do this myself, especially since I was surprised to see bits and pieces of bone intermingled with the ashes. I thought a cremated body would look like sawdust.

"Once the fragments are collected from the retort," Susan explained, "they go through a process to remove any metal. Then they're crushed."

I'm glad I took time to heal somewhat before dealing with Brian's ashes. These difficult details are things most of us don't talk about or even ask about. I'm in a better place now to hear and speak about the details.

At the city-owned public cemetery, I purchased a glass-fronted niche in the mausoleum, big enough for two urns. I wasn't sure if I would want my ashes to be placed in the same niche, but I thought it was a good idea to give myself, or rather my children, the option of putting me there. The niche was $1,600. When my mother passed away in 2012, she had pre-purchased the same size niche for $16,000. That's a mark-up of 1,000 percent in eleven years. *I guess someone must pay for the new wing of the mausoleum. Apparently, it won't just be the city. I would later congratulate myself on buying what I called the "double-wide."*

For Brian's internment, I invited family, a few friends, and the minister. We stood in a circle and took turns saying whatever we needed to say during this final good-bye, so nothing was left unsaid. I was prepared to be there however long it took for everyone to share their thoughts. I read "On Death" by Kahlil Gibran. The last five stanzas are my favorite:

> For what is it to die but to stand naked in the wind and to melt into the sun?
> And what is to cease breathing, but to free the breath from its restless tides, that it may rise and expand and seek God unencumbered?
> Only when you drink from the river of silence shall you indeed sing.
> And when you have reached the mountain top, then you shall begin to climb.
> And when the earth shall claim your limbs, then shall you truly dance.[7]

Alan, our minister, said a few words, followed by a prayer. The niche was on a wall, just shy of six feet off the ground.

After we completed our service, the attendant who had graciously stepped away from the area to give us some privacy came back and asked, "Who is going to lift the urn into the niche?"

This was not something I had thought about. I looked around at the group and no one was stepping forward. *Well, I guess it's me then.* The urn was too heavy to raise above my head, so Barry finally stepped forward to help me. We lifted the urn and positioned it in the middle of the "double-wide" niche, rather than to one side or the other. Brian got to sleep in the middle of the niche almost like sleeping in the middle of the bed when your partner isn't home.

For now.

CHAPTER 7

Call It What It Is: Suicide

Call it suicide
Don't fabricate
Just tell them babe
It was suicide
Don't sugarcoat it
Just let them know
—*James Arthur, "Suicide"*

According to *Merriam-Webster Dictionary*, suicide is the act or an instance of taking one's own life voluntarily and intentionally. After Brian died, I used the term "committed suicide," thinking it to be the correct way to explain that he had killed himself. I thought the phrase was universally accepted. When I started reading more about suicide, however, I learned from many publications that using the word "committed" was no longer accepted because historically, "committed" was used when the act of taking one's life was illegal. But suicide is no longer a criminal act in Canada. Suicide, including attempted suicide, was decriminalized in 1972. What's more, physician-assisted suicide became legal through Bill C-14, the Medical Assistance in Dying (M.A.I.D) Act in June, 2016.[8]

Most legislation regarding suicide or attempted suicide originates from religious doctrine that considered suicide a sin. In ancient Athens, people who killed themselves were denied normal burials and would be interred alone on the outskirts of town with no marker. In England, suicide victims have only been allowed to be buried in daylight since 1882. Before that time, people in England who died by suicide were often buried at night at a crossroad with a stake driven through their hearts. In France, the body was sometimes dragged through the streets and then hanged from the public gallows.[9]

Although some countries still classify an attempt or abetment of suicide as a criminal act, most countries in the Western Hemisphere have decriminalized it. However, in the Bahamas, a suicide attempt is still against the law. According to their penal code, Number 294, "Whoever attempts to commit suicide is guilty of a misdemeanour, and whoever abets the commission of suicide by any person shall, whether or not the suicide be actually committed, be liable to imprisonment for life."[10]

Attempting or abetting suicide remains a criminal offense in most Muslim majority countries, including The United Arab Emirates, Malaysia, Yemen, and Jordan. In Uganda and Kenya, countries that have predominantly Christian populations, attempting or abetting suicide is also considered illegal. Even in a mostly atheist or agnostic country like North Korea, suicide is illegal, but suicide rates are considerably low in North Korea because of the stigma of suicide. If someone attempts or abets suicide, the family may be ostracized and have their personal property confiscated by the government.

Many countries still make it illegal to assist or encourage someone to die by suicide, and a person's family may be penalized for helping a family member to die. In Romania, for example, a family member could face up to ten years in prison. In Russia, discussing suicide and methods of suicide, or even joking about suicide, may be censored on social media. Sadly, in 2019, the Moscow Times reported that the World Health Organization (WHO) ranked Russia third in global suicide rates.[11]

Euthanasia, the act or practice of killing or permitting the death of hopelessly sick or injured individuals (such as persons or domestic animals) in a relatively painless way for reasons of mercy, is also illegal in most countries. There is a subtle difference between euthanasia and assisted suicide. With euthanasia, it is generally a doctor who administers the lethal dosage. Assisted suicide involves the person ending their life with assistance from a doctor. It means the doctor hands over the lethal dose to the patient, and they administer it themselves.[12]

In the United States, suicide is not illegal, and there are currently eleven jurisdictions where physician-assisted death is legal: California, Colorado, the District of Columbia, Hawaii, Montana, Maine, New Jersey, New Mexico, Oregon, Vermont, and Washington. In most states, however, it is a felony to aid, advise, or encourage someone to die by suicide. A person who assists another person to die by suicide may even be charged with manslaughter.[13] Regrettably, Canadians with a documented attempted suicide have in the past been stopped from entering the United States, as US law allows for denying access to those with a mental health diagnosis.[14]

After researching the legality of suicide and the use of the words "committed suicide," I still had questions. How do you prosecute someone who is already dead? And why does modern Western society continue to use the term even though it is inaccurate? I can still often find the term "committed suicide" in magazines, television, and books. It's part of our common vernacular.

To make a change in how we describe suicide requires awareness and a willingness to change our language. I can see positive signs in that direction. For example, the Associated Press, a powerful force in our media, dictates the standards for appropriate language in most mainstream newspapers and magazines (but not academic journals). The AP has changed its stylebook to discourage the use of the phrase "committed suicide." Instead, it recommends alternative terms like "killed himself," "took her life," and "died by suicide." The media plays a big part in preventing suicide, and it is comforting to know they are creating best practices of what to say and what not to say when there is a suicide, including providing resources if someone is suicidal.[15]

Like most people, I learned how to talk about death and suicide from my parents, and they probably learned from their parents. I learned we were supposed to avoid these topics. In general, we use euphemisms to describe death: s/he "passed away," "crossed to the other side," or "went to a better place." Such euphemisms help us hold death at arm's length or cushion the reality of our own mortality. We also use these euphemistic phrases out of respect for those who are grieving, wanting to avoid causing further trauma.

Perhaps because most people feel a general sense of unease talking about death, we sometimes make light of it. Death itself seems so heavy, especially death by suicide. Usually, we don't joke about death directly to someone who has just lost a loved one, but I think we have all heard or maybe even spoken the terms, "toes up," "six feet under," "gave up the ghost," "bit the dust," "bought the farm," or "pushing up daisies." The challenge is, if these words are said in a public arena, you may not know who is in the room, and whether they are experiencing grief from losing a loved one or not.

If talking about death is something our culture generally avoids, then we especially avoid talking about suicide. Euphemisms we use to describe suicide reveal that mostly we believe the person who died was responsible for their death: "died by their own hands," "took their own life," "ended it all," and "managed death." Even less-desirable phrases used to describe suicide include, "kill themselves," "do away with themselves," and "off themselves." Being a survivor of suicide loss has made me more sensitive to how I speak about death and especially suicide. I want to be respectful to both the person who died and their survivors.

I admit that if Brian had not died, I would not be part of the conversation to change how we view and speak about death by suicide. I had never given any thought to how using this terminology suggested he had committed a criminal act. Since becoming more aware, I have made a conscious effort to say Brian "died by suicide." Over time, I have stopped saying the words "committed" and "suicide" in the same sentence. I didn't try to hide or lie about Brian's suicide. Having worked with suicidal youth over the years, I knew how even the word "suicide" carried a heavy stigma. Without that experience, I might have been tempted to hide or downplay how he died. I figured people would find out anyway, and if I named it, then others couldn't talk behind my back. It helped me to feel a sense of control rather than allowing someone else to take control.

People were usually respectful when I told them Brian died by suicide. I am glad I made the decision to name it right from the start. I think many were afraid to offend me and appreciated my lead in how openly I talked about it. It helped them to relax when they realized I was not going to gloss over the reality, lie about what happened, or fall apart at the word.

I strongly believe it's important to talk about suicide, so I typically don't correct people when they use the word "committed." I would rather encourage discussion about suicide rather than shut down the conversation about wording because I need to be right about how people discuss death or suicide. If it's a close friend, I feel more comfortable speaking up. My friend Laurie, for example, started talking about suicide and used the word "committed" several times before I shared my views.

"I prefer the term 'died by suicide,'" I offered. "Suicide is not illegal."

Laurie thought for a moment. "Wow, I never thought about using 'committed' before you said that." She paused. "I've used this term for so long it might take me a while to make a change."

"I get it," I replied. "It took me a while, and I really appreciate you making the effort to change your language for me. Thank you, my friend."

Laurie now uses the term "died by suicide," and then makes a point of telling other people how she changed her language after hearing me explain why I don't use the word "commit." She tells them how this change in vocabulary has altered her context around discussing suicide, and how she likes to make a stand for improving dialogue around suicide and mental health. There is power in words. When I tell people of my preference for "died by suicide," most have the same response I did: "I never thought of it like that before."

Simply, you do not know what you do not know.

In my recovery process, I made other decisions about language. Using the word "trigger" can itself be a trigger when the person who died by suicide shot themselves. Brian did not die this way, so it never crossed my mind the word could have such a negative impact on those survivors. Thankfully, someone in one of my Facebook groups brought up this concern. The moderators agreed that we should all refrain from using it. I have also heard of survivors who shudder when they hear the phrase "hanging around" because their loved one died by hanging. Since I never know what people have experienced, I do my best to refrain from saying either of these statements.

In making these decisions on how to talk about Brian's death, I always had to also consider what my children would want. When looking through the obituaries (which I do from time to time, along with looking through births, to see who is coming and going), death by suicide is almost never mentioned. Recently, I was moved by Wynonna and Ashley Judd, who in their initial statement on social media regarding the suicide of their mother, Naomi, on April 30, 2022, wrote, "Today we sisters experienced a tragedy. We lost our beautiful mother to the disease of mental illness. We are shattered. We are navigating profound grief and know that as we loved her, she was loved by her public. We are in unknown territory."

Shortly thereafter, they stated she died by suicide using a firearm. Clearly, they understood if they did not say it, someone else would.

When the time came to write Brian's obituary, I did not list his cause of death as suicide. I considered including it in the obituary but ended up conforming to social norms. I thought of my children and the repercussions they may face with making such a bold statement that would be documented for all time. *When they get older, what if they don't choose to be open about how their father died?* The bottom line: I didn't want to hurt their feelings. The irony of these thoughts is not lost on me. Here I am years later writing a book about Brian's suicide. Before starting to write, I asked my children if they were okay with me writing a book about their dad. Both gave me their blessing and encouraged me to finish the book. My daughter even did some editing for me.

After Brian's death, when school started again in January, I thought long and hard about how I could help my kids transition back into the classroom. I asked both if they would like me to come to their classroom to discuss our family's tragedy.

David looked at me, rolled his eyes, and said, "No way! I'm in grade eight. I'm not having my mother come to school."

I really hadn't expected him to accept my offer; I just didn't want him to feel left out. My true focus was on Jennifer, the child I was most concerned about returning to school. Since I had pulled Jennifer out of class for the last couple of days of school before Christmas, her grade five teacher knew of Brian going missing and his subsequent death. I thought of asking the teacher if it would be okay for me to talk to the children in the classroom about Jennifer's father's suicide. I wanted them to hear it from me that Jen's dad had taken his own life and what that meant. I also did not want Jen's teacher to be in an awkward situation if the topic arose and the children engaged in conversation about Brian's death. I thought that going into the class and being open and honest about what had happened would be the best approach.

I almost talked myself out of it. *What if they ask questions, I'm not able to answer? What if I start crying and cannot stop? Could my talking to the children make it even worse for my daughter?* Instead, the mother bear in me emerged, and I had a good talking to myself. *You can do this. You must do this.*

I appreciated that Jennifer's teacher supported my visit to her class. The children sat on the floor in the reading nook. I explained that our family had gone through a very sad Christmas because of Jen's father's suicide. I explained suicide to them and answered their questions.

"Why did he kill himself?"

"I really don't know why. I don't think we will ever really know why. I think it had to do with how much pain he was having. People who take their own lives are usually very, very sad. We all get sad sometimes. Mommies, daddies, and children. Sadness is a normal emotion. It often happens when the sadness goes on for a long time, and the person loses hope they will ever feel better again. Being sad does not mean you will die by suicide. Talking to someone when you are sad and letting them know how you feel is one of the best things you can do."

"Did Jennifer's dad tell you he was sad?"

"He told me he had a lot of pain in his back. He didn't talk about being sad, and he didn't talk about wanting to die."

I knew it would be important to talk to the children about suicide at a level they could understand. I did my best to answer their questions with short, simple responses. I didn't give them more information than they asked for. I encouraged them to ask questions and let them know it is okay to not be okay.

I also asked the children to be understanding if Jennifer was having a tough day. I expected some parents to call me to express their displeasure in what I did; but no one called me, and no one called the teacher. My intention was to make a safe space for my daughter by being honest and calling it by name: suicide. Later that day when we were at home, I asked Jennifer how she felt about my coming into the classroom to talk to her classmates.

"I think it was good; everyone was really nice to me today," she responded.

I think Jennifer was grateful she didn't have to hide how her dad died.

Calling it what it is had one other unexpected benefit. Through my honesty about Brian's death, I also opened the door for other people to share that they also had a loved one die by suicide. For example, about twelve years after Brian died, I shared about being a survivor of suicide to an audience of about one hundred people. Afterward, a woman from the audience approached me and said how inspired she was by my talk. Her son had taken his life two years ago, and she only told her immediate family how he had died. She told others he died in a car accident. With tears running down her face, she told me how concealing what really happened increased the burden she carried. She felt the pain of her son's suicide and the shame and guilt of her lies about how he died. I encouraged her to start telling her truth by confiding in some close friends. Through these conversations, she could reclaim some of her power regarding her son's tragic death.

I had this scenario happen over and over again. Whenever I mentioned how Brian died, probably one out of three people indicated either someone in their family or someone they knew had taken their own life. In this way, I'm happy to be part of changing the conversation around suicide, to reduce the stigma around speaking the truth of what had happened, and to remove any associated or perceived shame.

It is okay to talk about suicide.

CHAPTER 8

The Stigma of Suicide

We need to change the culture of this topic and make it OK to speak about mental health and suicide.
— Luke Richardson, professional hockey player and coach

Throughout my life, I've had times when I've needed to deal with suicide. Each time, I have felt the pain of the stigma that surrounds this issue, which has sometimes made me question my actions and reactions.

My first experience of suicide occurred when I was young. I heard stories about the murder-suicide that happened at the end of our street, but I did not know the family. Other than being a little scared to walk past the house as I got older (rumour had it that the house was haunted), I didn't have any meaningful connection to it. Suicide was something that happened to faceless, nameless people.

In 1974, when I was in high school, people were less willing to discuss suicide than they are now. It was a taboo subject. Suicide was something that happened to strangers that I didn't know, or I read about it in books or saw it on television. It didn't happen to close friends or acquaintances. Then three students at my school took their own lives within a three-month period. My friends and I were shocked that people our age who we knew and saw at school every day were gone. Although school administrators never publicly announced the cause of each death, whispers in the hallway said they died by suicide. The news spread like wildfire.

One of the girls was in my circle of friends. I had known Julia (not her real name), for four years. Her father was a minister. I remember Julia sharing about her father's shame for her when she bought the album *Jesus Christ Superstar.* Her father thought that album contained blasphemous lyrics. Personally, I never understood his protest about the words of these songs. Despite knowing about the severity of her family's moral codes, I had no idea of the depth of Julia's emotional pain. To me, she was always this cheerful, fun-loving girl with a mischievous grin. We never knew why Julia killed herself but, sadly, we decided Julia killed herself because of her father. Our circle of friends wanted someone to blame.

I never knew Julia's father, but I want to believe he loved his daughter immensely. They simply had different views on how to live life. I could never reconcile her death being solely the result of conflict with her father. Probably I felt this way because I had conflict with my father, and I didn't want to kill myself. I told myself there had to be more to the story. I wished Julia had been able to share with us, her friends, her true thoughts and feelings about her life. It was as if we never knew what was really going on for her.

Kids talked about Julia's suicide in hushed tones in the hallway. "Did you hear she killed herself last night?" This question was followed by shocked expressions, looks of fear, and uncomfortable silences. Inevitably, everyone wanted to know why. We had our theory. Others asked different questions. Did she have a fight with her boyfriend? Was she pregnant? Of course, we didn't discuss her death in the classroom. It was as if the teachers didn't want to broach the subject, possibly fearing that talking about suicide might open the door to copycat behaviour. The lack of discussion just emphasized how talking about suicide was not okay. And then it happened again, not once but twice.

Two seniors then died by suicide, one male, one female. I did not personally know them, but both were honour students who had many friends. Before this happened, I thought only loners disconnected from others died by suicide. My friends and I never talked about suicide until all of this happened. For the rest of the year, I cannot remember talking about much else. The three students' deaths affected all of us. It was as if we were always waiting to see who would be next.

Having three suicides within our school could be categorized as a suicide cluster. Fifteen years later, Madelyn Gould (et al.) would report that a suicide cluster is an excessive number of suicides occurring in close temporal and/or geographical proximity.[16] Clusters occur primarily with teenagers or young adults. Mental health is not contagious, but there is evidence to show behaviours can be copied and spread quickly within a group.[17]

Perhaps my experience with the three suicides in high school helped prepare me for the next tragedy, an even closer connection, one that truly shook me to my core. About a year after high school, my friend Amy dated a guy named Joe from our graduating class. I had gone to school with Amy for six years, and we became close friends through our love of drama. Amy was short and curvy with blonde hair and a bit of a European accent she denied existed. She was smart, funny, and had an incredibly compassionate heart.

Joe was a genius and a social outcast. He was tall and lanky with red hair and freckles. I don't think any of us knew what to do with Joe. He had always struggled to fit in and had been ridiculed by others because he talked in a way that no one could understand. Today he would be referred to as Sheldon Cooper from *The Big Bang Theory*. Back then, being different was even more taboo than it is now. Now we have a greater social awareness around how harmful bullying can be. But when I was growing up, we thought bullying was just "kids being kids." Now, I can't imagine the pain Joe experienced daily.

Amy looked past his quirks and had a brief relationship with him. When she decided they were not a good fit and broke off the relationship, he took his own life, but not before mailing her a long letter, pages full of how she had ruined his life and was responsible for his suicide.

After she received the letter, Amy showed up at the bank where I worked. Her skin was pale, and her eyes gave her a haunted look. She nervously asked if I could meet her for lunch. Amy looked like she was about to cry. I turned to my supervisor and asked if I could go to lunch immediately. We sat at an outside table in an area made for downtown workers to eat their lunch, set in the middle of the avenue, blocked off from traffic. The sun was shining, and it was a beautiful summer day.

"This came in the mail today. I want you to read it," Amy said, her hand shaking as she slid the manila folder across the concrete table.

"What is it?" I asked.

"Open it and you'll see" she replied, her voice barely audible.

There was no return address on the envelope. I pulled the letter out, and my jaw dropped when I saw it was from Joe. He had died only a few days before. My stomach turned, reading what seemed to be incoherent ramblings that blamed her repeatedly for how cruel she was to break his heart.

Amy and I talked at length about Joe, her decision to leave the relationship, and the letter. In the end, Amy knew she was not responsible for his death. She understood he was a troubled young man. Nevertheless, reading his letter was devastating for her. I have always thought that was the cruelest thing he could have ever done.

We weren't surprised Joe ended his life. It is unfortunate we are not surprised when someone who is considered "odd" dies by suicide. However, when someone well respected and revered dies this way, we are shocked by the news. For example, Robin Williams was famous, highly regarded, and loved by millions. When I heard he ended his life, my body went numb. Many years had passed since Brian's suicide, but the news of Williams' death sent me right back to the moment when I read my husband's suicide note.

Robin Williams? How could this be even possible? I first thought it was a hoax. Robin Williams was hilariously funny, wildly successful, and had amazing friends. It seemed to me he lived a charmed life. *Robin had it all. Why would he do this?* After his death, his wife, Susan, shared the results of his autopsy, indicating he had Lewy Body Dementia. Initially, he had been diagnosed with the early stages of Parkinson's Disease. How terrifying that news must have been to him. How scary it must have been for someone with such a brilliant mind and comedic talents to start experiencing a loss of capacity and control. As details emerged about Williams' long-term suffering with depression, I grew angry. We can be so compassionate when we hear someone has cancer or heart disease. We would never tell someone with cancer they aren't trying hard enough to beat it. We would never encourage someone in a wheelchair to use the power of intention to get up and walk. But when we hear of someone's mental health issues, we often feel judgement, apathy, or even disdain. We tell them to "Just get over it," or "You aren't trying hard enough to get better." In this way, we dismiss and minimize the enormous pain people with depression experience. We hold people with mental health issues to a different standard than those with physical disabilities.

Studies have shown that globally, 350 million people suffer from depression. According to the American Psychiatric Association, depression is a common and serious medical illness that negatively affects how you feel, the way you think, and how you act. Depression causes feelings of sadness and/or a loss of interest in activities once enjoyed. It can lead to a variety of emotional and physical problems and can decrease a person's ability to function at work and at home. Sadly, fewer than half of the people who suffer from depression will seek treatment.[18] Most of us want to feel normal, to not stick out too much, to feel accepted as part of the tribe. Due to social norms, it takes a level of courage to reach out for help because depression can be perceived as a weakness. In our competitive world, one that emphasizes the survival of the fittest, being considered a "weak link" could make someone feel incredibly vulnerable and scared.

The Oxford Dictionary defines stigma as "a mark of disgrace associated with a particular circumstance, quality, or person." Stigmatization comes from not understanding, not accepting, and fear. Fear of being stigmatized often prevents those struggling with mental health issues to seek help. Also, like too many people, they may not know or accept that their condition is biological and no fault of their own. Kevin Caruso, founder of suicide.org, explains: "Because of the stigma [the ignorant stigma, mind you] that still exists concerning mental illness, many people who need help do not seek it. Even though there is clear scientific data that indicates irrefutably that a physical connection exists with most mental disorders, many people still stigmatize others because they stupidly hold on to the misguided beliefs of yesteryear that people with mental disorders are weak or just lack will power."[19]

I studied suicide in college as part of my course work in psychology. I wrote a paper on the subject, which led to my desire to become certified in suicide prevention training. After Brian died, I became somewhat obsessed with searching for answers, mostly to understand why it happened. I wanted to break through the stigma attached to Brian's suicide, to wash it out of existence as if it were a dark stain on my clothing for all to see. I read books, went for individual and group counselling, and learned how to search the Internet for information. Whenever a news story, documentary, or article appeared referring to suicide, I gave it my full attention. I wanted to know all that I could on this subject.

I grew angry when I read an article on the stigmatization of suicide and how it plays out within the helping profession. An article in *The Atlantic* from January 2015 indicated that some psychiatrists avoid seeing patients who are at high risk of suicide because it is the number one reason for wrongful death lawsuits brought against mental health practitioners. The author went on to say the risk of successful malpractice suits is quite low, with clinicians winning up to 80 percent of these cases. After reading this article, I felt frustrated beyond words. If psychiatrists avoid patients and patients avoid psychiatrists, then the suicidal person who is reluctant to seek help and the practitioner who is reluctant to provide help creates a hopeless, vicious cycle.[20]

On October 10, 2012, the World Health Organization (WHO) called for the end of stigmatizing depression and other mental health disorders. In honour of World Mental Health Day, they also called for better access to treatment for those suffering from mental health disorders. The two main challenges for addressing and decreasing suicide across the globe include cultural taboos regarding discussing suicide and inconsistent data about suicide because many countries have not made suicide prevention and documentation part of their health priorities. People's unwillingness to openly discuss suicide may also lead to false reporting about the cause of death, particularly in countries where suicide is illegal, because the surviving family may be at risk.

The WHO Mental Health Action Plan 2013-2020 addressed the need for improved mental health services globally including a target of reducing the suicide rate in participating countries by 10 percent by the year 2020. In 2019, the action plan was extended to 2030, and in 2021, new and updated indicators and implementation options were added.

The plan has four main objectives:

1. to strengthen effective leadership and governance for mental health;
2. to provide comprehensive, integrated and responsive mental health and social care services in community-based settings;
3. to implement strategies for promotion and prevention in mental health;
4. to strengthen information systems, evidence and research for mental health.[21]

First, we need to talk about mental health and suicide. In some ways, I viewed Robin Williams' suicide as the last gift he gave to the world. If it could happen to him, no one is immune. His death prompted more discussion about suicide, depression, and mental health issues than at any other time I can remember. When a famous person dies by suicide, there can be a fear of contagion. According to *Newsweek*, when Robin Williams died, calls to suicide prevention hotlines increased dramatically. One month before his suicide, the National Suicide Prevention Lifeline received about 3,500 calls a day. The day after his suicide, the number of calls tripled; there were 50 percent more calls during the week that followed. On September 22, 2020, the US House of Representatives passed several pieces of critical suicide prevention legislation, including the National Suicide Hotline Designation Act, which establishes 988 as a unique, new, three-digit mental health and suicide crisis hotline. The new number is a critical step in providing services to those in emotional crisis and launched on July 16, 2022. In addition, in December 2020, the Canadian government unanimously passed a motion to implement a three-digit national suicide prevention hotline. Support for the motion was directly impacted by the rising number of suicides and attempted suicides during the pandemic. The hope is to break the stigma of mental health and eliminate barriers for those seeking help.

While these new actions are encouraging, the conversation around mental health and suicide often comes to the forefront immediately after the suicide of a famous person, and then, unfortunately, talk fades away until another death occurs. Fans hold vigils, post on various social media platforms in support of mental health, and other famous people weigh in on how they didn't see it coming. They all talk about how we need to change the conversation regarding suicide, but then they abandon the conversation until someone else dies by suicide. The cycle repeats.

A young woman I followed on social media wanted to make sure this conversation continued. She was a voice for erasing the stigma attached to mental health issues. Amy Bleuel, creator of Project Semicolon, made an indelible mark on the world—literally. She had a tattoo of a semicolon on her left arm to remind herself to keep going in life, even when she felt like stopping. According to her bio on the Project Semicolon website, Bleuel faced many obstacles in her life, including bullying, rejection, the suicide of her father, self-injury, addiction, abuse, and even rape. She chose the semicolon because that is the punctuation a writer uses when they could have ended a sentence with a period but decided not to stop. Bleuel said, "In literature, an author uses a semicolon to not end a sentence but to continue on. We see it as you are the author, and your life is the sentence. You're choosing to keep going." In April 2013, Bleuel encouraged others to use the semicolon. It didn't have to be a tattoo; people could draw one on their wrist and post a picture for others to see on platforms such as Facebook and Instagram. It's estimated that millions of people shared photos, drawn, or tattooed on their bodies as part of a movement to remove shame and stigma surrounding mental health.[22]

Tragically, Amy Bleuel took her own life in March 2017. Her willingness to speak openly about mental health and suicide inspired me. Not only was she willing to be vulnerable, but she empowered others to be in dialogue regarding their own journey and created a safe community for others to share. Bleuel made a difference in her short life.

R U OK, another powerful movement, started in Australia in 2005. This brilliant initiative, held on the second Thursday of September, began as a man's response to his father's suicide. This son believed that by creating connections with others, particularly those who are struggling, "We can create a world where we're all connected and are protected from suicide." The movement's message is both simple and profound, encouraging everyone to ask people around them the question, "Are you okay?"[23]

Many times in my life my Spidey senses told me something was amiss with a friend or family member, and I would ask them if they were okay. At first, I was reluctant to come right out and ask if they had thoughts of hurting themselves, or, more specifically, if they were contemplating suicide. I'm more willing to ask now. I can't take the chance of missing the cues, even if it makes me feel uncomfortable. I may be the one who gets them into dialogue before suicide becomes their only option. If I'm wrong, I'm okay with that. At least I asked.

I could see my close friend Heather showing signs of depression after a bad breakup with her boyfriend. She never wanted to go out. Instead, she preferred to stay home and watch television. When I did drop over to her house uninvited, Heather looked like she had not showered for several days. I was surprised she even answered the door. Reluctantly, she invited me in since I had driven halfway across the city to see her. After making small talk, I took a deep breath and began. "I'm really concerned about you," I told her. "Are you having thoughts of suicide?"

Heather's eyes widened and she promised me she was not suicidal. "Thank you for asking though," she said. "That takes a lot of guts to ask the question. Given Brian's death, I can see why you would ask me that question."

"I love you my friend. I don't want to repeat the mistake I made with Brian when I didn't ask him if he was suicidal."

"I get that," Heather replied. "I just need some time to get over my heartbreak."

"If you start to have suicidal thoughts, do you promise me you'll call?" I asked.

"Yes. I promise."

Typically, people who are contemplating suicide give clues, either through their words or actions, about how okay (or not) they really are. I asked my friends how they handle similar situations, and some have answered they don't want to give the person who is struggling any ideas. Trust me, if suicide is not on their radar already, chances are slim to none you're going to be the one who plants it in their consciousness.

Grief experienced from a loved one dying is hard enough. Grieving someone dying by suicide adds another dimension of difficulty for survivors. There is an added layer of shame and judgement, along with a fear they could bear some responsibility for the suicide of their loved one. On top of all that, they may now worry that suicide is hereditary, causing surviving family members additional anxiety—even panic.

In my case, I had to constantly tell myself I wasn't to blame and had nothing to be ashamed of. If people chose to shun or avoid me because of Brian's suicide, so be it. I wasn't in control of their reactions. Some people did retreat from my life after Brian's death. Initially, I felt hurt, but now I realize they were coming up against their own beliefs, opinions, and thoughts about suicide. Or maybe they just didn't know what to say. Researcher Jacqueline Cvinar explains that surviving friends and family must deal with a "complex psychological impact of the act," and this impact is "further complicated by the societal perception that the act of suicide is a failure by the victim and the family to deal with some emotional issue and ultimately society affixes blame for the loss on the survivors." Her work demonstrates that suicide is so stressful for those grieving that clinical intervention may be needed.[24]

When Brian died in December 2000, I didn't have access to the number of studies and books now available about suicide. I recently searched on Amazon using "books on suicide," which generated more than 1,000 hits. When I went to the library in 2001, I could find only eight books on suicide. Psychologists have since written extensively about suicide and how to support survivors. Suicide-attempt survivors also share their stories about why they tried to take their own life, and survivors of suicide loss share their stories of grief and recovery.

Fortunately, I did find a book that became my lifeline: *No Time to Say Goodbye: Surviving the Suicide of a Loved One* by Carla Fine, published eleven months before Brian's death.[25] Ms. Fine's story of surviving her husband Harry's suicide became the balm to my open wound. Her husband was a respected New York physician and took his own life in 1989. In her book, she talked candidly about finding her husband's body and the trauma she experienced afterward. She shared her journey of self-discovery and related stories of healing from others who were part of her suicide bereavement group.

Ms. Fine wrote: "Suicide is different from other deaths. We who are left behind cannot direct our anger at the unfairness of a deadly disease or a random accident or a murderous stranger. Instead, we grieve for the very person who has taken our loved one's life. Before we can even begin to accept our loss, we must deal with the reasons for it and the gradual recognition that we may never know what happened or why."[26]

She got me. I was not alone. Someone out there understood the pain, anguish, shame, and confusion I was experiencing. If she could survive and be willing to talk about her journey, so could I. I am eternally grateful for Ms. Fine's decision to go public with her story. Her willingness to share inspired me to share mine. It took years, however, to heal enough and feel ready to offer others my own perspective, wisdom, and encouragement.

Despite the prevalence of depression and other mental health issues, taboos against discussing them are still very strong. People can mobilize against a tangible disease. Think about breast cancer. We can see women with gaunt faces and sometimes disfigured bodies, wearing scarves to hide their bald heads after chemotherapy, and we can immediately empathize with their situation. These kinds of images propelled the marketing of wearing pink T-shirts and buying pink merchandise resulting in millions (if not billions) of dollars raised for research to find a cure.

But depression and mental health issues can't be visualized in the same way. We fear what we cannot see inside someone's head. The success of pink campaigns has been to mobilize women demanding change. Rallying to address mental health issues has not become as big of a business machine like breast cancer research—yet.

How do those of us directly impacted by suicide mobilize dollars for research to cure depression, bipolar disease, and other mental health issues that can lead to suicide? There has not yet been a global movement like the ALS Ice Bucket Challenge to raise funds. Groups such as the Stop Suicide Campaign, the Canadian Association for Suicide Prevention, and the American Foundation for Suicide Prevention are dedicated to raising awareness and support for these issues. In addition, Individuals have raised money in numerous ways, including social media campaigns, music festival events, and marathon races.

Since 2010, Bell Canada, a major telecommunications company, has held an annual campaign to raise awareness regarding mental health called "Bell's Let's Talk Day." This one-day advertising campaign occurs each January. Money is donated to mental health funds based on the number of social media and communication "interactions" that include a branded hashtag. Their goal is to focus on anti-stigma, care and access, workplace mental health, and research. Bell's total donation to mental health initiatives now stands at almost $130 million, with a plan to bring that amount to at least $155 million by 2025.[27]

The stigma of suicide has been reduced over the years through education and the willingness of those impacted to share their stories. There are closed Facebook groups where survivors can find support from other survivors. On websites such as Stop Suicide, The Mighty, and The American Foundation for Suicide Prevention, people can find information and resources. In Canada, the Canadian Mental Health Association has a suicide prevention department. They provide counselling for those who are suicidal and group bereavement services for survivors of suicide loss.

We are moving in the right direction, yet we have a long way to go. Opening the dialogue around suicide is the first step. Also, removing the shame and judgement around seeking help is key. Addressing bullying, especially cyberbullying, is a must. We need to adopt universal acceptance that it is okay to not be okay. As we continue the conversation around mental health, death, and suicide, the stigma will continue to dissipate.

When talking to a new person, I struggled to know what to say when it came to my marital status. Depending on the person and circumstance, I sometimes wanted to say Brian died of cancer, if only to elicit what I thought would bring more sympathy or so the conversation did not come to a screeching halt. I am not a good liar though, and I tried my best to stay in integrity by telling the truth. This is typically how the conversation would go:

"Are you married?"
"No, I'm widowed."
"You're so young; did he have cancer?"
"No, sadly, it was suicide."

Awkward silence. After a brief apology, the topic was changed, or the conversation ended. People just did not know what to say next. If they showed any interest in furthering the conversation, I was more than willing to continue. Most did not. They became uncomfortable, and I could see their eyes wandering, looking for an escape route. Some thought it best to try and say something positive, to cheer me up. Often, I was met with platitudes or clichés: you are so strong; God only gives you what you can handle. Those that did engage in conversation usually had a shared or similar experience and were more open to talk about suicide.

My decision to be open regarding Brian's suicide wasn't easy, but in doing so, I felt I was taking back my power. I won't lie. Since there is still a stigma of shame attached to suicide, at times I just want to stay silent. In retrospect, I'm at peace with my choice to tell my story. Talking about it, naming it, is the first step to remove the stigma and start the healing process. Through courageous, authentic conversations, we can become better informed and compassionate regarding suicide.

I choose to speak the truth.

CHAPTER 9

The Club No One Wants to Join

Yo, I know what you're goin' through
We all been there, shit, join the club
— *LeMarvin, lyrics to "Join the Club"*

I remember back in elementary school when teams were picked for a sporting event or a spelling bee. As others were chosen, the tension built inside me, and I prayed to be picked next, so I didn't have to suffer the embarrassment of being last. This feeling of not being in control of my destiny while others determined my fate has always bugged the hell out of me. I felt that way with Brian's suicide. His act determined my fate, forcing me to join a club I didn't want to belong to. I had no say in the matter.

According to the Center for Disease Control (CDC), there was a 30 percent increase in suicides between 2000 and 2018 and a decline in 2019 and 2020. The most recent statistic reveals 45,979 Americans died by suicide in 2020, (approximately 126 people each day or one every 11 minutes). Overall, suicide ranked among the top nine leading causes of death in the United States for ages ten to sixty-four. However, it was the second leading cause of death for those ten to fourteen years of age and twenty-five to thirty-four. The suicide rate among males was three to four times higher than among females. In 2020, 12.2 million adults aged eighteen or older reported having serious thoughts of suicide, and 1.2 million adults attempted suicide. Shockingly, in 2019, there were two and a half as many suicides as homicides.[28] Public perception is there are more homicides, probably due to the media coverage available. I respect the media providing privacy when there is a suicide, but when we are inundated with coverage of mass shootings and murder, it stands to reason we think of the threat of homicide instead of suicide. It's scary to think about a greater threat closer to home.

According to the CDC, for every suicide, seven to ten people are directly affected. For the purposes of this chapter, let's just go with the number eight and do the math: almost 46,000 suicides per year in the United States, multiplied by eight and you have over 368,000 people each year joining the Survivors of Suicide Club. That is more than the population of Anaheim, California and just under the population of Cleveland, Ohio.

The main source of data for suicide rates in Canada is the Canadian Vital Statistics Death Database that collects demographic and medical [cause of death] information annually from all provincial and territorial vital statistics registries. Statistics Canada has pointed out, however, that suicides may be under-reported in this data source, given the "difficult nature of classifying suicide and the time lag in determining this as the cause of death, which may vary from year to year and from one region to another."[29]

A Statistics Canada report from 2020 stated that eleven people died by suicide each day, or around 4,000 a year, and is the second-highest cause of death for young people between the ages of fifteen to thirty-four.[30] Multiply that by eight and 32,000 new members join the club each year in Canada. That is about the size of Pointe-Claire, Quebec, and more than Leduc, Alberta.

The World Health Organization estimates that more than 700,000 people die by suicide each year internationally. If we go with only eight people being directly impacted, 5.6 million people a year become club members. That figure is larger than Los Angeles, California and more than one-sixth the population of Canada. In other words, *every single year* an astounding number of people are impacted by suicide.

Joining the Suicide Survivors Club was not something I ever thought would happen to me. I am in good company. Of course, no one expects to join this club with its very costly admission fees. Once Brian died by suicide, I became a card-carrying member, and there's no return policy on that. Many supportive, caring people are in the club. But no one wants to be there, and it's heartbreaking when someone else joins.

This club is not widely discussed. Membership is typically kept a secret until someone else metaphorically raises their hand and divulges that they've lost a loved one to suicide. For me, when that occurs, I feel less alone. I know that person understands what it's like to be in this club. I don't have to explain myself as much. In my experience, sharing my story has opened the door for others to admit their membership and tell their stories. Most people don't want to talk about the experience but finding another club member can be healing. In fact, I believe a higher power has brought us together for just that reason. Sadly, we feel a connection that otherwise might not be there. I have experienced some amazing heart-to-heart connections with other survivors.

Even though we have a shared experience of being survivors, our journeys are quite unique. My experience of losing my husband to suicide is not the same as the experience of the mother who lost her daughter or the son who lost his mother. My experience is not even the same as another woman who lost her husband to suicide. I cannot profess to know what it's like to have a child die by suicide, and I pray that I never do. But there are elements of the experience that we can all relate to, including the social taboos regarding suicide, the guilt of not knowing the intentions of our loved one who died, and the distress, including guilt, of not being able to save or stop them.

I carried additional guilt for not recognizing the signs of Brian's depression and spiral to suicide. I had worked with suicidal clients over the years and spent countless hours counselling them, often talking well into the night just to keep them alive, either in person or on the phone. At the secure treatment facility where I worked, I spent numerous hours in the emergency room watching clients who had cut themselves receive stitches. Even though it was a secure facility, somehow kids snuck in razor blades and shared them with the other kids. After taking one too many kids to be stitched up, I decided it was time to switch gears. I was transferred to a desk job at the centre doing data entry during daytime hours. I needed to take care of my own mental health.

Three months before Brian died, a beautiful seventeen-year-old girl I had worked with while in secure treatment took her own life, shortly after being discharged. She came from an abusive home and had spent time in several foster homes where she was sexually abused numerous times. She had difficulty sleeping and loved to sit on the floor outside the staff office and talk. Even though the youth were supposed to stay in their rooms at night, my colleague and I broke the rules and let her sit and talk. It was a time when someone could listen, really listen to what she was sharing. She loved to talk and had the most infectious laugh. She had golden brown long hair, big green eyes, and enviably long eyelashes. It was her good looks and vulnerable nature that led to her being sucked into the world of prostitution. She was in our care to get her off the streets and help her start a new path. After being released, she returned to the streets and ended up taking her own life. My heart broke.

I was still grieving her death when Brian died. *How could I have not seen the signs in Brian?* I held myself to a higher standard. I blamed myself for not seeing what was right in front of me. *I was a trained professional for God's sake. How blind could I have been?* Many others talk about not seeing the signs. Let me tell you, it doesn't matter whether you know what to look for or not, it's hard to recognize or acknowledge the signs when it's someone you love.

Dr. Brené Brown, a renowned research professor at the University of Houston, says the difference between shame and guilt by explaining that guilt is adaptive and helpful, while shame is neither helpful nor productive. Guilt is "holding something we've done or failed to do up against our values and who we want to be." Shame is "the intensely painful feeling or experience of believing that we are flawed and therefore unworthy of love and belonging – something we've experienced, done, or failed to do makes us unworthy of connection."[31] Brown sums it up nicely in Dare to Lead by saying Guilt = I did something bad and Shame = I am bad.[32]

Brown refers to shame as the swampland of the soul. It's the little voice inside of us that says we are not good enough or has us ask ourselves, "Who do you think you are?" Shame is associated with addiction, suicide, eating disorders, and violence.

According to Brown, women experience shame differently than men. For women, shame is "Do it all and never let them see you sweat." For men, shame is "Do not let them think you are weak." I believe this fear of being viewed as weak led to Brian's suicide. He had started his own business in financial services and struggled to close deals with prospective clients. I was the main breadwinner, and he felt ashamed of not being a good provider for our family. With his love for all things military, that translated to "death before dishonour."

I tried my best not to accept shame or blame for what had happened. This was often easier said than done. Although I initially beat myself up for not seeing the signs, I believed I was not at fault for Brian's death. Anytime I started to slip, thinking *maybe I could have done something to change the outcome,* I gave myself a stern talking-to: *Who do you think you are?* For me, it was necessary to stay in dialogue regarding my thoughts and feelings as I went through a period of not trusting myself. Over time, my confidence improved, and I felt able to rely on my positive self-talk.

Brown's distinctions helped me understand why I carried guilt but not shame. I felt I could have done or said things differently or behaved in a different way. I could have been more empathetic. I felt guilt for my actions or inaction. To help with my processing, I spent time in meditation and prayer, looking to forgive myself. I sought out various healers who worked with me to resolve my guilt. One of the most powerful healings occurred during a regression therapy session. At the end, it was evident that guilt was the prominent theme. The therapist explained there are two kinds of guilt. One is true guilt, where your actions have directly caused harm. The other is assumed guilt, where you take on something out of your control as your own. It was an "aha" moment for me. I was taking on assumed guilt. Knowing that made it easier to let it go. On the other hand, I do not believe I am a bad person for not seeing the signs, for not creating a different outcome.

Three weeks after Brian's suicide, I was sitting in a restaurant with my two children having breakfast. Through the skylight came a dazzling sunbeam; as I stared at the light, I felt a surge of joy. It felt like a sign from heaven that everything was going to be all right. It was the first time since his death that I'd experienced joy, however fleeting. I reveled in the moment as the previous days had been so dark and full of grief that I didn't think I would ever experience joy again. I remembered a quote by Edith Warton: "There are two ways of spreading the light: to be the candle or to be the mirror that reflects it." In that moment, I saw the possibility of being a mirror, with the hope that someday I could be the candle.

Late that afternoon, I returned a casserole dish to a neighbour, who had been kind enough to bring us food in the days after Brian's death. Her son played on the same basketball team as David, and although I did not know her well, we had become friends sitting in the stands as we watched our boys play ball.

"How are you doing?" she asked with a warm smile.

"I felt joy for the first time today," I naively told her, thinking she would be happy for me.

Her face fell; her eyes changed from kind and understanding to cold and judgmental. She looked at me as if I were some sort of monster. How could I possibly admit to feeling joy when my husband had just taken his life? Guilt grabbed hold of me and held me in a vise grip. I quickly gave her the dish and made my departure.

At a time when I was so vulnerable, I looked to others to determine whether I was doing this grieving thing "right." I questioned for some time whether it was okay to feel joy and finally decided it was. In this case, a woman was following her culture and tradition of grieving that did not include expressing joy, and she reacted accordingly. Differences in culture or religious beliefs can have a huge impact on how someone navigates through their grief. That was her way. I needed to find mine.

One of the smartest things I did in the year following Brian's death was attend an eight-week Survivors of Suicide Bereavement Group provided through our local Canadian Mental Health Association (CMHA). I felt lucky to live in a city where these resources were available. Seven other people had also recently become part of the club. They each had their own story of what had happened. Some had been blindsided as I was, and several had been living with family or friends who had finally completed after numerous attempts. For those survivors, it was a nightmare never knowing if, as one woman put it, "Today was the day" that their loved one would complete their suicide. I cannot imagine living in such fear.

It's human nature to compare our stories with others. It's a comfort to hold up our own horror stories against others, a way to say "Well, at least I didn't go through that." I found myself listening to their stories and being grateful Brian did not die at home or in front of me or use a more violent method. In the end, the result was the same, but the way someone dies by suicide can vary dramatically. I was one of the few in the group that found a suicide note.

The group facilitator shared information regarding suicide and coping strategies. Although she had experience working with suicidal people and survivors of suicide loss, she had not personally gone through the experience. Nevertheless, she was able to provide a safe space for the eight of us, three men and five women, to share our journeys. It did not take long to connect. Three of the participants had lost a son or a daughter, the youngest being thirteen. One man lost his wife of thirty-eight years. One woman lost her father, and two other women lost their husbands.

At the first session, we selected a seat at a rectangular table in a medium-sized meeting room. After a round of introductions and some general discussion about what the group was intended to achieve, we each had ten minutes to tell our story of loss. Most of us had joined the club within the previous six months, so it was still fresh. The multiple boxes of Kleenex on the table saw repeated use.

Each week we looked at a different aspect of our lives. How were we handling finances? How were we managing with our families? What were we doing for self-care? We learned about the stages of grief and how to navigate feeling overwhelmed. We learned how being in dialogue was a key to feeling better.

At the end of the eight weeks, most said how much they would like to stay in contact and get together regularly. I knew this group had served its purpose for me, and I did not choose to stay connected. I felt my story had been heard. But I think about these people from time to time. I wonder how their journey has been, and if time has helped to heal their hearts.

Several years after completing the group, I was invited to attend a conference for survivors of suicide sponsored by CMHA. More than 200 people attended, each touched by suicide in some fashion. A local media personality was the guest speaker; I was impressed with her candor about surviving her brother's suicide. She talked about how she was blindsided and shared her experience of guilt and shame. She was one of us and took a courageous step to be vulnerable and not worry about her public image. Suicide is an equalizer. It can touch any family, regardless of their culture or socioeconomic status.

Anyone can be a member of the Survivor's Club. The good news is there are a lot of caring, supportive people who are already there. Survivors can now connect through social media. There are several private groups for survivors on Facebook, moderated by people with suicide loss experience. In each of the groups I participate in, people are encouraged to share what is coming up for them in this safe environment. There is no judgement or shaming. When friends and family no longer want to hear about the suicide, the people on these sites are willing to listen. There are longtime club members and those who are new. In my experience, each new person is welcomed with kindness and compassion.

I have witnessed great empathy and support, regardless of how long ago the suicide occurred. This is especially vital for those who live in areas where supportive resources are not available. I wish social media had existed for me when Brian died. I can only imagine the difference it could have made for me.

If you are a survivor of suicide, I encourage you to connect with others and talk about your experiences, feelings, and journey. Get professional help. Join a support group either in person or online. Get in dialogue, tell your story.

You don't need to go through this alone.

CHAPTER 10

What to Say When Someone Dies by Suicide

There is no grief like the grief that does not speak.
— Henry Wadsworth Longfellow

One of the questions I am frequently asked is, "What do I say to the surviving family when someone dies by suicide?" Although I do not have the magic answer, I often find it easier to tell them what not to say. Over the years, in talking with other survivors, I have heard of some horrific things people have said to them: "It's your fault he is dead." "You're lucky you don't have to bring flowers home to your wife." Or take what happened to me when a neighbour came over less than a week after Brian died to give her condolences. After sharing pleasantries, she finally uttered the words that stabbed my heart, "Brian was such a great guy. It's such a shame he is burning in hell right now." My jaw dropped. *Did she just say that?* Maybe she thought I shared her "Christian" viewpoint. *That is the least Christian thing anyone has ever said to me.* Too stunned to tear her a new one, I asked her to leave.

People say stupid things. Some make me shake my head and think, *"What kind of person says such a thing?"* In those moments, I struggle to believe people do the best they can with what they know. Instead, I see them as insensitive assholes.

What irks me the most, even today, is when I hear, "They took the easy way out." I cannot imagine the mental anguish Brian went through while making his plan. I choose to believe that is true for any person that dies by suicide. There is nothing easy about it. End of story. I also take umbrage when I hear, "They died a coward's death." Suicide is not a cowardly act, nor is it an act of bravery. It is the act of someone who is desperate. Someone who is mentally unstable. To say it is cowardly is perpetuating the stigma surrounding suicide.

In addition, if someone told a joke or a story involving death or even said, "I would just die," "I would kill myself," or "I could just slit my wrists" in a cavalier manner, I became extremely sensitive. Of course, they intended to be funny or were just exaggerating, but they were often unaware of the rawness I still felt from Brian's death and how such seemingly innocuous and common sayings hurt me deeply. I wanted to scream, "Don't you know my husband just killed himself?" or "How insensitive can you be?" But, of course, they didn't know I had not shared my story. My polite response was usually to nod and appear to let what they said go, suffering in silence.

I'm now less likely to let it pass. Instead, I calmly say, "My first husband died by suicide." Then I watch as they usually become very uncomfortable and apologetic. I want to think I'm not being passive-aggressive. I'm just trying to raise consciousness. Okay, I admit, maybe I'm a little passive-aggressive.

At Brian's celebration of life, I was apprehensive about what people would say to me. Most people wanted to say something; however, many seemed awkward or just didn't know what to say. "I'm so sorry for your loss," they'd begin, which seemed like the polite and politically correct thing to say. In the past, I've said the same to others who were grieving. Talking to someone who has just had a loved one die can be uncomfortable. Talking to them about their loved one who has just died by suicide ups the ante.

Saying "I'm sorry for your loss" may not feel enough, but I was never offended by it; I always felt grateful for the sentiment behind the statement. I did not subscribe to the thought that using the phrase was trite or cliché. I chose to look at the intent behind the message, and I preferred someone say that to me than nothing at all. I found silence more hurtful and awkward. I have used the phrase many times to others, and I usually followed it up by asking, "How are you doing?" If you are going with the standard lines, I prefer, "Please accept my condolences," or "You have my deepest sympathy."

My friend Dee cut through the crap at the memorial service.

She came up to me, gave me a huge hug, and said, "It really sucks he killed himself. I am really pissed off with him. How are you holding up?"

I immediately felt myself relax. Dee spoke my language. We had only been friends for a couple of years, but I found myself drawn to her instantly when we met. She was a no-bullshit, say-it-the-way-it-is kind of gal. Dee became my ride-or-die: she is my Louise, I'm her Thelma. At the service, I instantly connected with Dee's words. She said out loud what was playing in my head. I thought, *She gets me; she understands.* Dee didn't just say platitudes or what she thought I wanted to hear. I felt her authenticity and true concern for me.

Others at the service who didn't know me as well, like one of Brian's work colleagues, also showed their authenticity. Taking my hand, he looked me in the eyes and softly said, "I'm not just saying this. If you need anything, and I mean anything, please call me." He then slipped his business card into my hand. On the back of the card, he wrote his home number and drew a small heart. His heartfelt words moved me. He wasn't afraid to be real during a moment of tragedy.

Having someone say something, anything, was better than silence for me, if their intention was to be helpful, not hurtful. I was afraid others were judging me by Brian's actions. When people chose to say nothing, I interpreted it as them being judgmental, and I made up a story that they blamed me. Hearing people acknowledge Brian's death helped me to feel connected. I was hurting so deeply, and hearing words of sympathy or condolences made me feel less alone. I also really appreciated hearing others say:

I can't imagine what you're going through.
I'm so sorry you're going through this.
My heart is broken for you.
I'm thinking of you.
You're not to blame for what he did.
I don't know what to say. I just want you to know I'm here for you.

I felt the greatest connection with those who maintained eye contact when saying how sorry they were. Anyone with darting eyes seemed insincere, and I questioned their words. I sensed they were uncomfortable, and their nervousness made me uneasy. A great tip for centering yourself when having a difficult conversation (including an argument) is to stand with your feet slightly pointed inwards. This grounds your energy field and helps you to remain calm.

One of the greatest gifts people would give me was to just listen. I love the phrase "God gave us two ears and one mouth." People asked how I was doing and then allowed me to talk. They didn't interrupt and didn't try to fix it for me; they just listened. I like to think they were practicing the eighty-twenty rule. They let me talk 80 percent of the time, and they got the remaining 20 percent. Maybe they felt uncomfortable, but they allowed for silence while I put my thoughts together. Sometimes that meant allowing twenty-five to thirty seconds to pass before I could organize my thoughts. Widow-brain is a real thing. Thoughts take longer to process. Sometimes my friends had to generate conversation by asking open-ended questions such as, "What's your favourite memory of Brian?" or "Tell me about a time he made you laugh." I firmly believe healing only happens within conversations.

A technique my friend Dee used was to deliberately slow her breathing down when I seemed really scattered. I watched her take deep breaths, and I copied her. I started to mirror her breathing without consciously knowing what she was doing. It was only afterward when she explained what she was doing that it made sense why I felt calmer in her presence.

I appreciated it whenever someone would say Brian's name out loud. Just because he died doesn't mean his identity ceased to exist. Saying his name provided me comfort. When someone mentioned Brian by name, it did not conjure up painful memories. Rather, it kept his essence alive. I didn't want anyone to tiptoe around me because I was a survivor of suicide loss; the more authentic people were, the better. I also appreciated that no one took the opportunity to tell me how Brian said or did anything that they didn't like. I didn't want to know. If anyone had a story to tell about how they felt wronged, they kept it to themselves.

Friends showed they cared in so many ways. No one was an expert on death, suicide, or grief, but most people had experienced some form of trauma in their lives. Knowing that people cared and wanted to help was the most important thing. Those who were unsure of what to say or do, yet asked me how they could help, made such a huge difference; I felt loved and connected.

Being asked how I wanted to be contacted helped. If someone wanted to drop by, I appreciated a call first. I hated when people dropped over to my house. If the doorbell rang, I only answered it if it suited me. It added to my guilt when I dropped quietly to the floor, pretending I wasn't home. If I did meet someone for coffee or invited them over to my house, I often needed a short visit. I tired easily and found it an effort to maintain a conversation.

A couple of months after Brian died, I was still deeply in the throes of grief when a friend wanted to cheer me up and took me to a play. I sat in horror when the crux of the story revolved around the suicide of a main character. All I could hear was "blah, blah, blah. . . SUICIDE." My friend asked if I wanted to leave and apologized profusely, explaining she did not know the storyline of the production. I probably should have left, but instead, chose to sit through an incredibly uncomfortable two-hour ordeal. It was just too soon for me. Perhaps I was trying to prove to myself I could handle the situation.

In retrospect, I didn't make a good decision. I was pretending to be brave at a time while I was still very fragile. The impact of my reaction to the word "suicide" left me questioning myself for days. I wondered if I would ever be able to hear that word without having my stomach turn. I wondered if I would ever regain a sense of "normal" emotions, where I could feel sad but not overwhelmed by a gripping fear of falling into an abyss of grief. I wondered if other people who had not experienced deep grief could ever understand the torment of my heart and mind. I felt disconnected from others and myself. To this day, I try to be mindful of what I watch or read. I have yet to watch *Thirteen Reasons Why,* but I made a conscious choice to watch *A Star is Born,* and *The Girl from Plainville,* knowing the outcomes ahead of time. It's about making choices that support my wellbeing, depending on how I am coping at that time.

Holidays and special occasions (i.e., Valentine's Day) often seemed overwhelming. Sometimes it wasn't the date itself, but the days leading up to it. The anticipation I was going to fall apart on the special day was often worse than the day itself. Thankfully, my therapist told me I might experience anxiety prior to an anniversary date or a day that held significance for me, so I wasn't surprised when it did. For the first few years, each holiday, each birthday, each anniversary included a few days of worry before the actual date. I found the nineteenth of every month to be tough to get through as it marked the day in December Brian left the house and died. Only my kids and close friends knew I struggled with that day because the date on his death certificate stated the twenty-second, when his body was found. On the one-year anniversary of Brian's death, I basically stayed in bed, cried, and watched movies all day.

Although many friends said, just call if you need anything, picking up the phone seemed impossible. I was already feeling vulnerable and asking for help just made me feel even more so. When friends called and asked, "Can I pick up the kids after school?" or "I'm going to the grocery store. Can I pick up a few things for you?" the burden of asking for help was removed. The pressure was off my shoulders, and I could decide if I wanted their help or not. Initially, I would say, "No, it's okay. I don't need help." Thank goodness my best friend Donna gave me a stern talking-to and told me to smarten up and say yes.

If someone had no intention of helping, I preferred they didn't even offer. I may have been grieving, but I could smell an insincere offer a mile away. Platitudes weren't helpful. Many people said they wanted to help, but I never heard from them again. This contributed to my feeling of being forgotten. I already felt abandoned by Brian leaving us, and when some friends stopped calling, I saw their original offer of support as insincere. I decided in my head that being a survivor of suicide loss meant I no longer deserved to be their friend and my grieving was a burden.

If someone who offered to help couldn't follow through, I greatly appreciated a phone call letting me know. I understood people had busy lives and preferred they decommit or schedule a time that would work for both of us. Just like Brian, I didn't want to become a burden to my family and friends. One friend of mine (you know who you are) would drop off cards of encouragement or bars of chocolate into my mailbox. She wouldn't ring the bell; it became her way to let me know I was loved and in her thoughts. I am forever grateful for her kindness.

There is no set timeline for grieving. When someone dies by suicide, there are additional levels of grief, including shame and guilt. This complicates the survivor's recovery and can take a longer time. My closest friends allowed me to recount the suicide over and over, trying to make sense of what happened, looking for what I might have done differently that could have prevented Brian's death. They probably heard the same story fifty times and let me tell it again without interruption. I had good days and bad days. One day I seemed to be doing great and coping well, and the next day I was a mess. Grief came in waves. It was unpredictable, and even though my ability to cope increased, the grief never truly went away. It was the wound that never fully healed. The edges started to come together, but the smallest scratch could open it once again.

I mentioned at the beginning of this chapter that it was easier to tell people what not to say. My number one pet peeve was when someone said, "I know how you feel. My cousin took their own life." I was so sorry to hear about your cousin, but, honestly, you couldn't possibly have known how I felt. Everyone is unique, and no two people grieve the same way. Instead, I would have preferred hearing, "I lost someone to suicide as well; it was really hard for me." Then we could have a dialogue about our experiences. Starting off with, "I know how you feel" made me shut down emotionally and want to stop any further conversation with that person.

I knew my friends also struggled with Brian's death, and I was willing to listen, to a point. However, I couldn't make it okay for them. I didn't have the strength. I was too busy focusing on my survival and trying to make sure my kids were okay. If someone started making the tragedy about themselves, it was time for me to back away for a while. I needed to surround myself with people who could be fully there for me. That is so contrary to how I had lived my life. I had always been the one to listen, the one to support others. This was not that time. I needed to be on the receiving end.

The times I felt the safest to share was when I felt the other person wasn't being judgmental. I was devastated by Brian's death, and my greatest fear was I would be judged or criticized for his suicide. Fortunately, my close friends gave me the space to fully express myself without any fear of judgement. With them, I shared more, cried more openly, and felt more supported. This really helped my grieving process. These friends also didn't judge Brian. I couldn't tolerate hearing he was selfish or cowardly because I didn't believe that to be true.

My close friends knew all the details of Brian's suicide. There were a couple of people I considered acquaintances who wanted all the gory details. "Did you see his body?" "Did he shoot himself?" This made me uncomfortable, and I questioned why they wanted to know. Were they asking just to satisfy their morbid curiosity? In those moments, Brian's death felt like a train wreck where people were clamoring to see the carnage. If I thought the person was authentic and sincere, I gladly shared with them. If I felt they were rubbernecking, forget it.

I'd never heard the term "religious bromides" before this experience. After it happened, several people told me, "God only gives you what you can handle." Although they meant well, when I heard this religious cliché in the midst of my deep grief, I wanted to throw up . . . or punch this person in the mouth. In no way did I think God handed me this situation because I was strong enough to handle it. When Brian died, I believe God wept.

Other things I heard that were not very helpful included:

- *He's in a better place.*
- *Time will heal everything.*
- *Everything happens for a reason.*

Social media wasn't part of my world when Brian died, so I wasn't faced with announcing his death on Facebook or expressing my grief online. I now belong to several groups through social media where support for survivors of suicide is available. I have seen people at their kindest, offering support and a listening ear. I have also seen some really mean-spirited comments, the downside of being vulnerable in a public forum. If someone close to me died now, I would choose to avoid or be extremely careful with social media for a while. I still would seek out private groups for survivors of suicide loss. Otherwise, in those early days, I would just protect my heart.

When I hear someone has died, I never say anything on social media unless the people closest to that person say something first. It is their story, not mine to tell. Some people get a rush in being the first to post breaking news. However, saying R.I.P. on Facebook because you just heard a person died could be devastating to family members who have not been contacted personally.

Many people told me stories about Brian after his death, some that I had never heard before, and I really appreciated it. When David bought his first condo, his realtor happened to go to school with Brian in Montreal. *What are the chances this realtor knew Brian? Did he remember him?*

"I remember Brian as a basketball star and that he was pretty smooth with the girls," he shared with a wink.

Brian always described his younger self as being a smooth operator; this confirmed it for me. I loved it.

It made all the difference to me when friends and family connected with me on birthdays, anniversaries, and religious holidays. It's nice to know others acknowledged there was a "missing" on special occasions. They didn't worry that bringing up Brian's name would be painful for me, mostly because I told them not to stop talking about him. Donna must have every date that holds significance for me written in her calendar. Without fail, I get a call each year on not only my birthday but my anniversary with Brian and the anniversary of his death.

"Hey beautiful, just thinking about you today and wanted you to know how much I love you."

Maybe that's why Donna is my best friend. (I'll tell you more about our friendship in the next chapter.)

If Donna and her husband Tom were hosting an event, like a dinner party, or if they decided to catch a movie, they usually invited me without expectation or pressure to join in. If I felt like going, I did. If I didn't want to go, they never made me feel bad or wrong about my decision. I never felt like an outcast or a third wheel. On the other hand, I was no longer invited to participate in the dinner club Brian and I had gone to for several years. I guess the other couples felt a little uncomfortable having a single woman at the table. It hurt, but I realized our relationships were superficial at best. I still would have appreciated the invite so I could have been the one to decline. It's a good example of the little girl in me not wanting to feel rejected.

Having someone really listen to me without giving advice or coaching was one of the best methods of healing I experienced. It allowed me to get the thoughts circulating in my head out of my mouth. Having a friend willing to listen and respond only with "I hear that" made me feel supported and cherished. It also allowed me to tell my story and sometimes hear it newly for myself. It sounded so different when it was just in my head. I'm certain my closest friends heard my stories multiple times, yet they still acted as if it was the first time.

One thing I have learned about myself is that I don't like being told what to do. If I asked for advice or some coaching, that is another story. Then I was open to hear other opinions. If someone said, "This is what I think you should do," chances are I wouldn't follow the advice anyway. Hearing advice or coaching when it is not solicited is annoying.

If I chose not to talk about the suicide, I didn't need anyone to pressure me to do so. Knowing I had people I could rely on to talk to when I was ready to talk made all the difference. I wasn't looking for the magic answers; I just needed someone to listen.

No magic timeline shows when a grieving survivor will feel better. Everyone moves at their own pace through grief. Just because they smile doesn't mean they are out of the throes of grief. Never try to guess where someone is on their grief journey. It doesn't hurt to ask. They may be able to put it into words, or just maybe you'll listen once more to their story. The important thing to remember is not to give up on a survivor of suicide. Your love and support could be the very thing they need to find their way back to a sense of normality. They will never be the same as they once were, but you can provide love and support while they find and create their new "normal."

I am grateful for those who loved me enough to help me through this journey.

CHAPTER 11

My Village

It takes a village to raise a child.
— African proverb

Growing up, it didn't matter where I was in the neighbourhood. A mom or dad always looked out for me. No matter whose house the kids were in, the adults in charge were responsible and took care of us. We knew if we were ever in trouble, we could go to the nearest house for help. We also knew that if we did something bad and another parent saw us doing it, we were in trouble with that neighbor and later with our parents.

I loved this sense of community, and I worked hard to recreate it when Brian, the kids, and I moved into a new neighbourhood in 1992, allowing Brian to be five minutes from his office. The day after we moved into our new home, our doorbell rang.

"Hi, I'm Liz, your neighbour. I brought you a lasagna and a salad," said the pretty blonde woman, mid-thirties, standing on our front porch with covered bowls in her hands.

"Seriously?" I stood with my mouth open.

"Yeah, I figured you would be busy unpacking and might not have your kitchen set up yet, so I thought this might help," she explained.

Liz's gesture set the tone for our experience with our neighbours, and I made sure to pay it forward when new families moved in. I also showed up with lasagna and made a new connection. I loved this tradition in our neighborhood.

Liz, a single mom, had two boys around the same age as my two children. The kids spent hours playing together. Our houses were back-to-back, separated only by a fence. In no time, we sawed out a square hole in the fence for the kids to pass through. It made more sense than building a gate between the two properties.

Four months after Brian died, Liz invited the kids and me over for dinner one night. As we sat on the barstools at the island in her kitchen, she poured me a glass of red wine and told me she had something to discuss with me. She sent the kids to the family room to play and looked me in the eye.

"If anything happens to you, I'd be willing to take in your children," she said quietly.

Another mouth-dropping moment. "Are you kidding me? I asked, barely able to get the words out.

"Yes, I've thought about it. I love your kids, and I'd be willing to be their guardian," she said confidently.

I was beyond words. I started to cry. I had never been so touched by someone's generosity. Liz was not even family. She was a good friend, but we didn't even spend that much time together. Our kids were the ones who had the stronger connection. Liz was a principal at an elementary school. She loved running and travelling. She also loved painting her kitchen. Sometimes in the middle of the night, I'd go to the kitchen for a glass of milk when I couldn't sleep. Looking out the window I could see Liz, painting her kitchen once again. She said it was her therapy since her divorce.

"My brother and sister-in-law, Wayne and Gloria, have offered to be the guardians for my kids," I finally said. "We set that up before Brian died, in case both of us died in an accident. If for some reason my family is not able to take them, I'd be honoured if you would agree to be the alternative."

"That works for me," Liz replied, raising her glass of wine, and clinking my glass. "Let's drink to that."

Brian and I also built connections through working at the treatment centre and volunteering in the community. Brian not only coached community basketball but also soccer for both of our kids over several years. On a hot summer afternoon once a year, we rented a huge bouncy castle that was blown up on our driveway and ordered several thirty-six-inch square pizzas. We invited the neighbourhood children to join us. The moms and dads sat on the deck with cold alcoholic beverages in hand while the kids bounced. It was our way of giving back to our little village.

Brian and I became good friends with several couples that lived on our street and the street behind us. Our kids played freely between the houses, knowing someone's mom or dad had an eye on them. After Brian's death, many neighbours and friends showed up with food, primarily lasagna. Maybe that's because lasagna is comfort food, or everyone has their favourite recipe.

The kids and I lived on a lot of lasagna that first year. We even started to rate the lasagna to determine who made the best dish. I didn't tell my children who made the lasagna until after they had rated it. The winner was Kelly. (He did not get extra points because he was my boss.) After our "lasagna year," it was a long time before we wanted to eat it again. To this day, I cannot eat lasagna without thinking about that first year after Brian died.

We enjoyed spending time with Tom and Donna, who lived around the corner. Tom is more than six feet tall with light blonde hair, blue eyes, and a killer smile that accentuates his dimples. He's the kind of guy most women stop to take a second look at. Donna is shorter than me, with red hair and freckles, and eyelashes most women would envy. When she laughs, which she does a lot, her blue eyes remind me of the Mediterranean Sea. The four of us got together occasionally to play cards or have dinner. We considered them our friends. After Brian's suicide, they stepped up to the plate more than anyone else. Donna's support during the aftermath solidified my connection with her. She became my lifeline, my best friend.

Donna and I started walking together almost every morning from 5:30 to 6:15, a practice that continued for almost thirteen years. This time fit into both our schedules. I certainly would not be out walking so early in the morning if it weren't for Donna. Typically, I walked around the corner to her house and saw her silhouette as she stood in her doorway, waiting for my arrival.

"Good morning, beautiful," Donna said every morning while giving me a hug. *What did I do to deserve such an amazing friend?*

Our intention was to improve our wellbeing: to lose some weight, get some exercise, and more importantly, "Solve all the world's problems by 6:15." We took turns sharing. I usually expressed my grief, allowing the tears to fall in the darkness of the predawn. I never left the house without Kleenex in my pocket. Donna listened or "held the space" as I liked to call it. She didn't judge, she didn't make me wrong for the way I felt, and often she refrained from giving advice. When it was time for Donna to share, she talked about her job, her marriage to Tom, and parenting their two boys, Kory and Colin.

Sometime later after Brian died, I learned that Donna had become my "hub" in the neighbourhood. She knew I was feeling overwhelmed with neighbours calling to see how they could help, so she asked them to contact her instead to find out how I was doing and what I needed. She didn't want me to be bombarded with well-meaning people. *What kind of a person thinks to do that? I don't think I would.* Her kindness and support helped me to surface from the abyss. One thing I know for sure, Donna did not tell everyone to bring me lasagna. We laughed about how we were trying to lose weight, and I had a freezer full of the Italian favourite. Good thing we were walking.

Another neighbour, Holly, called one day shortly after Christmas.

"Don't plan anything for dinner," she said.

She showed up with a four-course meal for eight of us. All we had to do was set the table. "What a blessing!" I exclaimed.

Before heading out the door, she hugged me tightly and said, "I am so glad I could do this for you. The blessing is mine."

When we asked her to stay for dinner, she declined, leaving us to enjoy her gift.

My friends Geoff and Laurie also came through with an incredible act of kindness. Geoff had worked with Brian in the financial services industry. He and Laurie became our close friends over the years. They helped my husband plan my fortieth surprise birthday party at their house. I am forever grateful for their support when I had to go through all of Brian's business papers. They sat with me on the floor, sorted through the mess Brian had left in his office, and helped me deal with the tax department and securing payment on his life insurance policy.

Based on the coroner's report, which stated Brian's body had "the liver like that of an alcoholic," the insurance company determined that Brian had lied on his application form, and therefore, the policy was null and void. They refused to pay the claim. But Brian wasn't an alcoholic. He had taken close to sixty Demerol, so his liver was enlarged.

When I talked about this situation, most people were surprised that the insurance company would pay at all. They typically said, "I didn't know insurance paid out when a person committed suicide." Again, they weren't aware that the correct term is "died by suicide." Their words also echoed yet another myth associated with suicide. If an insurance policy has been in place for two years, most companies do pay out in the case of suicide. It depends on the policy. Brian knew this. He wrote his own policy because he had his insurance license as part of the financial services he provided.

I was stunned by the insurance company's decision. Not only was my husband dead, but now I was about to lose the house and possibly the car. How would I ever make ends meet? To say I was angry at Brian for leaving me in such a predicament was an understatement. *If you were alive, I would kill you,* I told Brian in my head. Angry thoughts, angry words.

In this situation, Geoff truly acted with grace. Along with his colleagues, he advocated for me to receive the claim. I had the cheque in my hands three days later. Although I was very frustrated with this insurance company, I chose to focus my energy on the gratitude I had toward the community of financial planners that changed the trajectory of my family's lives. This was my village.

Laurie organized a benefit for my children, so they'd have money to attend college or university. Sometimes I feel connected to Laurie as if we were sisters in a previous life. We just "get" each other. She put together a buffet dinner and silent auction in the gymnasium of the treatment centre where I worked. The benefit was held on St. Patrick's Day, only about ten weeks after Brian's death. She secured an incredible number of items for auction and nearly one hundred people in my community attended the event. I was overcome with gratitude and could not believe how many people wanted to support our family. To be honest though, I did feel guilty asking others to help me. I love to help others. Letting them help me is a whole different thing. I felt rather unworthy.

How did I deserve such blessings? I wish Brian could be here to see how much our friends and family cared. It reminded me of stories I had heard about raising a barn when a family had been struck by tragedy. Laurie secured a local chef to cook Alberta roast beef on a bun along with a multitude of salads and desserts. I will never forget the smell of the roast beef; it reminded me of Sunday nights when my mom cooked pot roast. That night, the community rallied and raised more than $17,000 for my kids' education fund. I was stunned.

At the time, I was very reluctant to be in such a crowd. The thought of it made me feel claustrophobic. I worried about being overwhelmed with people wanting to talk with me. I consider myself an introvert who has learned how to be a social person, but in my current state of vulnerability, connecting with others scared me deeply. In my process after Brian's death, I had learned that these fears were very normal. The best way to handle any possible "fight or flight" response was to pre-plan my escape route if I needed it. As soon as I got in the door, I scanned the room for exit doors. *I will only stay fifteen minutes*. Then when fifteen minutes passed, I committed to another fifteen minutes. Having that strategy helped me stay the entire evening. Toward the end, I wasn't even looking at the clock or the door anymore.

Overall, I felt comforted by the sense of community at the event. The number of people who came up to me, especially men offering to help in whatever way they could, not only touched my heart but made me realize I didn't have to go through this difficult loss alone. If I needed help fixing things around the house or someone to take my kids to one of their activities, someone was there. I knew their offers weren't just lip service. All I had to do was ask. Did I mention, however, that I have a difficult time asking for help?

Our nearby church also provided support. We had been members of this church for about six years. Brian and I were both raised in the United Church of Canada. At first, it took a while for our family of four to feel connected to the congregation because many members had been there for years or were raised in that church. But in the end, our efforts paid off. After Brian's death, I felt completely embraced by members of the congregation, especially the United Church Women's Group. I joined this group a couple of years before Brian died but chose to get more involved after his death. Washing dishes or preparing food alongside these women helped heal my soul. At one point, I even became the chairperson for our church board. Upon my retirement from this two-year position, one of the women from the group, Rose, presented me with a prayer shawl. It was colourful, inspired by Joseph and the story of his technicolour coat. Rose explained how with every stitch she made in the shawl, she said a prayer for me. I still use it to this day, wrapping myself in the love and connection from my church sisters.

Our children attended Sunday School, and as they got older, they participated in the youth group. Our young, vibrant youth minister named Jamie was like the Pied Piper. With Greek-god good looks and sandy-coloured curly hair, many of the young girls (and maybe a few moms) had a crush on him. He was only twenty-four, so he was young enough to connect with the kids because, in some ways, he was a big kid himself. He engaged the kids in fun activities while teaching them about being a good person and living a meaningful life. Kids loved him.

After Brian's death, we became more involved in church activities. All three of us landed roles in the musical theatre program. I performed as Golde in *Fiddler on the Roof* and Domina in *A Funny Thing Happened on the Way to the Forum.* Am I a great singer? Heck, no. I did it because it was fun, it gave me something to do with my kids, and it got me out of sitting at home doing nothing.

In *Forum,* David played the part of the young ingenue, Philia. By then, he was more than six feet tall. To see him in a dress and long blonde wig cracked me up every time. Obviously, our director had an amazing sense of humour. In the play, Philia was supposed to be awakened by the hero in one scene. During one performance, as David lay on a bench pretending to be asleep, his wig kept falling off. The crowd roared, watching him play the part so melodramatically, all the while trying to put his wig back on.

Not everyone feels a sense of community in their neighbourhood. It takes effort to get involved in organizations or programs in the community. Not everyone wants to go to church. Given our busy lives, it's easy to pull into the garage and close the door without stopping to connect with those who live around us. For apartment dwellers, other than saying hello in the hallway or elevator, how many people really get to know those living right next to them? For many, this way of living may seem to work, but having a connection with others is one of my driving needs. Most of us need connections, especially during the most difficult times of our lives.

Social connection can improve our physical and mental health and has been linked to an increased chance of longevity. It can help us to recover from diseases faster and may lower anxiety and depression. Those who build connections with others tend to have higher self-esteem, are more empathic toward others, and are more open and trusting, leading to increased cooperation. Brian and I made efforts to connect with our neighbors, church members, and friends before tragedy struck. As a result, my kids and I did not have to go through the journey alone.

I read a story on Facebook about Paige Hunter, a teen from England who acted to save lives. She tied forty notes of encouragement onto Wearmouth Bridge in Sunderland to let people know it's okay to not be okay. Many people have died by suicide at that bridge. Paige left notes such as, "Even though things are difficult, your life matters; you're a shining light in a dark world. Just hold on." "Fight with all you have; tomorrow is a better day." "Don't you dare give up on this life, NOT tonight, NOT tomorrow, NOT ever." People who went to the bridge to die responded to Paige's messages. At the time of the Facebook posting, she was credited with saving six lives. The fact that someone cared enough to leave words of encouragement had an impact—not only for the suicidal person, but as we know, for the families who could have become members of the dreaded club.

Don Ritchie from Australia is someone else who has inspired me. He and his wife lived on a hill above a cliff, considered to be a suicide "hot spot." For more than fifty years, Don watched out the window, and any time he saw someone who looked like they might jump, strolled down the hill to ask, "Can I help you in some way?" By the time of Don's death in 2012, he was credited with saving 164 lives. Many think the number was much higher. Incredible!

I am not suggesting we all need to be like Paige or Don, although wouldn't that be freaking amazing? We can, however, have a say in how we treat people daily. Say a kind word, open the door for someone, let another driver into your car lane without getting upset at them. (Okay, I'm still working on that one.) If each of us reached out in a kind way, created a gentler, more connected world, perhaps fewer people would feel disconnected.

Who is in your village? It may be someone you only know casually right now. Given the opportunity to step up, people can amaze you, like my best friend Donna. She stepped up her game, and then we became best friends after Brian died. She saw a need and was willing to become my safety net. Who could that person be for you? A close friend or a family member? Someone in your neighbourhood? Another survivor you met in person or through social media? I have read about some survivors meeting through Facebook groups and ending up becoming friends and travelling together. Maybe there is a survivors of suicide group in your area. Or maybe you will find the strength to start one. Don't discount anyone. Keep your eyes and heart open.

I encourage you to find and cultivate your village.

CHAPTER 12
The Other Chair

Don't forget I'm always there
So save for me an empty chair
— *"The Empty Chair" by Robert Longley*

During a social work class in college, we discussed how difficult it could be for some practitioners to seek help or counselling to deal with their own challenges. After the discussion, I told myself that if I ever needed help, I would not hesitate to get it. I'd be willing to sit in the other chair.

Over the years, I've had the opportunity to counsel victims of domestic abuse, sexual abuse, and traumatized children in care. When Brian died, it became clear it was time for me to take the other chair. I didn't hesitate. I knew I needed professional help to get through the pain and grief brought on by what happened. Friends and family were very supportive, and I wanted an expert in grief management on my team. Luckily, my benefit package at work covered counselling. I was prepared to pay out-of-pocket if necessary. I knew taking care of my own mental health was paramount.

Sharon and Bill, the people who helped us from the Police Victims Assistance Unit, gave me the contact information for a grief counsellor. A few weeks after Brian's death, I made the call to set up an appointment with Elva. Not only did she have more than thirty years of experience helping people deal with issues of grief and loss, but she'd also written a booklet about it that the city police and local funeral homes distributed to those in need.[33] After initial introductions, Elva outlined what would happen during our sessions. She then handed me a copy of her booklet. I immediately recognized the cover, flipped it over, saw her picture on the back cover, and did a double take looking directly at her. I had not connected her name with the booklet before coming. Sharon and Bill had given me a copy. At that moment, I knew I had been given a miracle. I was in good hands. I immediately started to relax.

In the beginning, I saw Elva every few days. She listened patiently as I poured out my story, poured out my heart, poured out my soul. She held the space for me to cry, to get angry, to be sad, and to find the moments of hope and string them together. I went through copious amounts of tissues as part of my process of healing. I knew survivors of suicide had a higher probability of attempting suicide or dying by suicide, so I wanted to do whatever it took to be there for my children and to stop what could become a legacy in our family.

I am usually a logical thinker and can remember events and sequences of events with little difficulty. While deep in grief, my logic became muddled. I had difficulty remembering what happened and in what order. I found myself wandering the aisles aimlessly in grocery stores because I could not remember what I came in to buy. I forgot to pay bills. I had to make lists of things I had to do each day because, after an hour, I couldn't remember the tasks. It was amazing I remembered how to drive.

I became frightened I might be losing my ability to think rationally. Having someone like Elva tell me I was right on track eased my mind. She assured me this was grief at work, and my memory loss would pass as I moved through the different stages. What I called my "muddled mind" wasn't going to be permanent. During this time, I considered my friends a blessing, but my therapist became my true lifeline. Elva helped me wade through the maze of my thoughts and emotions. She helped me feel safe. She encouraged me to feel the pain and gave me tools to cope.

Elva's office was rather small, furnished with three comfortable chairs so she could counsel more than one person at a time. For me, the three chairs were comforting because I imagined Brian sitting in the extra chair, listening to me telling my story. Sometimes, with encouragement from Elva, I looked directly at the other chair to express my pain and outrage. It was cathartic.

Sitting to the right of Elva, snotty Kleenex in my hand, tears falling down my cheek, I'd say between heaving breaths, "I am so angry at Brian right now. I have never been so angry in my life. If he were still alive, I think I could kill him."

"Tell me more about your anger," Elva said calmly.

I have said similar words to clients. I knew what she was doing. She was allowing me to explore my emotions. It was a totally different experience when someone else was saying the words to me. As a counsellor, I could observe clients struggle to identify their emotions and learn how to express them. As a client, I gained a new appreciation of how freaking hard that was.

"I cannot shake this anger; it seems all consuming. If even the smallest thing goes wrong, I blame Brian. It's his fault. If he didn't kill himself, my life would not be in shambles right now. What an asshole!"

"Why don't you look at the empty chair and tell Brian how angry you are at him?" Elva suggested.

The next ten minutes were filled with me screaming at the chair, Brian's face clearly etched in my mind. Admittedly, colourful words passed through my lips. I called him every derogatory word I could think of.

"You screwed our family over! You screwed me over!" I cried.

Elva didn't censor my rant. She kept nodding, handing me more Kleenex and when silence came said, "Is there anything more?"

This spurred me on to another rant, and then another. Finally, when I felt I had expressed all my anger, I cried and cried and cried some more. Releasing the anger in a safe place was the best therapy I received in my time with Elva.

As much as I was angry at Brian, Elva helped me to deal with the anger I held against myself. Anger for not saying the right words, anger for not listening to my intuition, anger for not being able to save him. Sometimes I got angry for being angry. At first, I was resistant to admitting I was angry at myself. It was easier to be angry at him. Staying angry at Brian allowed me to stay in a victim mode. It was tougher to look at my own behaviours because then it was up to me to make a change. I found my greatest healing in doing this therapeutic work.

After several months, as spring started to show her colours, Elva suggested, "Perhaps you would consider taking up gardening."

I cringed. I have never liked gardening and the thought of pulling weeds made me shudder.

"Maybe not right now," she said, observing my scrunched-up nose. "When you're ready, gardening can be very healing. Touching the soil, watching new life, taking care of living things can help take you out of your circling thoughts. I think it's one of the best strategies for working through grief. I recommend it highly," she continued.

I was not buying it. I remember as a child how my mother would make me weed the vegetable garden, and I grew to hate it. It would be many years before I attempted to take Elva's advice and learn how to garden. Now, every time I dig a hole to plant a seed, I think of Elva. Admittedly, I'm still not very good at it.

When studying social work, I read the works of Elizabeth Kubler-Ross, a pioneer who worked with terminally ill patients and their families. So I was already familiar with her theory that when a person is faced with a traumatic event, they might experience emotional responses called the five stages of grief: denial, anger, bargaining, depression, and acceptance.[34] In his 2020 book, *Finding Meaning*, David Kessler (who co-wrote a book with Kubler-Ross) added a sixth stage, called "finding meaning" or making sense of the loss and seeing meaning in it.[35] A person in grief may not necessarily experience these stages in any particular order, or even experience all five. I did pass through all five (some more than once) and definitely not when I expected. For example, I observed myself jump between not believing he was dead (denial) to feeling furious that he'd done this to me and our family (anger). These powerful, contradictory emotions taught me that survivors go through their own unique grieving process; there is no right or wrong way to grieve.

Recognizing the stage I was in gave me a reference point for the grief I was experiencing. Elva also listened and helped me identify which stage of grief I was experiencing in that moment. Having her describe what she saw helped me know where I was at in the process and helped me feel that I was having a normal response to my husband's sudden death.

I spent a significant amount of time in depression. I saw this in the vast amount of time I spent sleeping in front of the television eating large amounts of food. Although I knew I wanted to go on living for my children, there were times I just wanted to crawl in a hole and die. After three or four months of deep grief, I had the capacity to make the distinct choice to live. Following that moment of clarity, I made a point to set three small goals each day upon waking, something I continue to do to this day. I also started a gratitude journal that helped me focus on the many blessings I had in my life. Therapy with Elva and walking with my friend Donna were the biggest factors in moving through the depression.

David was so close to his dad that I feared he might die by suicide as well. I was prepared to fight for my son. Research indicated that I needed to pay attention to keeping him alive. The National Institute of Mental Health lists a family history of suicide and mental disorder as two risk factors for suicide. This list also mentions exposure to others' suicidal behaviour, such as that of family members, peers, or celebrities, as an additional risk factor. In other words, there can be a behavioural contagion effect. David chose to go for counselling as well. Losing his father at age fourteen had a serious impact on my son. My therapist's husband worked in the same office, and David found great comfort in working with him for about a year.

I became curious. Why were family members of those who died by suicide at a higher risk to kill themselves? I was stunned to come across the following in my research: "People who had known someone who died by suicide in the last year were 1.6 times more likely to have suicidal thoughts, 2.9 times more likely to have a plan for suicide, and 3.7 times more likely to have made a suicide attempt themselves. The pain of dealing with the loss of a loved one by suicide coupled with shame, rejection, anger, perceived responsibility, and other risk factors, can be too much to bear, and to some, suicide seems like the only way to end the pain. Some may feel closer to their loved one by taking their life in the same way."[36]

I can certainly identify with the feeling of just wanting the pain to stop, along with the feelings of shame and perceived responsibility. In addition, I had feelings of extreme guilt for not seeing the signs, not being able to stop him, and confusion as to his thought processes. When Brian died, I first thought I wanted to join him. I didn't think I could bear the pain. I can see why as survivors, we are more susceptible to taking our own lives.

During the first few months after Brian died, David and I would often talk into the wee hours of the morning. There were no topics considered taboo, and sometimes we spoke about death and what we believed happened after death, especially to someone who died by suicide. I believe the time I spent with David, along with the therapy he received, helped to save him from taking his own life. I felt tremendous sorrow and anger seeing how his father's actions had hurt my son deeply. It was a difficult journey for him to reconcile the pain. One night, David and I talked about our fears of someone else in our family dying by suicide.

"I'm worried about you. I can see you are so sad about your dad taking his own life that I worry every day you might do the same, just to be with him," I confessed. "Because Dad took his own life, we are both at a higher risk of doing the same, and I could not live if you died too."

David looked me straight in the eyes: "Mom, I promise you I would never kill myself. I could never, ever, do that to you. I can see what you're going through with Dad, and even though I am sad, I absolutely promise I would never do that."

"I promise I would never kill myself either. We have to be the ones to break the legacy of this family."

"Do you swear?" he asked.

"I swear. Do you swear?"

"I swear, Mom."

"Then let's pretend we cut our hands and make a blood pact," I suggested.

We each took our index finger and pretended to cut our opposite hand. Then we pressed our "cut" hands together to seal the vow. Looking at each other, we said together one more time: "I swear."

Jennifer was only ten years old and dealt with the suicide differently. When I tried to talk with her about her dad, she would usually answer quickly and then want to change the topic. I was reluctant to push the conversation. She attended family counselling in the beginning only because I made her go, but after a few sessions, she said she didn't want to continue. I don't think she connected with Elva, nor was she ready to discuss her experience of Brian's suicide. I honoured her decision, hoping she would go for help when she was ready.

I cannot say enough about the value of talking about my grief with my counsellor, children, friends, and family anyone I trusted and who cared. Without talking with someone else when I was grieving the most, I would have recycled the thoughts in my head and listened too closely to my inner monologue. If you are struggling with the idea of getting grief counselling, I urge you to find someone who can listen to your story and provide you with the guidance to work through your pain.

I am very glad I chose to sit in the other chair.

CHAPTER 13
What If?

We spend too much time living in the what if
and need to learn to live in the what is.
— *Ritu Ghatourey*

What if I hadn't gone to work the day Brian decided to die? What if I had just said, *screw it, work can wait; my husband needs me to stay home with him today!* What if I had trusted my instincts and come home for lunch that day? What if I had monitored the Demerol the doctor gave Brian for pain? What if I had recognized the signs of his depression? What if I had asked him if he had suicidal thoughts?

What if? What if? What if?

After Brian died, I played the "what if" game way too much. It became a way for me to fantasize taking different actions that may have led to a much different outcome. Even knowing that the result would not have changed, playing what if appealed to my imagination and desire to be in control. It also soothed any guilt I hung onto. I played the game by running mini-movies in my head, rewriting the script over and over with different scenarios and endings. Each time, the outcome fit my definition of a satisfying conclusion where Brian and I lived happily ever after.

In the beginning, I tortured myself about how the outcome of that fateful day might have had a different, happier ending—if only I had done something different. A part of me wanted to take responsibility for what happened, but why? What did I think I was? Psychic? Someone who knows what's going to happen in the future. No, no, and no. I do not possess superpowers.

At times in the months that followed, I sometimes found myself thinking there was some sort of mistake, and it might be someone else's body they found. After all, I identified the body over the phone; I never actually saw his corpse. I conveniently forgot that once Brian's body had defrosted, the coroner found his driver's license in his back pocket. I can now see that this defense mechanism of denial helped shield me from the shock of this traumatic event.

But what if Brian were here right now? If you asked him whether I had made a difference in his life, I believe he would tell you that I had. He would say something like, "She was a loving and caring wife and an excellent mother. As parents, we laughed together and worked hard to create a life for our children, for our family."

What he probably would not tell you, however, were the struggles we experienced, mostly with our finances and health. His mantras of "Never let them see you sweat" or "Everything is going to be okay" were meant to project to the outside world that everything remained above board. He never broadcasted our difficulties, and I'm certain he never talked with even his closest friends about things that troubled him. Instead, he kept his troubles deep inside, especially during the last year of his life. Brian didn't even share his pain with me. My husband had been raised to keep a strong upper lip. He never wanted to be a burden to anyone.

Raised as the oldest son of a war veteran, Brian learned early on men do not show weakness. It's their job to be the strength of the family, the protector and provider. Although his father was always kind and loving to his grandkids and me, Brian often commented on how his father, as he aged, seemed different from the man who raised him. His dad became softer, gentler, less rigid. We talked about how both our fathers were strict disciplinarians, and how they had high expectations for us to succeed. Brian alluded to something happening between him and his father, but when I asked him what transpired between the two of them, his reply would be, "I don't want to talk about it." I always suspected it stemmed from a quarrel regarding Brian's decision to stop working toward his first university degree.

After his death, I had a lot of *what ifs* about that possibly pivotal conversation in our kitchen when he told me he felt like he was a burden to our family. What if I had recognized what Brian said as his way of telling me he was contemplating suicide? What if I had asked more questions and used that moment as an opportunity to explore what he was really thinking and planning? What if our conversation had triggered the teaching from my social work training that he shouldn't oversee his own medication?

Sometimes my iterations of the *what if* game ventured into more bone-chilling territory. In this more sinister version, I asked: What if he considered a murder-suicide? What if he burned the house down or crashed our car so we would all perish? Part of me thought that scenario never would have happened. Brian never would have considered taking us all out with him, would he? As much as I wanted to believe that to be true, I had to remember that he was heavily medicated, depressed, and emotionally and mentally unstable, even though I didn't recognize the severity of his condition at the time. At the end of playing this *what if* game, I gave silent thanks to Brian for taking his own life—not mine and our children's lives, too.

I prefer to believe that if Brian *did* think about taking us all out, his thoughts would have been coming from a place of love. He would only have done it to protect us from the pain of his death. We were a tight-knit family. I will never believe he ended his life to see us suffer. He only wanted to end his own suffering. I will never know if this murder-suicide scenario existed in his thoughts. I just know it existed in mine.

Statistics indicate that men complete suicide four times more often than women do. Although men between the ages of twenty to thirty die by suicide in alarming numbers, men between forty and sixty years old kill themselves most often.[37] Brian fell into that demographic, at the age of forty-six.

Why are men more likely to kill themselves? If we consider the support systems women and men put in place for themselves, most women have at least one girlfriend to talk to. I know I had many. Brian, like many men, had few, if any, close friends. For me, talking with a girlfriend, sometimes over a glass of wine, allows me to release my stress by sharing about my life and listening to my friend share hers. Women are more determined to find girlfriends who are like them and make them feel a sense of belonging so they can express themselves.

In general, when we think of men getting together, we think of conversations focused on external affairs, not personal experiences or feelings. Men are also pressured to be financially and professionally successful, often at the expense of developing relationships. In addition, according to Dr. John Ogrodniczuk, a professor and director of the Psychotherapy Program in the Department of Psychiatry at the University of British Columbia, men in the early stages of depression tend to behave self-destructively, abuse alcohol or drugs, engage in promiscuity, drive too fast, or practice other risk-taking behaviours. Because men are conditioned to hold their thoughts and emotions inside, they can become hostile, abusive, or isolate themselves from other people. Ogrodniczuk states men tend to talk about their emotional problems in terms of *stress* rather than experiencing sadness or feeling down. There is a reluctance to being vulnerable. Rather than discussing their emotions, men tend to act out instead. It usually takes men longer to seek help, either from a friend or a professional.[38]

What if men could openly talk about how they feel? Our society places expectations on men through messages like man up, suck it up, don't be a pussy, and don't show emotion. Boys are taught not to cry because people generally view it as a sign of weakness. Although women are growing more vocal, through movements like #MeToo, in many ways, men are not encouraged to fully express their thoughts and emotions to friends and family members. They are socialized to be tough, and any sign of vulnerability can be seen as a sign of weakness. As a result, according to the Toronto Men's Health Network (TMHN), it is easier for men to acknowledge physical symptoms rather than emotional ones.

There is a movement for men I would like to draw attention to, The ManKind Project, started in 1985, whose mission is to create a safer world by growing better men. According to their Facebook page, this not-for-profit men's organization offers men the opportunity to explore their lives, overcome obstacles, create new choices, and embrace a healthy, powerful and peaceful masculinity. The project states they have a presence in twenty-one nations offering peer-led support groups and programs for men.

Another resource, HeadsUpGuys, led by Dr. Ogrodniczuk through the University of British Columbia, supports men in their fight against depression. Their website provides tips, tools, and information about professional services, including those related to suicide. It also provides a self-check depression screening tool. Although not a diagnosis, this self-check test can be used to determine if a man is experiencing depression. If he is, then he's encouraged to seek professional help.

In addition, David Deida dedicates his writing to exploring the difference between the feminine and masculine. His ninety-five-minute audio recording, "Beyond Success and Suicide: How Men Grow from Burden to Freedom," focuses on transformational work for men. I believe if Brian had been freer to talk about his own pain and challenges—as a husband, a father, a man—he might still be here today.

Eventually, I stopped playing the *what if* game. It became time to move on. I chose not to live my life looking in the rearview mirror. The responsibility for my own life and happiness rested with me. Right or wrong, good or bad, they were my choices, and I had to deal with the aftermath. As time went on, my relationship to making choices became easier. The choice itself may have been hard, but I didn't beat myself up about it anymore. I became gentler, more forgiving with myself. I now ask myself, *What if I stick my head in the sand when life gets shitty?* Maybe that's what I choose to do. *What if I make bad choices?* They are my choices to make and my mess to clean up. I want to be as accountable to myself as possible.

The universe provided me with a learning opportunity. If I chose not to learn the lesson, I may have attracted similar experiences, so I could have another go at learning that lesson before moving on. In other words, I learned that I cannot go back and rewrite what happened that day or the days leading up to Brian's suicide. I can, however, pay attention to the lessons life teaches me and do my best not to repeat the tough ones.

Will I make mistakes ever again? Absolutely. Will I make choices that are not in my best interest? Probably. Will I sometimes play the *what if* game? Perhaps. What I can tell you is that I now have a greater awareness. I'm able to stop myself, take a breath, and say,

I am grateful for the power to choose.

CHAPTER 14

Going Through His Stuff

Mostly it is loss which teaches us about the worth of things.
—*Arthur Schopenhauer*

Why are some of us so attached to our belongings? We keep clothes that no longer fit, books we've already read, and mementos of our life experiences long after they've served their purpose. Sometimes we think we will get back into those jeans, reread that book or look at our mementos when we have more time. Of course, some of us are better at being unattached than others.

I've come to understand that nothing has any meaning except what we give it. We each see the world through our own lens based on our experiences, beliefs, values, and opinions. When my grandmother gave me a necklace, I thought of her gift as being better than the crown jewels. Was my grandmother's necklace expensive? No, she gave me a piece of costume jewelry. But I placed immense value on the shiny green gemstones with gold trim because I believed my grandmother gave it to me as a symbol of her love.

When someone dies, their stuff stays behind. For family members, the questions come up: What do we do with it all? What does it mean to us? Which items mean the most to which individual?

Almost daily after Brian's death, I went to his closet just to smell his shirts. Somehow, that made it seem less real that he was gone. *How can his smell last so long?* I felt comforted knowing his clothes still hung in the closet and remained in his drawers. Over time, though, I knew I needed to figure out what to do with all his belongings. I needed to sort through them and determine what to keep, what to give away, and what to throw away.

Brian's clothes smelled of Old Spice. I tried giving him expensive cologne as a gift for Christmas or his birthday—he still loved Old Spice. It took me a while before I even wanted to wash my sheets because having his scent beside me as I slept comforted me. Slowly, the scent in his closet faded, but I could still make out his distinct odour. It always reminded me of time we spent together. I desperately wanted to remember those good times. Like when we walked hand in hand through the bird sanctuary looking for eagles or cuddled together in the hammock we received as a wedding gift that hung from the old May tree in the backyard. Or when I went to the school where Brian worked to tell him we were pregnant with our first child. I couldn't wait for him to come home. I needed to tell him as soon as I found out. As we stood in the middle of the school hallway, he turned a bit grey at first, then smiled broadly as he swept me into his arms and gave me a long, slow kiss.

About six months passed before I could even consider getting rid of any of Brian's belongings. I had been too deep in grief and too busy making sure my children were okay to deal with his things. Besides, I felt I would be dishonouring Brian's memory even to consider giving his possessions away. During the first few months, I wasn't ready to take on such a herculean task, choosing to wait until I felt strong enough to start. Friends offered to help me sort through his clothes and put them in bags for a local charity, but this task was something I wanted to do myself. I wanted to take my time, feel the feelings, experience the memories that came up, and cry if I needed to. I didn't want to feel rushed or be mechanical about this process.

I felt more emotional purging his clothes than I ever did when I discarded my own. I didn't think that would be the case. Making decisions about his clothes felt very final, and I didn't want to let him go. I also didn't want to regret letting something go, only to wish later that I had kept it.

Once I developed the courage, I started to pull out his shirts, suits, ties, and sweaters, piece by piece. Brian had simple tastes. Other than a couple of business suits, he felt most comfortable in Nike sweatpants and T-shirts. Every time he went to an air show, Brian had to purchase either a ballcap or a T-shirt. The Canadian Snowbirds, F-18s, Harriers—if the shirt had a picture of an airplane on the front, Brian happily wore it. If he had to be more formal, he usually chose a funky tie. He favoured ties with images of Yosemite Sam, Bugs Bunny, or for special occasions at Christmas, the Grinch who stole Christmas. He had ties with basketballs for coaching and ties with money symbols for meeting with a client. He used his clothes to show his quirky, fun-loving side.

With each item, I did the sniff test to see which held the strongest scent. I put those aside. This process took me the better part of a week. Did Brian have a lot of clothes? Not really. But taking my time, holding each piece, and reminiscing about the memories it brought up helped my healing process.

He loved some of his sweatshirts, especially two he purchased during the Calgary Winter Olympics in 1988. They were identical white sweatshirts with colourful flags of the world stitched at odd angles all over them. He wore those two shirts until they were threadbare. I wasn't a fan when he bought them, and as they deteriorated, I liked them even less. Every time they ended up in the laundry, I prayed they would finally fall apart so I could throw them out. No such luck. They were well made and lasted twelve years. Over the years, I had tried to convince Brian to toss them out, but he refused. Throwing them out myself was more painful than I would have imagined. You'd think I'd be relieved to get rid of these threadbare eyesores, but instead, it hurt.

I told my children to keep any of their father's clothes they wanted. My son chose Brian's leather jacket, a sweatshirt, and some ties. David also picked the poppy my husband wore every year on Remembrance Day to remember his dad. Jennifer only wanted a couple of ties. When she went away to college, the ties remained in a box where they still sit in my storage room.

I also gave David the black onyx ring his dad wore almost daily. One day he came home from school with the ring crushed. Shocked, I asked him what happened. He told me he slammed the locker door repeatedly on it until the ring was destroyed.

Trying to stay calm, I asked, "Why did you do that?"

"I don't know," he whispered as he looked down at the floor, as if preparing for me to yell at him.

"Were you angry at Dad for killing himself?"

"I'm not sure," he said.

Maybe subconsciously, David felt he could express his anger toward his dad through this ring. He immediately regretted doing it.

"It's just a ring," I assured him. "If that's what you needed to do, so be it."

Years later, I asked David if he wanted me to get the ring fixed. He said no, the ring would bring back memories of his outburst of anger. For some reason, I still have the ring in my jewelry box. I'm still not ready to part with it because Brian loved the ring, and I loved Brian. Maybe someday I'll be ready to let it go.

Going through Brian's stuff included tackling his office. When it came to paperwork, Brian was one of the most disorganized people I knew. Self-employed as a financial services manager, his office often had stacks of paper on the floor. I didn't have a clue what to do with it all. As previously mentioned, Geoff and Laurie helped me take care of the paper disaster.

Brian was also an avid reader. Our bookshelves were filled with novels, biographies, history books, and literally hundreds of books about airplanes. To call Brian an airplane fanatic would be an understatement. He had photo albums full of pictures of airplanes in museums and at air shows. (Just in case my kids, especially my son, wanted them, I held on to those albums for almost ten years before finally letting them go.) After David selected a few history books—several on airplanes—he and I filled twenty boxes to take to the secondhand bookstore. I backed the vehicle up to the door and opened the hatch to the van. A man pulled up beside me at the same time and looked into my vehicle as he walked to the door to see what I was dropping off.

"Hi there, I notice you have a lot of boxes of airplane magazines in the back. Do you mind if I look before you drop them off?" he asked.

I gently lowered the box of magazines onto the floor of the van.

"Do you love airplanes?" I asked, hoping he would say yes.

"Airplanes are my passion. I came here today hoping to find some magazines I don't have yet," he explained.

David pulled on my sleeve, "Mom, this is the janitor from our school. He and I have talked about airplanes before."

The man then turned to look at David for the first time. "Oh, hi, David. Is this your mom?"

"Yes. These magazines belonged to my dad. You know he loved airplanes too," David added.

"I want you to take all the magazines," I offered. "Brian, my husband, would be so happy to have someone who loved airplanes have these magazines. Please take them as my gift."

"I couldn't do that. Let me offer you something for them," he replied.

"Ten dollars. For all of them."

"You know they're worth a lot more than that. There are boxes and boxes of them," he resisted.

"Ten dollars. Not a penny more."

It made me happy to know something that meant so much to Brian went to someone who would truly appreciate and love them as much as he did. I couldn't have planned this exchange any better.

I kept pictures of Brian displayed throughout the house for several years. I wanted my children to feel connected to their father and didn't want to hurt their feelings by removing them. I finally decided that to move forward and create space in my life for someone else, I needed to remove all his pictures from common areas. It took me six years to get to this place. Before removing any pictures, I wanted to get the blessing of my children. I wasn't sure of the impact my action would have on them. By then, David was twenty and Jennifer was sixteen. At dinner one night, I broached the subject. "I want to talk to both of you about something I'd like to do. I will always love your dad, and I need to remove his photos from around the house," I said cautiously, expecting pushback from one or both of them. "I feel I cannot move forward with my life, and possibly a new relationship, when his photos are throughout the living room and kitchen." They were both fine with my request.

I started in the living room where there were two large, framed pictures. One, a couple shot of the two of us: I wore a formal sequined dress, and Brian sported a dark grey suit. The other photo, my favourite, the one I had selected for his service, a head shot of Brian taken at an air show, sporting aviator sunglasses and flashing the smile that always made me weak in the knees. I spent several minutes staring at each photo. My heart felt a little squeeze as I placed them in the storage box. Then I headed to the kitchen to remove photos out of plastic holders held by magnets to the refrigerator. Then I went down to the family room and finally to our bedroom. One by one, I placed the pictures in the box, and with each placement, I told Brian I loved him. It may seem like a weird ritual, but it helped me create new space in my life. I put the box in the downstairs storage room. I didn't want the box in my bedroom closet since I wanted to keep the energy of my bedroom clear. The kids both kept photos and memorabilia from their dad in their bedrooms.

Early on, one of the toughest things I needed to change was my husband's recording on our answering machine. Sometimes I phoned our home number just to hear Brian's voice. Finally, my dear friends told me it *creeped them out* calling my house and hearing Brian's voice on the message. It was a simple greeting: "Hi, you have reached Brian, Cathie, David, and Jennifer. We are not able to come to the phone right now. Please leave your name and number and we will get back to you. Thanks, have a great day!" We had talked about whether to put a goofy message on the answering machine like many of our friends had but decided it best to go with boring and generic in case a client called for Brian.

I resisted recording a new message, and then the weirdest thing happened. The voice recording disappeared. It just vanished. In a panic, I called our telephone provider to see if they could retrieve it.

"Hello, this is Carol. How can I help you today?" the operator began.

"This might seem like an odd request, but it is critical I retrieve the voice message that was on my phone."

"I'm sorry, ma'am. I don't think that we can do that for you."

My heart started to race.

"You don't understand. My husband died, and I need to hear his voice. I call myself every day just to hear him. I need you to find the voice recording and restore it. I am begging you."

I talked faster and higher as the quiver in my voice turned into panic.

Silence.

"Let me put you on hold, and I'll see what I can do."

It seemed like an eternity passed as I listened to the dreadful elevator music in the background, holding the receiver in an iron grip.

Finally, Carol returned to the call. "Good news, we can restore the voice message immediately."

I wanted to jump through the phone and kiss her.

"Carol, you are a lifesaver!"

It's amazing how people will find a way to help.

I kept Brian's voice message for another couple of months. That gave me time to prepare for the change. When I was ready, and only when I was ready, I asked David to record a new message. After I changed the message, I wept. That was my biggest crying session since Brian died. It became one more layer of letting go.

Over the years as I went through the house, I found more of Brian's stuff tucked away. I discovered a binder containing his innermost thoughts that he had written while taking personal development courses. I could have read through his book and maybe gotten a glimpse into past wounds Brian might have suffered as a child. I immediately realized the content might answer many of my questions regarding his years growing up. I had taken the same courses and knew the kind of work involved in healing the past. Maybe something would tell me about his relationship with his parents or siblings something he never divulged to me. After much contemplation, I chose to destroy the book without reading a word. If Brian didn't want to share past hurts with me when he was living, I didn't feel justified in reading them when he was dead.

Nearly two decades later, I now have only one box with some of Brian's belongings. I still need to decide what will happen with that last box. If neither of my children wants the contents, it will be time to let it go. Through dealing with Brian's belongings, I have learned that what I hold on to is just stuff. When my mother passed away, I went through the same experience. I still have a few pieces of her clothing, and from time to time, I give them the sniff test. I can still faintly smell her perfume.

I am currently practicing letting go of attachment to my belongings. I'm motivated to purge as many of them as possible, including any notes or writing I have kept regarding past hurts I have already let go. Most of those hurts are in this book, anyway. I spent the first half of my life accumulating things. I hope to spend less than the last half of my life getting rid of most of it. I want to live more simply and make it as easy as possible for the person who must sift through my stuff when I die.

I do wonder, though, will anyone sniff my clothes?

CHAPTER 15

Can We Get a Dog?

I have found that when you are deeply troubled, there are things you get from the silent devoted companionship of a dog that you can get from no other source.
Doris Day

After lunch on Christmas Day, three days after Brian's body was found, I was washing dishes in the kitchen when my ten-year-old daughter asked me with a wide smile, "Can we get a dog?"

I almost dropped the plate in the sink, totally unprepared for her question. Her father had just died. It was the last thing I expected to hear. Over the years, my kids had asked for a dog, but our answer had always been no, as Brian was allergic. Now that he was no longer with us, I imagine that in the mind of a ten-year-old, his absence meant opportunity.

I wasn't sure how to interpret Jennifer's question. I knew she felt devastated that her dad had died. She had been his *tiny dancer.* Over the years, they cranked up the music and danced around the house with her feet perched on top of his, spinning from room to room. As he read bedtime stories to her, Jennifer snuggled next to him. He also coached her soccer team and often played with her and her dolls. They were close.

I knew Jennifer was hurting. The last thing I wanted to do was to say something that might make her feel wrong for asking. I also had no intention of caring for a dog right then. I loved dogs, but I feared the responsibility. At the time, I could barely imagine raising two children on my own.

"We'll have to wait and see," I told her, exactly what my mom always told me when she didn't want to give a definitive answer.

The conversation about getting a dog persisted, mostly driven by Jennifer, but soon she enrolled her brother in her quest. She also involved other family members, who told me getting a dog would be *great therapy* for our family. When I was a young girl, I had desperately wanted a dog. I even gave my dad a puppy for his birthday when my next-door neighbour's dog had a litter. But my dad told me he refused to take care of a dog and made me take it back, which broke my heart. I didn't even realize returning a birthday present was an option. Since that time, I never lost the desire to have my own dog, so my resolve to remain a pet-free home already appeared to be on shaky ground.

My determination wavered. Pardon the pun, but Jennifer was like a dog with a bone. Every time we saw a puppy, she looked at me with her *puppy-dog eyes* and said, "Pleeaasse, Mom?" Every time, I took a deep breath, told myself I couldn't handle one more thing, and once again said no. Then one day, almost two years later, my children and I went out for lunch to celebrate my niece Shannon's wedding anniversary. Most of our extended family attended. Afterwards, on the way to my brother's house for cake, we *happened* to go to the pet store to pick up food for Shannon's dog. I say *happened*, but somehow, I think this outing may have been planned.

My kids loved going to the pet store and surveying all the animals, especially the dogs. While chatting with my niece, Jennifer ran up to me. "I found him! I found our dog!"

She took my hand and led me over to the little window where two Maltese Yorkshire Terriers were playing. "That's him! That's our dog," she declared. In her eyes, I could see she expected me to see what she already knew.

I still did not want a dog because I knew two things. First, despite their promises, my kids wouldn't take care of the dog. I would end up with all the daily dog duties. Second, someday I might have to make the decision to end the dog's life. I wanted nothing to do with either of these major responsibilities. I wasn't ready to make such a commitment. To my daughter's great disappointment, we left the store without the dog. The silence in the car ride home spoke volumes.

At my brother's house, the campaign to change my mind started in earnest. Everyone—including my mother, children, sister-in-law, niece, and her husband—worked together to beg, plead, and promise the moon, if only we could get THE DOG. I felt like the worst mother EVER.

Finally, I caved.

We hopped in the car and drove back to the pet store. When we got to the window where the dog had been, it was empty. The kids were devastated. *Great. I really screwed this one up.* However, a door to the back room had been left open a crack. I peeked inside. I could see a staff member putting *our* dog into a kennel.

Pushing the door open, I said, "Excuse me, has someone bought him already?"

"No," she said, "he's part of a group of dogs that are going to a birthday party in hopes that they'll find a forever home."

Thank God.

I asked if they could take a different dog to the party so we could purchase this one.

She smiled and said, "Of course," as she placed him in my arms.

I remembered watching a dog expert on TV explaining how to tell if you have a dog who will be obedient. You flip them on their back, and if they remain passive, that is a trainable dog. I held him like a baby with his four legs in the air. He became completely passive, looking up at me on his back, his big brown eyes staring into mine. Smart dog! He had obviously watched the same episode and knew this trick would find him a forever home.

Just as I signed the papers and ran the credit card through at the till, another family with two children younger than mine came to ask about the same dog. They had done the same thing, gone away to think about it for a bit. The children were loud and hitting one another. Once they heard the dog they wanted had been purchased by another family, their behaviour escalated. If we had not returned at that moment, the family with the seemingly spoiled kids would have adopted our dog. *We saved you, buddy.*

On the way home, I saw a sign for the transit system: Park and Ride. Looking over my shoulder into the back seat of the car, I asked, "Do you like the name *Parker* for our dog?"

"Yes! We love it," they agreed enthusiastically. Honestly, I think they would have said yes to calling him "Poopieface." They just wanted a dog.

Before we could take him home, our little puppy needed to be neutered and get all his shots. I was on my way out of town for work, so when I got back five days later, I picked Parker up and brought him home in the small dog kennel my sister-in-law Gloria had given me. I unstrapped the kennel from the back seat, held it securely in my left hand, and opened the door that led to the family room. David, Jennifer, and my mother were waiting for the dog's arrival. I don't even think they said hello to me. I handed the kennel to David; he unlocked the door and reached in to gently pull Parker into his arms. The lovefest began. The kids finally had a dog. They took turns holding, petting, kissing, and taking him out to pee (a novelty that quickly wore off). As I looked at my kids and the complete joy on their faces, I questioned myself: *Why did I feel I had to wait so long? Seeing them be happy is everything I want.* Jennifer finally took a break fawning over Parker. She came over to me on the couch, threw her arms around my neck, looked me right in the eyes and said, "Thanks Mom, you are the best... mom... ever." *I wonder how long that distinction will last?*

People had told me that dogs could help people heal. After we adopted Parker, I looked up some medical research on the subject. According to Animal Behaviourist Takeumi Kikusui of Azabu University in Japan, gazing into your dog's eyes lowers your blood pressure and raises your oxytocin, also known as the "love hormone."[39] Oxytocin is also associated with empathy, trust, sexual activity, and relationship-building. Your oxytocin levels rise when you hug or have an orgasm, and increased levels can have a positive impact on depression and anxiety. Owning a dog can also reduce isolation and increase your physical activity. I certainly felt more present and calmer when petting Parker on my lap.

In fact, it filled my heart to have this little furball get so excited when we walked through the door. Even if we had only been gone five minutes, Parker did what affectionately became known as the Ear Dance. Typically, we entered the house and climbed the stairs to the dining room where he anxiously awaited our return. He pushed himself along the carpet with his ear to the ground. Parker could cover quite a distance, but usually he went in circles for a minute or two, taking turns with which ear he pushed to the ground. Then he gave us lots of kisses and followed us from room to room.

At the pet store, they had told us that being part Yorkie, his legs would not be strong. We would need to lift him onto the couch or bed. The first time we left him alone while we went out for dinner, we set him up in the kitchen with a four-foot high wire kennel positioned around his bed. To our surprise, when we returned, Parker greeted us at the door, wagging his tail. He had climbed the wire fence, wiggled through the banister, jumped onto a bookcase in the family room on the level below the kitchen, onto the couch, and finally sat waiting for us by the garage door. It turns out, our dog could jump. Often, he took two or three stairs at a time, ears flying as he soared through the air, a free spirit. Over the years, we called him Houdini or Bolt because if he had the chance, he would make a run for it.

Although he passed my initial test of obedience at the pet store, this dog had no real intention of letting me be the master. Shannon acquired a puppy about the same age as Parker, and we decided to take our dogs to obedience class for six weeks. Shannon's dog, Tyson, was a star pupil, and the instructor encouraged her to sign her dog up for level two. As Parker's owner and trainer, I failed obedience class. Silly me, I thought the class meant to teach *him* how to behave. I was so wrong, not to mention embarrassed.

"Come back and take level one again; maybe next time Parker will start to obey," said our instructor, trying to keep a straight face.

Yeah, and pigs will fly. We never returned.

As I predicted, Parker became my dog. I walked him most mornings, bathed and fed him, and let him sleep on my bed. Usually, in the middle of the night, he burrowed under the covers and became my hot water bottle, especially during the winter. When my children grew up and left for college/university, he became my close companion, comforting me again as I learned to live alone without them.

As much as my children begged to get a dog, I made the conscious choice to get Parker. Faced with the possibility of losing something, I questioned if the value it would bring could be worth the risk. Taking risks seemed way too scary sometimes. In doing it anyway, I expanded my possibility to love again. I wasn't ready to fall in love with a partner, so having Parker allowed me to practice loving something outside myself. He also reminded me daily that I was lovable.

For fifteen years, one month, and twelve days (5,521 days total), Parker was my dog on this earth. We adopted him at five months old. When he reached fifteen-and-a half years old, I had to make the heartbreaking decision to put him down—the day I dreaded since bringing him home. Parker could no longer see well, so he kept running into walls. His back legs were no longer reliable enough to hold him up. He had accidents in the house, even when he had just been outside to relieve himself.

I saw both my mother's and father's bodies after they passed away, but I had never experienced watching a living thing die before. I considered not being in the room when Parker was put down, but I thought I might have residual guilt for letting my dog die without me. I admit to having a bit of curiosity and a lot of fear. *What would it be like to see the process firsthand? Would I break down emotionally? So what if I did? Could this be cathartic for me to face death, perhaps my own mortality?*

I made the decision. David happened to be in town for work, so it seemed like the best time to schedule the appointment with the veterinarian. Before taking Parker to the vet, I took him for a short walk and cooked him some lean ground beef. He gobbled it up and licked his bowl to a clean shine. David arrived and I opened the kennel for Parker. He scooted in, knowing an open kennel door meant we were going on an adventure. We spoke little on the way to the veterinarian.

The waiting room was full, mostly with dogs, but there was also one cat. Parker shook in my arms, something he always did whenever he went to the vet. *You have no idea what is about to happen, my little buddy.* After a few minutes, a vet technician told us our room was ready. Her name tag said Becky. A metal table sat in the middle of the small room. I was struck by how sterile the room looked and detected the odour of bleach. I expected it to smell more of stale urine. I lifted Parker, and we spread a blanket over the cold, metal surface. My stomach churned. The thought of what was about to happen made me physically ill.

Becky told us the vet would be there in a few moments.

"Please take your time saying your goodbyes. When you are ready, just stick your head out the door and let us know," she said kindly.

I'm grateful they didn't rush us. We had the time to say everything we wanted before the vet came in.

I held Parker's face in my hands and said, "Thank you for being such a good dog. You helped me on my journey to love again, and I am grateful for your love. I'll miss you, my little buddy."

I could barely see; the tears were coming so fast. My heart felt like it was breaking down the middle.

David took Parker into his arms. We wiped away our tears, kissed our little guy, and after what seemed like ten minutes, I opened the door, looked down the hallway, and nodded to Becky who was now behind the front desk. She nodded back at me and mouthed, "I'll be right there."

Within two minutes Becky was back in the room, along with the vet. The veterinarian took her stethoscope and listened to Parker's heart. She explained she would give Parker a needle that is like a sedative, but also contained the lethal dose of meds that would end his life.

"Are you ready?" she asks.

I looked at David, then nodded. The technician turned on the electric shaver and removed fur from Parker's front right leg while the vet prepared the cocktail.

Parker was shaking, and I petted him over and over.

"It's okay, it's okay, it's okay," I repeated.

The vet looked at me once more, and I nodded before she injected the needle.

"It's okay, it's going to be okay."

In a matter of seconds, Parker's body went limp. I held on to the side of the table as I started to feel a little faint. A minute later, the vet put the stethoscope to Parker's chest once again, checked his eyes, and declared him gone.

After a few minutes of silence, we wrapped Parker in the blanket and David lifted him into his arms. We made our way down the hallway, out the back door, and out into the crisp fall air. In silence, I opened the back hatch of the SUV, and David laid Parker's wrapped body on top of some cardboard I kept in the vehicle. We made one stop on the way home, and as we got out of the vehicle, we saw the most magnificent sunset. Brilliant rose and orange hues danced across the clouds as golden rays of sunshine burst through, creating an explosion of colour. It was magical. It was as if God has painted a picture just for us to see. I said a quick prayer of thanks. *What a send-off. Thank you, God, for giving me this dog.*

I felt guilty making the decision to end Parker's life and probably put it off longer than I should have. If I thought he would get better, I would have scooped him up and changed my mind. I felt like such a liar. Telling him he was going to be okay? I realized the soothing words were for me, not him. I needed to hear it would be okay. The words eased my guilt.

As difficult as it was to lose my dog, I remember the joy and healing he brought me and my children. I am grateful for the unconditional love he gave me every day. I am grateful for the Ear Dance and the cuddling under the covers on a cold winter's night. I am grateful for the indomitable spirit of this dog, who taught me to exceed others' expectations and not buy into the limitations they may impose, to express joy with wild abandon, and to be willing to leap. Most of all, I am grateful Parker taught me I am worthy of love and that I can love again.

I ask myself, *Would I get Parker again? Would I choose to experience the deep sense of loss with his passing? Would I expose myself to watching his little body fail him? Would I love him enough to let him go?*

My answer is simple: in a heartbeat.

CHAPTER 16
The Rings

With this ring, I thee wed and make you mine forever.
To have and to hold until the end of time.
— *Hank Snow, "With this Ring"*

When I saw that Brian had left his wedding ring lying on top of the manila envelope, I knew in my heart that Brian was not coming back. He had never once taken off his wedding ring during our fifteen-year marriage. He prided himself on his commitment to never remove it. Whenever a discussion of wedding rings came up with family or friends, he held up his left hand and proudly exclaimed that it had never left his finger.

The day after I found his ring, I held it and stared at it. I slowly turned the gold band over and over with my fingers, studying the colour, the small diamond in the centre, and the small scratches embedded in the band. I remembered that shortly after getting married, I showed off my rings to someone at work. As I held them up to the light, I noticed a small mark on the gold band. I was distressed that I had already scratched my ring, until an office visitor who was in the throes of a nasty divorce, said, "Better a scratch on your ring than a scratch on your soul." *Ouch.* Now the scratches on Brian's ring made me think that I would forever have a scratch on my soul from his death.

I gingerly slipped his ring on my left-hand ring finger so it would touch my wedding ring. It was much too big to fit securely on my finger. I couldn't wear it without the risk of losing it. I couldn't wear it without the risk of losing it. I had suffered enough loss, I didn't want to lose his ring. I cried, heaving monstrous tears. I opened my jewellery box and created a space for his wedding ring to rest. At that moment, I didn't want to think about what to do with it. *Maybe one of my kids will want it when they get older.*

So, what importance do I give to rings?

Growing up, I dreamed of the day I would get married and wear a wedding ring. I held the dream of being connected to and loved by one person close to my heart. A wedding ring symbolized belonging to someone. I remember my mother reading fairy tales to me; someday my handsome prince would ride up on his white steed and present me with a diamond that would take my breath away. I fantasized about others commenting on its brilliance, and all would know that I was truly loved.

As a young girl, my mother sometimes let me try on her wedding and engagement rings. I dreamt about what my rings would look like. When I grew older, my mom gave me my paternal grandmother's wedding ring. I cherished it but didn't wear it as I thought the single diamond in an antique setting looked too dated.

So much for fairy tales. When Brian proposed, he didn't even have a ring to offer me. Knowing he had a very limited income, I offered to take the diamond out of my grandmother's wedding ring and have it placed in a new setting. We agreed that when we had more money, he would buy me a diamond. The engagement ring and wedding ring fit together like a puzzle. My grandmother's diamond stood out in a simple but uniquely shaped golden band. Although it wasn't anywhere near the fantasy I had imagined growing up, I still loved my rings, and I loved Brian more.

The morning after our wedding, we were lying in bed talking. We put our hands side by side to look at the rings.

"I will never take this off," he said.

"Neither will I," I replied.

He managed to keep that promise, or so he said. No matter what he was doing—working on the car, playing sports, swimming, washing dishes—his wedding ring didn't come off, as far as I knew. He declared it a symbol of our union, our love, and our commitment. I, on the other hand, did not fulfill that promise. My rings sometimes came off when I washed dishes or changed a dirty diaper. I could always justify my decision. As time wore on and after the birth of two children, I put on weight, and my rings simply would not come off. I think he liked that; probably the only thing he liked about my weight gain.

Even though I couldn't remove my rings, I liked keeping them on after Brian's death. It helped to ease the pain of him being gone. The vows we said at our wedding were in *sickness and health, 'til death do us part.* I wasn't ready to fully accept his death. As mad as I was at him for taking his own life, I still wanted to belong to him. I wanted others to know that I belonged. I didn't want to be alone. Our vows meant until we were both dead. Marriage meant forever.

My mother also kept her rings on after my father died. It seemed to me that older, widowed women who had been married a long time tended to do that. My mom survived my dad by twenty-eight years. It influenced my decision to keep my rings on. It symbolized her love and commitment to my father. I wanted my children to know that even though Brian was gone, I still loved their father and held my commitment to him.

I continued to wear my wedding rings for several years: part denial that Brian had died and part protection so I would not attract attention from other men. At first glance, I looked like a married woman. I didn't want to admit I was a widow. A woman in her forties without wedding rings usually means she has never married or is divorced. I didn't want to explain to potential suitors that my husband had died because typically the next question was, "How did he die?" *Ugh. Too much work.*

I needed to work out my own pain and raise my kids. I told myself that I didn't have the time or energy for a new relationship, that men couldn't handle a woman with so much baggage. No man would want to take on a partner grieving because of suicide. Taking off the rings meant freedom to pursue another relationship. I wasn't ready for that. I wore my rings as a shield to protect me from being hurt again.

Many times, friends asked, "When are you going to lose the rings?"

With the extra weight I had put on since getting married, no amount of soap and twisting was going to get them off. I declared that when ready, I would lose weight and the rings would come off naturally. This would be a sign to my friends of my readiness for another relationship.

Four years after Brian died, I thought I was ready to move forward with my life. Maybe I would meet a nice guy and start dating. I would take it slow; I wouldn't jump into anything too fast. I went on a diet. I cut back on carbs and sweets. I started exercising. I walked with Donna. In about five months, I lost thirty pounds. *Good for me! You've got this girl! Congratulations!*

Stepping out of the shower one day, I dried myself off and noticed soap residue on my left hand. As I wiped my hand with the towel, my rings felt loose. Holding my breath, I cautiously twisted them and watched as they slid down my finger. I took them as far as the base of my fingernail. My heart started to race. I stared at the deep indent on my finger where they had rested for so many years. I could either take the rings off completely or push them back on. I cried as I slowly pushed them back into the indent. I was not ready.

It took me less than three months to put the thirty pounds back on.

Was this a conscious decision? No. Deep down, I wasn't ready, and above all, I had more work to do on myself. I told myself it wasn't time yet. Fear held me in a tight grip. Fear of being hurt again, of loving someone only to be left behind, of taking a risk. *What if someone showed interest and when I tell him my husband died by suicide, the air gets sucked out of the room, he loses eye contact, and the conversation gets awkward? What if I give my heart to someone, and maybe they don't die, but they leave me?* I held on to my story: no one, not ever, would love me as much as Brian did.

The following year I went to a personal development course in Los Angeles. As I entered the room and scanned the participants, a short woman standing by her seat in the front row drew my attention. About my age, she sported spiky, bleached-blonde hair and was dressed casually in jeans and a tie-dyed T-shirt, with a scarf wrapped around her neck. I, too, am a front-row gal. Why pay all this money for registration and travel and not take advantage of getting the most out of my experience? Her cool attire and seat choice made my move to approach her an easy one.

"Hi, is this seat taken?" I asked.

"I saved it for you," she said with a wink.

We introduced ourselves. My soon-to-be new friend, Gail, lived in Colorado on a communal property consisting of ten houses with a main building that held the kitchen and dining area. The community pooled money for groceries, and each household took turns making three meals a month. Gail owned a couple of alpacas. *That is so cool!* She talked about the benefits of living in a community.

Living with others who believe in sustainable living had been something I had considered for some time.

"I love having my own home and knowing when I travel for work, my house is taken care of and so are my animals," she shared proudly. "I'm so happy I decided to join this community."

Gail owned a business focused on people's health and wellness.

Part of the course included partner work, and I found myself sharing at a deep and vulnerable level with Gail. She spoke her mind, and I found her to be genuine and compassionate. Before long, we finished each other's sentences. I was amazed at how quickly we established a friendship. We talked about how we probably knew each other from a previous life, and then we laughed. Do you know that quote about people being brought into our lives for a season, a reason, or a lifetime? We were brought together for a reason.

We spent the next four days of the workshop together, working as part of a group, learning how to live more successful lives, pushing ourselves and each other to become the best we could be. We talked about living a life of purpose, of dreaming big, of embracing risk. I told Gail about my life, about Brian's suicide five years ago, and how I wanted to be in a new relationship but feared putting myself out there again. I told her about my rings and the time they almost came off, but I had sabotaged myself to make sure they stayed put.

"Just cut the fucking things off," she said.

I sat there stunned at her words and felt tightness in my chest. My breathing became shallow. She said it again, slowly, "JUST...CUT...THE...FUCKING...THINGS... OFF!"

The idea had never crossed my mind. I could just make the decision to take them off. That scared me.

Would it be sacrilegious to cut the band?

What would others think?

Would Brian be mad?

Was I ready?

What if I cut the rings off and then changed my mind?

I thought about it for what seemed an eternity; in reality, less than a minute had passed.

"Okay," I said, taking a deep breath, "I'll do it."

"Let's go!" she said, abruptly standing up from her seat.

"Where?" I asked.

"To the jewelry store to get them cut off."

"Now?"

This shit was getting real.

"Yes, now," she said firmly.

I barely knew this woman but trusted it was the right time, the right place, with the right person. We headed to the mall within walking distance of the convention centre. With each step, I told myself, *it's time, it's time.* The jewellery store we found was empty, not a customer in sight. *Perfect, I don't need an audience.* Except for the soft, piped-in music, silence permeated the space. Perhaps the nonstop chatter in my head blocked out all other sounds and kept me in my own zone.

We walked up to the illuminated display case filled with wedding and engagement rings, sparkling and shiny, waiting to become a symbol of love for a new bride. The irony was not lost on me.

Gail boldly told the young clerk, "Cut these rings off her finger."

The jeweller's eyes widened, and she looked surprised at Gail's candour, but quietly went to the back of the store and returned with a pair of jewellery clippers. I didn't even know they existed. The salesclerk looked at me and asked if I was sure.

I took a deep breath and in a quiet but firm voice said, "Yes, please cut them off."

The jeweller slid one side of the clippers under one ring and snip—the ring broke in half. She looked at me with one eyebrow raised as if to ask if she should continue. Tears started falling down my cheeks. I nodded. She snipped the second ring. Done. I pulled the gold pieces away from my finger and put them on the counter. My new friend held me as I let the emotions flow. My body shook with heaving sobs. I cried. I cried hard. I had just released the symbol of my marriage that I had held onto with such determination.

I am a firm believer that nothing has meaning except for the meaning you give it. Letting go of the physical reminder of my marriage was one thing; I still had work to do to let go of the emotional connection to it.

I had given the symbol of the rings so much meaning that removing them proved to be gut-wrenching. Since the rings had been so tight on my finger, the indent left behind took a long time to go away. Over time, as I changed my mind about needing to have the rings, I found myself wishing my body would hurry up and erase the indentation. I put my wedding ring pieces in my jewellery box, nestled safely beside Brian's. From time to time I took them out to look at them. Over the years, I considered having the gold melted down and made into a new piece of diamond jewellery. Redesigning gold and diamonds seemed easier than redesigning my heart.

A part of me resented Brian for never buying me a diamond ring. Several years before he died, I had told him that I wanted him to buy me a diamond. He agreed to do it, but it never happened. After he died, I saw a news article about how a company could take the cremated ashes of a loved one and compress them until the ashes formed a man-made diamond. I thought about it for a bit—maybe this could be the way Brian could give me a diamond. I never followed through. I imagined he would find this idea a little funny since we shared the same dark sense of humour.

On a cruise to the Caribbean in 2009, I bought myself diamond earrings in St. Thomas: three rows of three tiny diamonds in a square cut in each earring. When I showed them to my niece Krista upon my return, she said, "Oh, you bought no-man diamonds."

"What the heck are no-man diamonds?" I asked.

"I have some myself. No man bought them for me; I bought them myself."

Hmm, what a great concept: not relying on a man to buy me a diamond!

When others have asked me about the best time to remove your rings after a spouse dies, my answer is always the same: it's different for every person. What was right for me may not be right for someone else. Only they will know. I do encourage other women, however, to only remove the rings if they want to. What others think about them wearing their rings is not their concern—none of their business. Even though Gail boldly told me to cut off my rings, I wouldn't have done it based solely on what she said. I was ready; I just needed someone to nudge me to act on a decision I had already made. I needed her help to get past the fear.

I chose to take off the wedding ring Brian gave me. Nothing more.

CHAPTER 17

The River of my Dreams

For life and death are one, even as the river and the sea are one
Khalil Gibran

I've always had an interest in dreams. What do they mean? Is it a way that our higher self helps us work out issues in our life? Are they messages from a higher power? Or are they purely for our entertainment or to stimulate curiosity? Why do I remember some dreams and not others?

A few months after my father died in 1984, I had a dream where I was walking against the current of a river in thigh-high water. There were people in front and behind me. I didn't recognize anyone as we walked in unison, but I sensed I was with friends and family. We followed a slow, rhythmic pattern. Walking against the current required a certain level of energy.

After a few minutes, I spotted my father lounging on a very large, flat rock in the middle of the river. He sprawled comfortably in the middle of the rock, his legs outstretched as he leaned back on his forearms with his head tilted back to receive the shining sun. He wore beige shorts and a white T-shirt. His face shone with contentment and peace. It had been such a long time since I had seen my father with a smile on his face. He had been sick for so many years before he died that I had forgotten what he looked like when he smiled. My dad looked happy, clearly enjoying his experience.

"C'mon Dad. We have to keep walking up the river," I explained, somehow sensing that was the instruction we were all supposed to follow.

"I think I'll just sit on this rock and watch the people go by," he responded lazily.

"No, Dad, we need to keep walking," I insisted.

Maybe he didn't understand the importance of the instruction.

"You go on ahead; I'm going to sit on this rock and enjoy my time here," he replied with a broad smile.

Reluctantly, I continued my journey up the river. All around me, the other people continued the slow, steady pace, as if all knew what we were supposed to do. It was our destiny. Why did they understand the plan and my father didn't? I looked back to see him basking in the sun, and then the camera lens pulled back for a panoramic view. I could see multiple rocks up and down the river with people sitting on them. Sometimes they sat alone; sometimes several people shared the same rock. Suddenly it made sense. Moving up the river depended on each person's choice. Some chose to keep moving upstream. Others chose to bask in the sun on a rock. No right or wrong, no judgement—each person was either walking or sitting.

When I woke up, I remembered the dream vividly and felt a deep sense of calm. For the first time since my father died, I felt at peace with his passing. My dad had so many health problems and suffered physically, emotionally, and mentally. I always wished he would find peace in death. I saw this dream as a gift and felt gratitude for the experience. I had struggled with his death and questioned whether he found peace. I took the dream as a sign that he had.

A few months after Brian died, I dreamt again of walking with others against the current of a river. Again, we were thigh-deep, walking steadily and rhythmically toward our destination. This time, instead of a comforting image, one image became very distressing. I saw Brian trapped on the side of a deep riverbank with branches and briar wrapped around his body, holding him prisoner. His body was covered in cuts and scratches, his face contorted just as it had been in the weeks before his death. When he saw me, he pleaded for me to help him. I couldn't, an unseen force kept me moving forward. No matter how hard I tried, how hard I strained, I couldn't talk to him, I couldn't do anything for him.

I awoke crying. I felt such a deep sadness and complete helplessness. If only I could have helped him release the bonds that trapped him! The dream reflected my feelings of helplessness in real life. I felt profound sadness that I couldn't help him while he was alive or in death. All I could do was pray that he'd be free of the bonds that held him. I prayed that he would realize what had happened, and somehow that awareness would help him be released from his agony.

What does a dream about a river mean? I looked in several resources and found one in the Dream Bible online (dreambible.com) that made sense to me: "To dream of crossing a river represents an obstacle of uncertainty, difficulties you need to overcome, or unwanted situations. Unpleasant situations that [are] temporary. Crossing a river symbolizes moving through a phase prior to achieving a goal."

My dream reflected the helplessness I felt being a single mother. I had two children experiencing deep grief that I needed to support. I had to manage money, something Brian had done for our family. I questioned whether I was making good choices for myself and my kids. I had anxiety facing new situations; my life became one uncertain moment after another. *Will I screw up my kids? Will I run out of money? What if I die and they become orphans?* That final question became my greatest fear.

I thought about the dream for several weeks. I couldn't erase the image of Brian crying out for me to help him. I finally decided that other than prayer, a daily practice, I couldn't do anything more to help him. I needed to focus on myself and my children. I decided to behave as if I were strong and hoped it would happen. Using the power of intention to create a new possibility, I told myself over and over, even when I didn't believe it, that I *will* provide for my family. It became my daily affirmation.

I have seen Brian a few more times in dreams over the years. One time I was walking through a high school corridor, and students were bustling between classes. Brian walked toward me and smiled. He appeared about thirty years old, his age when we first met. He wore a tweed jacket and looked like a teacher. He looked happy. His face showed no more pain or struggle. It looked like he had found himself again. He turned and walked away, into the crowd. It's funny; we had often discussed that he would make a great high school teacher.

Three years after Brian died, I went white-water rafting with a group of thirty people on what would have been my eighteenth wedding anniversary. Although I love sitting by water, dipping my feet in the ocean, and swimming in pools, I never imagined going white-water rafting in the Rocky Mountains. As part of a personal development course that I took to help move forward in my life, I agreed to fully participate in whatever they threw my way. So, what the heck, I put on a wetsuit, a life vest, and a helmet. It was exhilarating. On the International Scale of River Intensity, the rapids were a Class 3 or 4, which is something between getting wet and getting soaked while experiencing drops and small waterfalls.

Along the way, we pulled our rafts to the shoreline and climbed a cliff and walked to a bluff that overlooked the river. There were no rapids below us and no rocks. The instructors challenged us to jump off one of two cliffs. One measured fifteen feet above the river, and the other about twenty-five feet. We had a choice to jump into the rushing river individually or with a partner. Once in the river, we could swim to a shoreline about thirty feet downstream and climb the cliff again.

Before the jump, we met as a group and talked about the significance of taking this *leap of faith*. I took to heart what one of the instructors recommended: "If there's anything you feel holding you back in your life, release it into the river." How fitting, I thought, remembering my past dreams.

I decided to do the smaller jump first. Standing with my toes inched over the natural ledge, I looked down into the water and saw an opportunity for healing. I also felt tremendous fear. The instructors said to jump in silence, or at least as quietly as possible. I hesitated briefly, staring into the rushing water below me, and then took one huge step off the ledge. I hit the water much sooner than I expected.

The cold water shocked my system. The river comes from glacier run-off, so I expected it to be cold. Not that cold, though. A second or two passed before I popped back onto the surface and felt the current carry me downstream. I quickly swam to the shoreline and started my ascent up the cliff. This time I decided to do the bigger jump.

As I stood in line for the big drop, the woman in front of me turned around and said, "How about we hold hands and jump together?" She looked as nervous as I felt. Typically, my instinct is to help others, to make it okay for them. This was not one of those times. This jump meant far too much to play the nice girl and take care of someone else. I was taking care of me.

"Sorry, I need to do this on my own. Maybe someone else would like to jump with you."

Her face looked a bit defeated, but she nodded and asked the woman behind me, who gladly accepted her offer. I felt proud for choosing in that moment to focus on my needs. I knew I only wanted to jump off the higher cliff once and make it count.

Twenty-five feet above a river does not sound very high but standing up there looking down into the deep blue, rushing water below proved daunting. An Olympic high diving board is only seven feet higher than where I stood. I had always been in awe watching those high-dive competitions. This would be the closest I would ever come to doing that myself.

One by one, people took turns jumping. The time came for me to step onto the large flat rock that jutted over the river. I stared at the rushing river below. The extra ten feet made the river look a whole lot farther away. The sun hid behind a cloud, making the river look darker, more ominous. I shivered as the cool wind pressed against my body, still wet from the last jump. I smelled the pine trees, fresh rushing water, and clean mountain air. I breathed in deeply and said a little prayer. As I jumped, I mentally released my marriage into the water. Jumping into the river became one of the most spiritual and freeing experiences of my life. This time as I floated back to the shoreline, I felt lighter, as if a huge weight had been released.

Loading back into the rafts, we continued our journey down the river in silence. I imagined that most people, like me, were quietly contemplating their experience. At the end of the journey, all thirty of us stood in a large circle to debrief. The leaders asked us to share our experiences of white-water rafting and jumping into the water off the cliffs. Each person took a turn sharing when they felt it was their time to talk.

The woman who asked me to jump with her said, "My son is addicted to heroin, and I don't know what to do. I can't make him stop. He doesn't want my help. Today I released my need to control him. I love my son, and I realize I can't save him; he has to want to get help."

A young man said, "I was unfaithful to my girlfriend of three years, and I haven't been able to tell her. I love her and want to marry her. I released the guilt and shame I've been living with, and I'm ready to tell her the truth."

About half of the people spoke before I felt ready to share.

"Today would have been my eighteenth wedding anniversary. My husband, Brian, killed himself three years ago. The past three years have been harder than any of you can imagine. I would say my life has been hell. I want to change my story. I don't want to live in a hellish experience anymore. Today when I jumped into the river, I released my marriage. I let Brian go."

I told the group about the two dreams I had, one with my father and the other with Brian. One person in the group suggested that this rafting trip could be the perfect way to change my story surrounding my anniversary. She was right. In the previous three years, I had been so sad on this day, but today, I had created a new memory; I had done something to reframe the day. To this day, I always remember white-water rafting on my anniversary.

Whenever I'm sad or someone I know dies, I am called to the river. The rippling sound of water as it flows over rocks soothes my soul. I love the motion, watching the power of the water push its way downstream. If I lived closer to an ocean, I would prefer to go there to hear the waves crashing. Often, I take my chair and a book and sit beside the river, knowing the sound of the water holds great healing energy for me. I don't feel a great need to jump into the river again. If I can't get to water, I find a substitute.

When I was in the Caribbean in 2009, I purchased a rain stick, which is a percussion instrument made from a hollowed plant stalk that's sealed at both ends and filled with seeds or pebbles. When the stick is held upside down, the pebbles cascade, creating a sound like rainfall. Once all the pebbles reach the end, the stick is then turned over again, and the sound continues. The origin of the rain stick is unclear but has been linked to Indigenous people using them in their spiritual practice to summon rain. I have found using the rain stick to be very healing. Listening to the sound of the rain stick can quickly calm my anxiety or unease.

For me, water in all its forms is healing. Having a hot shower soothed my soul. Whether it was feeling the cleansing power of the water or allowing myself to have a good cry as the water poured over me, I felt more connected to myself. I could get lost in the moment, get out of my head, and let go of the myriad thoughts and emotions that overwhelmed me.

If I didn't have the opportunity to jump into a hot shower, I held my hands under running warm water whenever I felt anxious or overwhelmed by my emotions. After a few minutes, I could feel the tension and anxiety start to drain out of my body. On nights when I had difficulty sleeping, running my hands under warm water helped me relax before slipping back into bed and nodding off.

A couple of years ago, I started floating in a sensory deprivation tank about once or twice a month. Hydrotherapy has been around for thousands of years, and float tanks have been around since the 1950s. Stepping inside the tank and shutting the door felt like crawling into a cocoon. I would opt to keep the coloured lights and gentle music on until I situated my body in the water and waited for the gentle ripples to subside. Then, pushing the on/off button sent my world into complete darkness, unable to see where the water stopped, and the edges of the pod started. The idea is to float in the water and cut off as many sensory inputs as possible. I typically would float for sixty minutes, allowing myself the time to deeply relax. I didn't have to worry about time as the lights and music would come back on at the sixty-minute mark. I was able to let go of responsibility and worry. It was a form of meditation for me.

Will I dream about the river again? I don't know. Maybe I don't need to because I received the lesson about choice. I now choose to take time to rest and embrace the moment with my face to the sun.

I choose to embrace the ebb and flow of my life.

CHAPTER 18

Walking Over Hot Coals

Can one go upon hot coals and his feet not be burned?
— Proverbs 6:28

I have a driving need to learn new things, and what interests me the most is learning about people. What makes them tick? Why do they behave in different ways? One of the best ways I discovered to study human nature is to look at myself and figure out what makes me do what I do. For example, why do I procrastinate? I discovered I get a rush from waiting until the last minute, working frantically to complete my task. When I produce the result, I get a feeling like there's a magician saying, *Ta-da!* This way of acting satisfies my need for challenge and excitement. I can either meet these needs constructively or destructively. When I'm conscious of my actions, I can choose to have those needs met constructively.

My quest for knowledge is one of the reasons I decided to study social work. Looking at human behaviour and our ability to navigate change fascinates me. After graduating in 1980, I worked as a crisis counsellor at the local women's emergency shelter, followed by helping teens transition from the child welfare system into independent living.

In 1984, a friend told me about a weekend workshop scheduled in her city, San Diego, which was getting great reviews from her friends. She asked me to take the course with her. The workshop, Live, Love, Laugh, facilitated by Jack Canfield, fueled my love for self-discovery. Today most people recognize Jack as one of the two authors of *Chicken Soup for the Soul*. At the time, I had never heard of him, as Jack would not become a household name for several years.

Shortly after we started on Friday night, Jack asked where people had come from to take the course. Many said San Diego and the surrounding area. A couple of people came from Los Angeles, and someone travelled all the way from San Francisco.

I put up my hand and said, "I'm from Canada."

"What? Canada?" said Jack, his mouth hanging open.

"Yes, Canada."

"Did you come all the way from Canada for this course?" he asked, with astonishment "I have never had anyone travel so far for one of my workshops."

"Yes, my friend told me the course could change my life and would be worth the trip," I added, hoping the course would be worth the money I spent.

No pressure, Jack.

Jack did not disappoint. Through that workshop, I discovered I loved personal development courses. They fit hand in hand with the studies I had done through social work. During that workshop, we created a list of goals that we wanted in life. While I had often thought about this, I wasn't aware of the power of intention. Writing my wishes and desires down made them more real; I declared to the Universe *what I wanted most.* That was the first step; how I got those things would follow.

On the top of my list, I wrote, *being married and having two children.* I had started dating Brian a month before. A week before flying to San Diego, Brian told me he loved me. While writing that list of intentions, I realized I wanted to marry this man. We married less than a year later.

Three years into our marriage, Brian and I had an opportunity to attend a four-day workshop, The Pursuit of Excellence, offered by a well-known personal development company, Context International. I had shared with him my powerful experience with Jack, and he agreed to give the course a try. Our lives changed after that experience: the way we communicated with each other, addressed conflict resolution, and understood responsibility and accountability. We learned about the Law of Attraction and setting our intentions to create success. We practiced saying positive things about our future. We embraced change. Brian even won an award. His peers voted him the person who made the greatest change in their life by becoming more authentic.

Going through these courses helped us to be congruent. Being on the same page, or so I thought, was one reason why I never imagined Brian would die by suicide. We had all the tools for creating successful lives, yet over the years, old habits resurfaced. We stopped communicating in the same way. We used to lie in bed and talk for hours about everything. Over time, we often didn't sleep in the same bed. We stopped speaking our truths to each other. We became focused on survival: paying the bills and working hard to take care of our family. Conversations we did have usually centered on the kids.

We stopped dreaming. We forgot the power of intention. When travelling on an airplane, the safety instructions include the importance of putting your oxygen mask on first. We forgot or consciously chose not to do that. The biggest breakdown in our relationship came from pretending we had everything under control, when clearly, we did not.

Fast-forward twelve years after taking the Pursuit workshop. Deep down, I was angry about having to work nights and not getting much sleep. I was pissed off that due to our weak financial situation, I still needed to work even though I felt quite ill. I wanted Brian to be more successful. I resented when he chose to watch TV or read a book instead of building his business. I thought Brian didn't take his responsibilities seriously and relied on me to bring home an income. Neither of us liked to fight, so we remained silent when there needed to be communication. Instead, the tension between us grew. In retrospect, I can understand why Brian didn't want to tell me he lost his job. In his mind, he probably didn't feel safe to do so.

After his death, I knew I had to do something to get myself back on track. I had made the decision to live, and now I needed to build my tool kit once again. Three years passed before I felt ready to sign up for another personal development course. I had focused entirely on taking care of my children, ensuring that bills were paid, that we had food on the table, and that the kids did well in school and stayed involved in extracurricular activities. Taking time for myself seemed selfish. Finally, I realized if I did not put on my oxygen mask and take care of myself, I wouldn't be able to take care of my family. That meant taking out the magnifying glass for a good look at myself. *What worked for me? What didn't?*

I'd been living in survival mode, exerting the least amount of energy to get through each day. I wasn't good at managing money and made several bad investments. I was notoriously late when paying bills. I told friends I would call them and then conveniently forgot or found an excuse not to phone. Being self-indulgent or having my own pity party became easier than maintaining connections. I watched too much television, ate too much junk food, and although I cleaned the house, the yard was a disaster. I needed to get my life together. That meant looking at where I was sitting in my comfort zone.

We all have a range of things we will accept into our lives, and if things happen outside that range, we will do whatever it takes to get ourselves back into our comfort zone. That works if your life is totally working for you, and you aren't interested in making changes; but I wanted more. More love, more money, more happiness, more connection. I have a sign on my wall that says, "Nothing shifts until you shift." That meant becoming the best version of myself.

Remembering the positive impact of personal development courses, I decided the time had come to continue my journey. I have done some interesting and crazy things in different courses, using each opportunity to learn something new about myself: completing high ropes courses, managing white-water rafting, sitting in sweat lodges, performing on stage, breaking boards with my hands, and breaking an arrow with my neck. Yes, my neck.

To create a breakthrough in eliminating self-defeating beliefs, I participated in one exercise that involved putting the pointed end of a wooden arrow into the suprasternal notch, otherwise known as the hollow at the base of the neck. Another person held the other end steady, not pushing into my neck but not allowing the arrow to slip. *If this arrow does not break in half, it could go straight through my neck and kill me.* The program facilitator had demonstrated how to do this, their arrow broke, and they did not die. I can do this; I want to prove to myself I can do this. You are not going to die. You are not going to die. Once I calmed my mind and felt ready, I took a step toward my partner. I watched as the arrow first bent upwards and then snapped in half. A surge of adrenalin rushed through my body. For a moment, I felt invincible. Tears rolled down my cheeks as I savoured the incredible feeling of freedom from fear. One of the greatest lessons I learned is that I'm tougher than I ever gave myself credit for.

One of the greatest experiences of inner strength involved walking on hot coals—for just short of 11 metres (36 feet)—two separate times. To get a visual of that distance, most bedrooms are about 3.6 metres (12 feet) long. Imagine the length of three bedrooms back-to-back. Had I known this is what the course entailed, I likely wouldn't have gone. I would have talked myself out of even trying what I considered to be a very scary experience.

At the event, the fire walk team started preparations early in the afternoon. They methodically piled wood several feet high on a section of dirt where grass used to grow. They carefully stoked the fire and ensured no embers left the bed they created as the flames burned down into coals. About midnight, the coals would be hot enough. The path of red-hot embers would become our path of transformation. As participants, we went through training and mental preparation for several hours with the program facilitator.

"We are about to embark on a transformational experience like nothing most of you have ever done before. We are going to walk on fire," he said slowly, pausing deliberately after each word for greater impact.

It took a few seconds for my mind to catch up with what he just said. I started to feel pins and needles up and down my arms and legs. My heart started to race with excitement. I felt paralyzed with fear. Now I know why my friends who had taken the course had shared the value they got but remained silent about the details. By the end of the pre-fire walk training, I still had some fear and nervousness but felt part of something bigger. Doing the walk with so many people helped to make me feel safer. Safety is paramount. Prior to attempting a fire walk, proper instruction for the mind and body is critical.

The clock struck midnight on that cool, cloudy night at the base of a mountain range. The air felt crisp; a light rain fell earlier in the evening, but not enough to put out the burning coals. Aside from the glow of the embers, flashlight beams illuminated the path as we followed the assistants to our destination. As we neared the area of the fire walk, the smell of burning coals reminded me of the charcoal barbecue we had growing up. I always loved that smell. Now, the smell jolted the realization my feet would be in contact with those coals. I shivered.

The volunteers stood in silence, in reverence for the ceremony that was about to take place. The facilitator repeated the instructions one last time and asked each person to verify they understood what they were supposed to do. A first-aid station was nearby in case anyone's feet burned.

I removed my shoes and socks, placed them alongside a couple hundred other pairs in the designated area, and took my place in the long line. Out of respect for the person walking the coals, everyone was silent. Inching forward, alone with my thoughts since we weren't talking, I felt nervous and nauseous. *It's dark; maybe no one will notice if I slip out of line and into the forest. Wait, it's dark and who knows what animals lurk in the forest. Maybe I'm safer walking over hot coals.* I watched person after person take their turn, some moving faster than others. *I'm getting closer to the front of the line. What the hell was I thinking taking this course? What will people think of me if I chicken out?* Each person stated their intention for the walk before taking their first step onto the red hot coals. I watched as, one by one, people did their walk. Once on the other side of the sizzling runway, the surrounding crowd erupted into cheers, acknowledging the accomplishment. *I want people to cheer for me like that. I want to be celebrated too. That won't happen unless I walk.*

After a considerable wait, I walked toward the starting point of the hot coals. The grass leading up to the path was cold and wet. Two assistants stood like sentries blocking access to the coals. Beforehand, we had each selected someone to receive us at the end of the walk. This served two purposes: to focus our attention on another human being during the walk and to have someone to celebrate our success upon completion. The facilitator suggested choosing someone we had a close connection to. I chose my dear friend Tom to receive me. His wife, my best friend, Donna, stayed home to take care of their boys while Tom and I shared this experience. She attended the next year. He stood facing me on a mat of grass at the end of the path that could bring me freedom. His bright orange shirt and light blond hair shone like a beacon in the glow of the embers. I looked directly into his eyes and saw the love and belief that I could do this. I could hear the crackling of the coals, and in the distance, an owl hooting, I quivered in anticipation. *Just focus on Tom. Don't think, don't think, don't think.* Tom looked intently into my eyes, which calmed my nerves, giving me strength and courage. He nodded at me, as if to say, "You've got this. I'm here for you." I knew if I just focused on Tom's steel blue eyes, his energy would draw me across the coals.

I decided to walk fast, with purpose and intention, to make the journey safely. I took a deep breath and exhaled out the years of self-doubt that I knew were no longer part of me. Across the burning coals I went, inwardly chanting cool ice, the mantra the instructors suggested to help us mentally. I couldn't feel the heat. It almost felt like walking on ice. The smell of smoke filled my nostrils. I heard a soft, crackling sound under my feet. Pop, pop, pop. The sound of the sizzle made me move faster. My lips and throat were dry; my stomach quivered. Every cell in my body stood at attention, on high alert.

About thirty seconds later, I fell into Tom's arms. He embraced me tightly and kissed my cheek, whispering loudly in my ear, "I'm so proud of you!"

Then we were hooting and hollering, jumping up and down.

"I did it! I did it!" I screamed.

The crowd broke their silence and erupted in cheers and congratulations. The noise from their cheering reminded me of a football stadium. I was celebrated as if I had completed the winning touchdown. The process was repeated over and over for hours as more than 250 people completed their fire walk. Each person was celebrated equally.

I was euphoric. I walked on FIRE! I had no fear; I could breathe again. I felt my soul expand beyond the confines of my body. I was one with everything: the wind, the mountains, the air, the fire. I didn't know where my body stopped, and the surrounding space began. The feeling lasted several hours. I was on such an energetic high that I couldn't sleep. I felt directly connected to source, to God. Through meditation, I had experienced an expansion of consciousness, but that was the first time I experienced such a oneness with the universe in a conscious state.

I had one spot on a toe that ended up with a blister the size of a pea, but otherwise, my feet remained unscathed. Others who were not so lucky (or perhaps not as mentally prepared) burned their feet. They were assisted immediately by trained first-aid staff. So yes, there is danger in fire walking. Preparation and mental focus are key to a successful walk.

The next year, David decided to take the same course, and I volunteered to support him on his journey. When time came for his fire walk, he angrily looked at me as if to say, "What the hell have you gotten me into?" He looked really scared, and the momma bear in me wanted to rescue him, but I knew this was not about me. David had to decide for himself; I didn't pressure him in any way. He could choose to do the fire walk or not. He chose to walk and picked me as the person to receive him.

I cannot remember another time when I was as proud of my son. Watching him stand on the grass at the beginning of the walk, looking deep into his eyes and sending him all my love and support was a defining moment. Although eighteen years old, I still saw him as my little boy. At that moment, I saw him as the man he had become. I knew the demons David had faced with the death of his father. Through unconditional love and support, I wanted to support him in finding peace of mind.

I looked directly into his eyes and gave a slight nod. Seconds later, he was in my arms, both of us crying and hugging, hooting and hollering, celebrating his victory. My fire walk had had such a profound effect on me that I wanted the same for him. David assured me it was life-changing for him.

After all the participants completed their walks, the volunteers had an opportunity to do the same. We all chose to walk, and I naturally asked David to receive me. Looking into his eyes as I started my walk, I was overwhelmed with love and pride, feeling so empowered that I could get through anything. This time, nervousness existed, but fear did not. I felt more excited than afraid. My body vibrated with anticipation of walking on hot coals in front of David. I wanted to set a good example for him and show him I could take on anything, even a fire walk.

Walking on hot coals was never on my bucket list. If anyone had ever said to me someday I would do a fire walk, let alone do it twice, I would have told them they were nuts. But when the opportunity arose, I didn't hesitate. I saw fire walking as a way I could prove to myself I had great inner strength.

My experience with the fire walk helped me realize the power of my mind, that I had the ability to overcome self-limiting beliefs. Before my walk, I saw myself as weak, the one who hid in the shadow of her husband. The one who didn't have the courage to become successful, the one whose voice didn't matter. Only after the fire walk did I start in earnest to deal with my past hurts and find my voice. Walking on fire changed my way of thinking about myself. I had been figuratively walking on hot coals for years. I felt burned. Burned by past traumas, burned by Brian's lies, burned by his death, burned by having to raise my children alone.

Literal firewalking became a metaphor for my life. I tapped into a fierceness I didn't realize existed. I noticed how I have control over my mind. When facing difficulty, I could tap into the feeling I had crossing the finish line and relive the mental conditioning required to get there. I could set my mind to do whatever I choose. For the first time after Brian died, I could honestly tell myself I was going to be okay. *You've got this* became my new inner dialogue. To this day, whenever I find myself saying, "I can't," I remember the fire walk and what the experience taught me: *Actually . . . I can.*

You don't need to experience a fire walk to get this lesson. Each person who chooses to walk on fire needs to determine their motivation. I walked to prove something to myself. I faced fear in a way I thought was unimaginable. But fire walking is not for everyone. I use my walk as an example of stepping out of my comfort zone to challenge myself in a different way, to learn something new about myself. Taking a step out of your comfort zone will feel very uncomfortable and scary. Take baby steps. What could that look like for you? Perhaps your step is creating new friendships because most of your friends are couples, and you don't always want to be the only single person in the room. Maybe you choose to take a course or learn a new skill. Or you decide to volunteer and help someone else, so you aren't constantly focusing on your own pain. Maybe it's taking control of your finances or your eating habits. Or just maybe, it's simply getting out of bed, washing your hair, and walking out the front door. Whatever you choose to take on, remember: You've got this.

CHAPTER 19

Forgiveness

Forgiveness is a gift you give yourself.
Tony Robbins

When Brian took his own life, I asked myself, *Will I ever be able to forgive him?* Although my faith talks about the importance of forgiving others or of turning the other cheek, I felt at a loss about how I could possibly get to a place of total forgiveness. I have forgiven many things over my life, but this one seemed like the Mount Everest of transgressions.

When I was twelve years old and in grade eight, our home economics teacher decided to have us plan and host an afternoon tea for our mothers. This event would be the culmination of all we had learned in baking, setting a *proper* table, and serving. In the seventies, girls studied home economics and boys studied shop, which included carpentry and fixing small appliances. Back then, that was the norm. Allowing either boys or girls to choose outside the predetermined courses was not an option.

So, here was our homework: invite our mothers to this afternoon tea. In retrospect, it should have been an easy task. My mother didn't work outside the home, and I knew she would be available. The tea should have been an experience that would create a memory for my mother and me that we could talk about in the years to come. Instead, something else happened.

Grade eight girls can be the most vicious, self-centered, and arrogant creatures on the planet. When I reached grade eight, I stopped being a shy, meek, young girl. I found new friends and discovered a voice I did not know lived inside of me. I credit Bob Houston for initiating my transformation. Bob stood almost six feet tall and had an athletic build, a result of being a jock. His dark hair swooped over his forehead, and he had the habit of running his hand through his thick bangs to smooth his hair back. Bob was a cool kid. Everyone in the school liked him.

Near the end of grade seven, in the middle of the hallway, with kids bustling around us, Bob grabbed my shoulders, shook me, and said, "You are a nice person, but you are so quiet. You need to speak up more. I want to hear what you have to say."

He then walked away. *Did I just dream that? Did Bob Houston just tell me to speak up? He thinks I have something important to say. Oh my God!*

Time stood still for a moment. I looked around to see if anyone paid attention to what had just happened. It didn't seem anyone even noticed. Over the summer, I decided to grow out my hair from the pixie cut my mom had made me wear. I saved babysitting money and bought some new clothes. New jeans and a purple angora sweater with big white polka dots became part of my new look. I would no longer wear the handmade blue shift my mother sewed for me. I would return to school in September as a New Me.

When school resumed, I wanted to find new friends. A new girl showed up the first day, and I set my sights on friending her. Nancy was boisterous and funny and in no way shy. *She will be my new best friend. I can learn to come out of my shell by hanging out with her.* Turns out we shared a similar sense of humour and connected almost instantly. *Perfect, she doesn't know the old Cathie; she only knows the new me.* Compared to shy, mousy Cathie, this newfound persona felt exciting and edgy. I watched the cool kids be cocky and self-centred and thought I had to behave the same way to become one of them. I took more risks with Nancy, including stealing alcohol from my parent's liquor cabinet when they weren't home. I no longer wanted to be just the *good girl.* I started talking back to my mom, thinking I was becoming a badass.

I decided not to tell my mother about the tea because she was too old. She gave birth to me at forty. This meant she was about fifteen or more years older than the other moms. I felt embarrassed. I had met my friends' mothers, and they were cool. My mom was not. She wore dresses from the sixties and liked polyester pants. She didn't work outside the home until I started high school. Conversations with my mom often centred around what happened that day on *Days of Our Lives.*

My friends' moms worked in offices and had up-to-date clothing. I saw my mom as very old-fashioned and boring.

Several days passed with no mention of the tea. I thought about inviting her and then decided she would never find out. Finally, Mom approached me after I came home from school one day. "Nancy's mom told me today about an upcoming tea at your school," Mom started.

"Yup," I replied indignantly.

Here we go.

"You never mentioned it. Were you going to invite me?" Mom asked cautiously.

"Nope," I declared, followed by a minute of silence. When Mom did not respond, I followed with, "Because you're older than the other moms."

My mother turned and went to her bedroom. I spent a minute or two silently congratulating myself for speaking the truth. *Boy, I sure told her.* Then I heard something I will never forget: the sound of my mother sobbing. I had never heard her cry like that. It was a deep, guttural sound. The sound of heartbreak.

The sound of my mother crying cut through the arrogance, the self-righteousness, the mean girl I had become. I knocked on her bedroom door, and after what seemed an eternity, she said I could come in. I opened the door to find my mother lying on her bed, her pillow soaked in tears.

"I am so sorry, Mom, so sorry," I choked out through my own tears.

Mom remained silent, still wiping her tears with a monogrammed linen hankie. She looked at me, and the tears started once more.

"Please forgive me. I am so sorry I hurt you," I begged.

I loved my mom so much and to see her like this broke my heart. *I did this to her. When did I become such an asshole?*

My mother sat up on the edge of the bed and took a few minutes to calm down. Her tears started to slow. My parents slept in twin beds, so I cautiously sat at the end of Dad's bed, too afraid to come closer.

She took a few deep breaths and said, "I forgive you. I forgive you because once I said something to my father in anger. He had lost his left arm in a machine at the bakery where he worked. His arm got caught, and they had to amputate it at the elbow. One day he asked me to pass the butter. I was upset at something else, but I took my anger out on my father that day. I sarcastically said to him, 'Why, are you a cripple?' He glared at me with stone silence. I realized my mistake immediately and begged for his forgiveness."

Mom smoothed the blue quilted cover on her bed and patted the space to her right, motioning for me to sit beside her. I immediately moved over.

She laid her hand on my leg, looked me in the eyes, and said, "My father never forgave me. Six months later, he died of pneumonia at the age of thirty-nine. I will never forget how horrible I felt to not be forgiven, and I promised myself if any of my children said something they regretted and asked for forgiveness, I would most certainly forgive them. So, I forgive you."

I fell into my mother's lap and cried loud, ugly tears. We cried together. I felt such shame for what I had done and such gratitude I did not have to experience the pain my mother did when her father refused to forgive her. I promised myself I would never intentionally say or do anything to hurt my mother again. I felt a visceral shift in my body, humbled by the love of my mother.

Forgiveness is a choice. Forgiving is something we do for ourselves to move past something that has hurt us. *Merriam-Webster's Dictionary* defines forgiveness as the act of forgiving, which is to cease to feel resentment against [an offender.] Research on forgiveness backs up the need to forgive by showing the result of not forgiving. Holding in anger and resentment can have a huge impact on our bodies—physically, mentally, emotionally, and psychologically. Studies have shown repressed emotions can lead to stress. Stress is one of the top reasons we suffer from disease, sometimes leading to death.

According to a *Psychology Today* article, "Forgiveness can lead to health, improved relationships, better sleep, and overall well-being. Forgiveness is linked to lower mortality rates, lower cholesterol, lower blood pressure, lower cortisol (the stress chemical in our brains) and a lower likelihood of developing cardiovascular disease. Forgiveness may even support a healthier immune system."[40]

If forgiving is to cease feelings of resentment, Bert Ghezzi made a strong case for it when he said, "Resentment is like a poison we carry around inside us with the hope that when we get the chance, we can deposit it where it will harm another who has injured us. The fact is we carry this poison at extreme risk to ourselves." Nance Guilmartin, author of *Healing Conversations* and *The Power of Pause,* says to get curious, not furious. I love that. Her advice fits in with my belief that I can learn from everything that happens in my life. Things happens for me, not to me.

Let me say that again. Life happens *for me*, not *to me*.

Guilmartin talks about how we put deposits into our resentment bank account, consciously or unconsciously, and coming from a place of curiosity allows us to look at what we don't know we don't know. This is also known as our blind spot. The hurt may not go away immediately, but maybe it will soften, and then we can choose what we want to do. Stuff it back down or heal it.

Forgiveness isn't about letting someone else go free and clear. When you forgive someone, you allow yourself to escape past restraints. As best-selling author, Max Lucado, once wrote: "Forgiveness is unlocking the door to set someone free and realizing you were the prisoner!" In other words, we don't forgive for the benefit of the other person, we forgive to heal ourselves. Our mind has a way of taking hurts and traumas and storing the vibration of the connected emotion in our cells, right down to a quantum level. The act of forgiveness allows us to release the trapped negative energy. The saying, "You can forgive but not forget" is somewhat true. However, releasing the energy brings us to a state of neutrality. When we think about the hurt, we acknowledge it existed, but there is no longer an energetic charge. Forgiveness transforms us.

In the Heart Sutra Meditation, Deepak Chopra teaches that every decision we make is a choice between a grievance and a miracle. We can choose to live in anger and resentment or to forgive and let the hurt go. When a grievance comes up, Chopra recommends calming the mind through mindful breath and saying, "I let go of the grievance and I choose miracles." Say this over and over several times while breathing deeply.

The Mahatma Gandhi Peace Memorial sits a few blocks from the Pacific Ocean, at the Self-Realization Lake Shrine in the Pacific Palisades. A portion of Gandhi's ashes rests in a one-thousand-year-old stone sarcophagus, encased in a brass-and-silver coffer. A golden lotus archway, known as the "wall-less temple," stands in front of the memorial. The arch is white, accented by blue tile, with four blooming golden lotuses on top. The spring-fed lake in front of the memorial is surrounded by lush gardens, including waterfalls and exotic flowers. White swans grace the lake in front of an old Dutch windmill. Paramahansa Yogananda, the only person outside of India to receive some of Gandhi's ashes, founded the site in 1950. Throughout the ten-acre site, people can meditate on benches. Some just sit there to take in the beauty of the surroundings. Thousands of people visit Lake Shrine every year.

Throughout different visits to the city, I sat on those benches and meditated on Gandhi's nonviolent teachings. He once said, "One should forgive, under any injury. It hath been said the continuation of the species is due to man's being forgiving. Forgiveness is holiness, by forgiveness the universe is held together. Forgiveness is the might of the mighty, forgiveness is sacrifice, forgiveness is the quiet of the mind. Forgiveness and gentleness are the qualities of the Self-possessed. They represent eternal virtue."[41] Powerful words from someone I admire deeply. So my question became, *how can I forgive Brian, regardless of his action, regardless of feeling injured? Is that why I had to learn about forgiveness from my mother?*

One of the things people look for when considering forgiveness is an apology. Hearing "I am sorry" helps to justify the hurt and starts the process of healing. The offender takes accountability and acknowledges their role in an action deemed hurtful. For me, when someone says I'm sorry, my feelings are validated, and I feel heard. Their words reach across the abyss they created and their intention to mend the brokenness between us is extended. It is very hard for me to hold a grudge once the other person says they are sorry. If there is something I did or said that caused hurt for the other person, I will apologize as well.

So how do you forgive someone who is no longer around to say they are sorry? Reading an "I'm sorry" in Brian's suicide note did not have the same impact on me as looking directly into his eyes when he was alive and having him apologize. Although I appreciated that he left me a note, and I believed him when he said he had been faithful, I wasn't ready to accept his apology. It felt somewhat hollow. I feel the same way when someone writes me an apology in an email. The words don't connect the same way. I don't see the person's body language or hear the tone in their voice. I can't tell if the apology is authentic or not, so it doesn't impact me, or it impacts me much less than someone who has the courage to apologize in person and make amends.

I could only imagine how Brian wanted me to hear his apology. I could have chosen to dismiss his words, telling myself he didn't really mean what he said. Instead, about a year after his death, I sat quietly in my comfy chair in the living room, with no one else at home, to intentionally create forgiveness. After a short meditation, I visualized him sitting in front of me, taking my hands in his, and looking into my eyes. I pretended he spoke the heartfelt words, "I. Am. Sorry." After a few minutes of allowing those words to resonate in my body, I replied aloud, "I forgive you." Then, I allowed myself to have a good cry.

Silly as it may seem, I felt better. Without this exercise, I do not think I could have gotten to a place to forgive Brian. I did not forgive him right away. It took several years before I could finally say I forgave him. The forgiveness exercise started my path to forgiving him. I did not forgive Brian to absolve him for taking his own life; I forgave him so I could go on living mine. How did I know when I had forgiven Brian? When the thought of his suicide filled me with compassion, not anger.

There is no right way to forgive. Everyone is unique and must find a method that works for them. Here are some suggestions from my process of forgiving Brian:

- I said the words "I forgive you" silently and aloud. Sometimes that meant saying the words while looking in the mirror and watching my expression. Doing this had greater impact than just saying the words in my head.
- I told someone else, in my case, Donna, that I forgave Brian. Sharing my decision to forgive helped me to be accountable for my words and helped make forgiveness my reality.
- I used another person as a proxy. I had a friend stand in as Brian as I looked into her eyes and declared, "I forgive you." Powerful stuff.
- I wrote a two-page forgiveness letter addressed to Brian and then created a burning ceremony. I said some prayers and placed the letter in the burning fireplace. By burning the letter, I felt an energetic release of residual negative energy. Of course, a campfire or a large tin can (preferably outside in a safe area) can work just as well.
- I watched several videos on forgiveness meditations including one from Hawaii called Ho'oponopono (my favourite) on YouTube.

Ultimately, to fully do this work, I needed to forgive myself. I needed to forgive myself for not stopping Brian. I needed to forgive myself for not even considering he could be suicidal. I needed to forgive myself for being so angry and for all the nasty, angry things I said about Brian in the first few years after his death. I needed to forgive myself for not managing my money very wisely, making bad investments, and not taking better care of my well-being. Sometimes I found it much easier to forgive Brian than myself. I used to allow negative self-talk to overrun my ability to forgive myself.

Werner Erhard, the founder of EST, now known as Landmark International, proposed a concept that helped me in my forgiveness. He said if you wanted to forgive yourself for something, you had to give it space to exist. Not doing so would result in resistance. What you resist, persists. I am going to say that once again because it was a huge game-changer for me:

What you resist, persists.

That made sense to me. If I wanted to rid myself of guilt over my anger, I needed to acknowledge it and allow space for its existence. Only then could I choose to release it.

Erhard also said, "You cannot be complete in a relationship with any person whom you do not admire and respect as he or she is, and as he or she is not, rather than the way you think she is or would like her to be." He explained further that "Self-forgiving, and self-accepting, is an essential part of being complete in relationships. If there is something about your past that you are ashamed of, or guilty about—if there is something in it that you are hanging on to—if there is something there that you are using to burden another person—that will prevent you from being complete in your relationships.[42]

I knew I wanted to be complete with my relationship with Brian so I could move on to another loving relationship. To do so meant not only forgiving Brian but forgiving myself. I used many of the same strategies I mentioned above to work on forgiving myself.

Over two decades later, for the most part, I have forgiven myself for anything I said, did, or didn't do that contributed to Brian's suffering. Just when I think I have fully recovered from his suicide, something else will come up, and like layers of an onion, I need to peel back another layer. For instance, as I watched my son

David say his wedding vows, a wind blew on my neck, and I imagined it was Brian. I don't think it was intentional, but there was an empty chair in the front row beside my new husband where we sat. The thought that Brian wasn't there to see his son get married made me melancholy. Later, at the reception, as David took my hand onto the dance floor for the mother-son dance, tears fell for how proud I was of my son, as well as for the absence of his father. Brian should have been there. Times such as these are when I miss Brian the most.

Louise Hay writes on her website (louisehay.com), "The act of forgiveness takes place in our own mind. It really has nothing to do with the other person." There is a lot of anger, resentment, and hurt in the world. What would the world look like if we were able to release the hurt, the pain, and the suffering we experience and practice forgiveness? I believe if we granted forgiveness to each other and ourselves more often, we would all experience greater peace, joy, and love.

Ultimately, forgiveness is a choice. It is ours to make.

CHAPTER 20

Ready to Love Again

Someday you'll find someone special again.
People who've been in love once usually do.
It's in their nature.
—Nicholas Sparks

Growing up, I bought into the fairy tale that each person has one special someone that they will fall in love with and then live happily ever after. Watching Disney movies and reading romance novels led me to believe that the trick involved finding that one person. I kissed several frogs before I met and married my handsome prince. Never in the fairy tale did it say that the prince would take his own life and that the princess would have to rewrite the story.

We all bring a certain level of baggage from our past experiences into any new relationship. I knew after Brian's suicide I had a lot of baggage. A bit of baggage might be inevitable, but I wanted to bring a carry-on, not a moving van. I was also willing to accept someone else's carry-on, but I didn't want someone to back up their truck into my life and use it as a dumping ground.

The truth is, I feared being hurt again. Brian's death cut me so deeply that I doubted if I could recover. I had a lot of work to do on myself before I could ever be ready for a new relationship. So I kept working on myself, peeling back the layers of hurt and pain. I had a lot of love to offer. I just needed to be willing to open my heart again. I found love once. Maybe I could do it one more time. I still carried a glimmer of hope.

A couple of months before cutting off my wedding rings in 2004, I had a profound experience in opening my heart. It set the stage for being ready for that important moment. In the darkness of a movie theatre, sitting at a matinee by myself, I watched Gerard Butler play the lead in *Phantom of the Opera*. Something in his voice and the story affected me to the core. I physically felt my heart expand. I became mesmerized by his performance and after returning home, started searching the Internet for anything I could find on this Scottish actor. It wasn't sexual (okay, maybe a bit of fantasy existed for me), but I credit Mr. Butler for helping me to reawaken my heart. I went back to the movie theatre and watched *Phantom* twelve more times. Each time, my heart opened just a little bit more. Sometimes I dragged a girlfriend to the theatre; mostly I went on my own.

Until opening my heart, if any man showed interest, I didn't notice. I was oblivious to innuendos or second glances. I held on to my story that no man would want me with the amount of baggage I had. My belief in this story kept my rings on my finger for four years.

Five years after Brian died, I attended a course in Las Vegas focusing on finances. *Did I mention I'm a self-development junkie?* I wanted to learn from experts how to win at the money game. In the course, multi-millionaire entrepreneurs taught us how to achieve financial freedom. The common theme? Change your mindset, change your financial future.

Approximately five hundred people attended the five-day course in the large ballroom at the Flamingo Hotel. Most were from the United States, but there were a lot of Canadians and several from Europe and Thailand. People ranged in age from their early twenties to a woman in her eighties.

On the first day, the facilitator asked us to move about the room and talk to several people about what we wanted to create in our lives. I talked with a young man in his twenties from Denver. There is no ocean where he lives, but the term *surfer dude* crossed my mind. He had just started in multilevel marketing and wanted to hear how to make his first million dollars. *Good luck with that.* I had tried several times to run a business through network marketing and had failed miserably. Even though my cynicism kicked in, I did my best to keep a poker face and not show my doubt. I wished him well.

The second person I connected with looked like a Jewish rabbi. He was relatively short, dressed in black, and had a prayer shawl. His hat and long beard resembled those of Hassidic Jews. He clasped my hands in his and looked deeply into my eyes.

He said, "I have a message for you."

This took me aback, but I listened to what he had to say.

"Your new life partner is going to be attracted to the brightness of your soul. Your energy is like a bright yellow light. He will not be able to resist you. It will be like you are a magnet drawing him to you. This I tell you will come to pass."

I stood frozen in silence. I had not even told this man my relationship status, or that my husband had died, and yet he gave me this message. I had cut off my rings more than a year earlier, and the indent in my finger had faded. Perhaps he looked at my ring finger? I looked at his nametag: "Howard." Ironically, Howard was my father's name and Brian's middle name. The name Howard translates as "noble watchman."

I thanked Howard for his message and quickly looked for my friend Andrea who is Jewish and from New York. I told her about Howard and his message.

"I want to meet him. Let's look for him!"

She grabbed my hand, and we searched through the crowd of five hundred. Nothing. We continued to look throughout the three-day course. No amount of scanning the room helped us find Howard. He had vanished. Could he have been an angel? Sent to give me hope? If so, where would I meet this new man of mine?

Upon returning home, I felt a new sense of possibility. Maybe my new love really did exist. The fear of being hurt remained, but I held on to Howard's words as a sign something new was on the horizon. I just had no idea when. How would I know when the right person came along? Maybe it was the guy who smiled at me as we stood in line at the gas station waiting to pay for our gas. Maybe it was someone I already knew. I kept my eyes open for this man to appear in my life.

In 2006, I convinced Donna, another friend, to fly with me to Scotland for the inaugural Gerard Butler fan convention. About one hundred women from around the world converged in Glasgow to celebrate his career, hoping to meet him in person. Unfortunately, he was filming the movie *300* in Montreal and was not able to attend. He did videotape a special message in the middle of the night before the convention and had it sent by FedEx, so we could watch it the next day at the convention. Instead of meeting Gerard, I got to meet his mom, his stepdad, and a few of his relatives, who were a bit surprised at how many women would travel the globe for a member of their family. Looking back on this now, it seems crazy. At the time, it made perfect sense in my healing journey.

Two years later, in 2008, both of my kids moved away from home to attend school in Ontario. Until then, I had not fully experienced loneliness. In the quiet of the house, with only the dog to keep me company at night, I longed for companionship. By then, Brian had been gone almost eight years, and I had not gone on a first date in more than twenty-four years.

Many times, when a friend asked whether I had started dating again, I found myself saying I wanted to be in a new relationship, but I didn't know how to start. I was almost fifty years old, and meeting someone new seemed insurmountable. Everyone had a piece of advice. Often, they suggested online dating as the route. Take my hairdresser, Lin. We became close over the years, and I knew as soon as I sat in her chair, the inquisition would start.

"So, are you dating yet? Why not? You are an amazing woman with lots to offer. You need to get yourself out there and find someone, girl!"

Lin was in her mid-thirties, single, and a serial dater. She met most of her dates online, but secretly held on to the hope that her friend, a guy, would realize that she loved him deeply and would feel the same.

One day she said, "I suggest eHarmony. It takes a while to fill out the questionnaire, but I've met some amazing guys through the site. Or you could try Match.com or Plenty of Fish."

Since my kids were in Ontario, maybe now was the time to step into the dating arena. I really didn't like the idea of joining a website where men could look at my picture and profile. When Lin explained eHarmony to me, it seemed a safer way to go. *Maybe having to answer all the questions will weed out the duds.* I spent several hours answering the multitude of questions that would enable their computer to match me with a compatible man. I prided myself that my answers were flirty, but cheeky. I wanted someone with a great sense of humour. I could add a picture to my profile following eHarmony's recommendation. I chose not to. I was afraid that someone would judge me based on my looks. *I will dazzle them with my witty comments; they don't need to see what I look like to be interested.*

After the site connected me with various men, I received numerous requests for either a picture or more information about me. I chose not to answer. As I scrolled through the possible matches picked just for me, every single one of them stood beside a motorcycle. *What's that about? Reliving your youth?* When I filled out the questionnaire, I had not said I liked guys on motorcycles. If anything, I found bikes a turnoff. My brother had been in a serious motorcycle accident years ago, and I swore I would never get on one. I took it as a sign I was not ready to date. I cancelled my subscription and started to wonder if I would ever be ready. Maybe my destiny involved being single for the rest of my life. I started to discount what Howard had said to me. Perhaps I was never going to find love again.

A week later, at a personal development awards banquet, I chatted with a man at my table. He was about my age, with salt-and-pepper hair and deep, dark brown eyes (my favourite). After initial pleasantries, he shared that his wife had died from cancer. *This is a sign he wants to know if I'm married; that's why he brought up his marital status.* Well, not really. We talked for a few minutes about surviving her death and his journey to find love once again. When I say we talked, I mean he talked, and I listened.

After about ten minutes of listening to his story, I shared that my husband had died, but when I said the word "suicide," his expression changed. He no longer looked me in the eye but instead gazed around the room. The conversation became very stilted.

"I'm going get a drink before the bar closes," he said quickly before bolting out of his chair.

He never asked if I wanted a drink. When he returned, he chose to sit at a different table. This reinforced my biggest fear about finding a new relationship. *Well, that sucked. So much for finding a new man. Men cannot handle my story. Men are weak assholes.* I was afraid of being judged harshly by Brian's actions. *No man will be willing to accept me as the widow of someone who died by suicide.*

Despite this belief, I refused to lie about Brian's suicide. Anyone worth being with needed to be strong enough to deal with the reality, hear the words, and support me in my journey. At the end of the night, Mr. I-cannot-handle-your-stuff left with a pretty petite blonde. *Good luck, hon. I hope you're a good listener. He has a lot of grieving to do. He also likes to hear himself talk.*

Beyond fearing a man could not handle my story was my fear of being sexual again. In the year before Brian died, our sex life could be described as nonexistent. It had been a long time. The thought of getting naked with another man scared the crap out of me. But my sexual desire hadn't diminished. I wanted to be sexually intimate once again. When I first slept with Brian, I carried about twenty pounds of excess weight. Now, after two kids and years of grieving and comforting myself with food, I carried an additional fifty pounds. *Who would want to see me naked? Who would want to sleep with me?*

While chatting with a friend two weeks before my fiftieth birthday, almost eight years after Brian's death, our discussion sauntered into the area of sexuality. She knew I hadn't dated anyone since Brian's death and asked me point blank, "Do you use a vibrator?"

I could feel my face flush. We were good friends, but this topic seemed taboo, something uncomfortable to talk about.

"No," I replied.

"Well, we're going to get you one for your fiftieth."

Yikes. Totally out of my comfort zone, so I let my friend take the lead. She took me to a home-based party hosted by a "sexologist," as she coined herself. I found her presentation informative and fun. I made my purchase of the most expensive vibrator she had (my birthday present to myself), and the sexologist delivered it in person to my house in a plain brown box.

The moment the vibrator arrived I was a bit surprised to realize I felt shame about wanting to be sexually satisfied. The kids had moved out, so thankfully, they weren't there to ask questions when the package arrived. I cautiously opened the box, read the instructions, and then promptly put the vibrator into the blinged-out pink box I purchased through the sexologist to store my toy. I didn't jump into bed and use it right away. I had to talk myself into it. It took a couple of glasses of white wine and a steamy romance novel for me to open the box and give the vibrator a test run.

Sex, like suicide, is a conversation where many people shut down. I am no exception, and luckily, the older I get, the more open I become. Shows like *Sex in the City* made it more acceptable for me to talk about my sexuality. Like Samantha in the show, I named my vibrator B.O.B., my Battery-Operated Boyfriend. The more BOB and I hung out, the more comfortable I became taking care of my own pleasure. Slowly the shame subsided, and I became more open about discussing sex with my girlfriends. I was surprised to hear how many of my friends, even those who are married, have their own BOB. They take responsibility for ensuring their own sexual needs are met; they don't always rely on their husbands. *Who knew? I should have bought a BOB a lot sooner!*

I had a huge fear of my kids finding BOB. I thought it would be too awkward for them if they did. So I instructed one of my nieces that in the event of my death, her one job involved driving 300 km to my house to destroy the evidence. She promised she would. I have since released her from this promise.

Over the next couple of years, I continued to talk about wanting to find love but did absolutely nothing to look for it. My social interactions were typically with married friends, and I did not seek activities that might have put me in the pathway of single men. I did go on a cruise with a group of people in 2009 and did meet a very nice man. We flirted with each other, nothing more, but after the cruise, I never heard from him again. I saw this connection as an opportunity to practice flirting. I had not flirted in so many years; it felt good to know I could do it.

In 2010, my best friend Donna and I went on a four-day girl's trip to New York city. As we sat in an Irish pub called Paddy Maguire's one night, she said, "Let's make your list."

"What list?" I asked.

"The list of what you want in a new partner."

Donna jumped off the bench seat and walked up to the bar to grab some paper. She came back with a marketing flier that was blank on the back. So, over a couple of pints, we created The List.

"The first thing I want is a spiritual man," I declared.

"Good, write it down," instructed Donna.

"Stands in his purpose," I added, remembering a course I took called Sex, Passion, and Enlightenment.

Women are looking for a man who knows what his purpose is in life. Men are looking for a woman who nurtures him.

Over the next two hours, I completed most of my list:

- Fun
- Sense of humour
- Kind-hearted

- Compassionate
- Open-minded
- Financially stable
- Likes adult children
- Generous
- Handyman
- Ready for a relationship
- Smart
- Strong family values
- Romantic
- Great in bed

I might as well ask for what I want. When we got back home, I showed my list to other girlfriends and asked them if I had missed anything. Could they see something I couldn't? In all, my list had thirty-seven items. I tucked it into my purse. I wanted it close at hand in case I thought of something else to add. I keep it in my purse to this day, in case I'm telling a single woman or man about the process. I pull out the ragged piece of paper in the hopes that person might be inspired to do the same.

I used my mother as a reason I could not pursue a relationship. She lived to be ninety-three years old and resided independently in a seniors' complex. Mom still had a kitchen and did all her own cooking. I took her grocery shopping every second week and often made extra when I cooked to toss into her freezer. She had someone come in every other week to clean when she no longer could push the vacuum or clean the floors.

When Mom wasn't taking art classes or exercising at the local swimming pool, she led six other seniors in a weekly workout session in the common room in her building after the city cut programs for seniors. She loaded up the basket of her walker with soup cans and a boom box. I suspect I got my resiliency from her.

Mom stayed with us every second weekend, three weeks at Christmas, and another three weeks in the summer. Her scheduled activities usually occurred during the week, which left her weekends free. Once my kids moved out, it left a space for one-on-one time with my mother. This made it even more difficult to envision being in a relationship, fearful that Mom would get pushed aside. During those weekends together, I sometimes lamented how I wanted to find love again and someday be married again. My mother loved clichés and would inevitably answer, "If it is meant to happen, it will happen."

During her last Christmas, in 2011, Mom showed me that she believed I could love again. When I was a child, she had made me a personalized Christmas stocking big enough to fit the Raggedy Ann doll she had also made for me. She spent countless hours hand-stitching designs on the front with my name stitched in bold red letters across the top. Everyone in the family then wanted one. Over several years, my mom made everyone their own stocking, including my dog, Parker.

One year she made a stocking for my niece's boyfriend. I commented to her that if I ever married again, I wouldn't have a stocking for my new husband. It didn't feel right to use Brian's Christmas stocking and just change the name. I also worried that my mom would die before I met another man.

After we had opened all our presents on that Christmas morning, my mom asked mischievously, "Isn't there one more present behind the sofa?"

Jennifer jumped up to grab the box and seeing my name on the label, handed it to me. I unwrapped the present to find a shoebox with a card on top that said, "I BELIEVE." I opened the box to find a large red stocking with hand-stitched designs on the front. No name adorned the top. Mom explained that when I met the right person, I could put his name on the stocking. Her belief touched me deep in my soul. If she had faith that I could find love again, then perhaps I could believe it too.

Sadly, the following summer, July 2012, Mom died of heart failure. In October of that year, my management position got restructured. It had been a hell of a year, losing my mom and losing my job. Feeling lost, I looked for a way to find structure and support. From experience, that meant either counselling or another personal development course to get me back on track. I knew that, left to my own devices, I might spiral into depression. Six weeks later, I reattended a course offered through Excellence Seminars, called The Wall. I had taken the course twenty-four years earlier. The Wall is designed to enhance your relationship with yourself by identifying the walls where you stop yourself from getting what you say is most important to you. With all the changes happening in my life, I decided to pull out the mirror one more time and look at what direction I wanted to pursue and where I might be stopping myself. Now that my mom had died, what excuse did I have left to stay single?

During the course, I finally made the decision to allow myself to love again. I had said it before, but finally realized I just couldn't let go of my marriage vow of "'til death do you part." Subconsciously, I had held on to the belief that it meant both Brian and I had to die. Even though I released my marriage into the river, I found a residual belief that continued to hold me back. I had to choose to love again. Nothing would happen until I made this conscious choice.

In January 2013, I drove to Edmonton to attend a one-day course called "The Year of Your Dreams." The course is intended to help you create your stake for the year, just as a pioneer would stake their claim many years ago. By the end of the one-day course, each person writes a saying on a wooden stake indicating their intention for the year ahead. To figure this out, the day is full of exercises and introspection. We were instructed to get up, move around the room, and tell three people our goals. I briefly thought of *Jewish Howard,* my mystery angel with the message of finding love again.

From across the room, I saw a handsome, older man walking toward me. He looked tall, probably about six foot two or so, with hair more salt than pepper. Plaid shirt, black pants, running shoes, glasses. When he saw me walking toward him, he smiled at me not only with his mouth, but also with his eyes. He walked with confidence, head high, shoulders back. The little voice in my head immediately said, *Oh, he's already married. There is no way this man is not married.* I shook his hand, a good, firm handshake (something very important to me), and we introduced ourselves. As he said his name, Dick, I looked at his name tag to be sure. I had never met anyone named Dick before. *That takes balls,* I thought, inwardly smiling at the irony of my words.

I proceeded to tell him the three things I wanted to create: "I want to have a life partner, as I have been widowed for twelve years and have not had even one date. I want to find a new career or job opportunity as my job got restructured. I want to lose weight and get fit."

Dick looked intently into my eyes and said, "Those are great goals. I want a wife."

The room stood still as I looked into his blue eyes. He went on to say other things, but it was like Charlie Brown when the teacher talked. Wah, wah, wah. *Did I hear him correctly? Did he just say he wanted a wife? Maybe I imagined him saying that.* Who says that? We finished our conversation, shook hands, thanked each other for sharing, and moved on to the next person.

Later, during a short break while getting myself a cup of tea, Dick sidled up beside me and started asking more questions. "You mentioned something when we were talking that you were interested in spirituality," Dick began. "I would be interested to hear more about what that means to you."

What the hell! This guy is asking me questions. He seems interested in me. Did I say something about spirituality? I don't remember those words coming out of my mouth. I don't remember what the heck I said. As he spoke, Dick had such calmness to his manner. Did I mention his captivating blue eyes? I found out that we lived in different cities about four hours apart.

The facilitator called everyone back to their seats.

"Let's talk later," Dick said with a wink.

I sat at my table and shared with the gal next to me that I had just met someone, and he seemed interested. "Let's see if he comes over after the session to talk to me," I said, hoping he would and scared that he wouldn't.

I liked his energy. It seemed as if we had known each other before.

At the end of the day, Dick came over and asked if we could exchange phone numbers. He said he would call me by the end of the week. I touched his arm and said, "If you don't, I will be calling you."

I'm not in the habit of touching people I don't know, especially men. With Dick, it just seemed natural.

He called the next week. We talked for about an hour. He called again the next week and a couple of times the week after that. Each time, our conversations got longer. Then the phone calls became more frequent, almost every night. We became friends. Not living in the same city turned out to be a blessing. The distance led us to get to know each other in a way that provided safety for me.

I never realized that the name that displayed when using my land line had both Brian's and my initials with our last name. After dating for four months, Dick asked me to change the name that came up on the display. I had not been aware of that tiny but impactful leftover, since no one else had ever mentioned it. Little things like that can get overlooked. I was happy that Dick was able to tell me it bothered him, and I was able to make the change right away.

We saw each other about twice a month, often meeting for coffee in Red Deer, halfway between us. After dating for about four months, we were walking in a park after having coffee at our regular rendezvous spot. We started talking about what we really wanted in a partner. It seemed the perfect time to show him *The List.* I pulled it carefully out of the secret pocket in my wallet, unfolded it, and handed it to him. He slowly read each item and seemed to read it over and over.

Finally, I said, "You have every quality I am looking for."

He smiled and replied, "You don't know if I'm any good in bed yet."

I blushed.

In true Dick Godfrey fashion, he winked and said, "I am."

He met everything I had wished for on the list except one: "loves to dance." I decided not to make it a deal-breaker. The most important quality I wanted was honesty. Dick was one of the most authentic, honest people I had ever met. I would take that over almost anything else. He was never scared by my being the suicide widow, and his strength and compassion inspired me.

We agreed to date exclusively for one year. At that time, if we didn't feel we were a match for marriage, we would part so each of us could find our *person*. In January 2014, we returned as a couple to the Year of Your Dreams course. The facilitator asked people to come on stage and share the results we created for ourselves in the past year. When we raised our hands, she suggested we come to the stage together, as a couple.

We got on stage, and I shared first. My stake for 2013 said *Queen of Abundance.* I created the intention to manifest more money, more love, more career opportunities. I talked about how I found a new job as an assistant manager for a pie company (quite a departure from social work), a new relationship, and new possibilities by deciding to write this book. Dick's stake read *Be the Tree.* He had wanted to create deeper roots in his relationships with his three adult children. He shared that he did not accomplish his goal because he spent so much of his free time building a relationship with me.

"Instead of spending more time with my kids, I had the honour of getting to know and fall in love with this beautiful woman here."

He reached into his back pocket and pulled out an engagement ring.

"I cannot get down on one knee because of my bad knees, but…will you marry me?"

There was a collective gasp from the seventy-five people in the room. Several pulled out their phones to videotape the proposal.

"Yes, yes, I will marry you!" I exclaimed, tears running down my cheeks.

We had come to the end of the trial period. I expected an engagement; we had agreed we wanted to spend the rest of our lives together. I just did not expect it to be in front of a crowd.

In our discussions about the possibility of getting married, we talked about rings set in silver as I didn't want another gold band. The ring Dick placed on my finger was silver with tiny diamonds surrounding the square-cut stone. Several weeks after our engagement, I glanced at a vision board I had created before meeting Dick. The documentary *The Secret,* talks about the power of taking your intentions and creating a visual display. I cut out pictures from old magazines depicting my innermost desires and pasted them on Bristol board. I filled my vision board with images of places I wanted to travel, my dream car, healthy living, and a lot of happy couples, including wedding shots.

The board included a picture of a stunning engagement ring. The solitaire diamond was square-cut surrounded by tiny diamonds, with more tiny diamonds on each side of the band. I froze in awe as I compared the engagement ring on my finger with the image on my vision board. They were identical! I had set the intention of an extraordinary engagement ring, and it manifested right onto my finger.

We were married ten months later in a fun, loving ceremony attended by our friends and family. I chose to sell my home and move to his acreage. I wanted the experience of living in the country. I didn't realize what a transition it would be. I love the tranquility of my new home, but sometimes I swear I can hear the jingle for the old TV show, *Green Acres.* Albeit cliché, taking the girl out of the city proved to be easier than taking the city out of the girl. At the time of this writing, we have been husband and wife for over seven years.

Eight years passed between meeting Howard and finding my new love. I believe Howard was an angel sent to tell me that I would find love again. I believe that messages come our way from a variety of sources. The important thing is to pay attention and believe.

The journey from Brian's death to finding love again was not an easy path. There were certainly bumps along the way. I consider myself blessed to have found love twice in my life. My view of love has matured. I no longer look for someone else to make me happy. I no longer hide behind my husband; I feel free to express my thoughts and opinions. I chose a partner who supports my need to travel, spend time with my girlfriends, and take time away from working a nine-to-five job to write a book. Regardless of my journey—from a loving marriage to trauma and grief, to being sad and lonely, cynical of ever finding love again—the desire to love and be loved remained.

I didn't give up.

CHAPTER 21

How Can I Ever love Christmas Again?

It came without ribbons, it came without tags,
It came without packages, boxes or bags,
Maybe Christmas he thought doesn't come from a store
Maybe Christmas perhaps means a little bit more.
— *The Grinch Who Stole Christmas by Dr. Seuss*

Someone asked me if I felt guilt about celebrating the holidays without Brian. Honestly, I don't think I did. I felt sadness and regret that he missed some of the most amazing times of our children's lives. Seeing their faces light up at the excitement of Santa or of opening a present left me with mixed emotions. I delighted in watching them be happy, yet inwardly I felt sad that Brian could not see it for himself. Because Brian died just before Christmas, I experienced sadness, sometimes even depression during the holidays, but no guilt.

Christmas was always my favourite time of year. As a small child, the excitement of Santa landing on the rooftop with his reindeer, magically sliding down the chimney, and leaving beautifully wrapped presents enthralled me. In a family where we did not have much more than the essentials, my parents made a special effort to decorate the house, prepare the Christmas baking, and ensure all four children had several presents waiting under the tree. When I had children of my own, I loved creating a magical Christmas experience for them. Even if we didn't have much money, I somehow found a way to follow the traditions my parents created.

I continued to love Christmas, even when tragedy struck. On Christmas Eve 1988, while two months pregnant with our second child, I stood in the kitchen of the group home we managed, blood running down my legs. I cried out to Brian, who, though distraught himself, calmly arranged for other staff to care for the children while he took me to the nearest hospital. My doctor arrived and after a brief examination said I had lost the baby. After a surgical procedure and an overnight stay in the hospital, I returned immediately to the group home. Then on Christmas morning, I acted as if nothing tragic had just happened for me and my husband. At the time, it seemed more important to create a magical Christmas for the children, who did not have moms and dads to go home to over the holidays.

In other words, I did not take time to grieve; I just kept going. I knew that Christmas would never be the same. Six months later, I found myself curled up on my bed in a fetal position, crying uncontrollably. I could pretend only for so long; the grief had finally caught up with me. Given that so much time had passed, I thought I had escaped going through the grief process. I was wrong; I had just stayed in the denial stage a long time. Finally, I worked my way through the other four stages of grief regarding the loss, although it took the better part of the year. After that, each Christmas I thought about my lost child and allowed myself to feel sad. But the miscarriage did not stop me from loving Christmas—until Brian died by suicide just before that holiday.

Many thoughts went through my head after the university student found Brian's body on December 22nd, but I distinctly remember this question: *How can I ever love Christmas again?* The fact that Brian had died just before Christmas made it all even more devastating. I wanted to scream at the top of my lungs that he died during a holiday I held sacred, a time where I had already experienced some trauma. How dare he! He knew I loved Christmas. He knew I had a sad memory connected to this time. *How cruel could he be?* That argument may hold some weight if suicide was logical, or if Brian could have considered the impact of his death on me. I fully believe he could not see past stopping his pain. At that point, he felt suicide was his only option.

That Christmas became a blur. I don't remember very much from Christmas morning. Presents were opened, stockings unpacked, and family members kept my coffee cup full. I think some Bailey's got added into the mug. On and off throughout the day, we talked about a memorial service for Brian. One of my nieces, Krista, took both of my children to a matinee movie to provide a distraction from the sorrow.

Later in the afternoon, as we prepared the holiday dinner, I remember vividly hearing You Jerk by Kim Stockwood on the radio. I started singing as loud as I could. Kim sings about not being able to put into words how much of a jerk the other person is being. I didn't relate to her line about feeling better now the person was gone. Rather, the chorus spoke to me. When the part came where she sings, "You jerk," I screamed the words. As loud as I could. Not the nicest lyrics, but I found it so liberating to scream them, so cathartic. My family encouraged me to yell if I wanted to.

"Go for it," Sandra told me, "Get it out."

My mom and brother nodded approval. Once the song finished, my niece pulled out her iPod Nano and let me listen to the song and sing the lyrics over and over until I felt complete. It really helped.

About a month after our first Christmas without Brian, my friend Liz invited us to go to Edmonton with her and her two boys. We went to West Edmonton Mall which features a massive waterpark. While the kids frolicked in the waves and slid down the monstrous waterslides, Liz and I sat on wooden beach chairs along the shoreline.

She advised, "Over time, grief does get easier to deal with."

Liz had gone through a painful divorce and had experienced the death of a close friend. At the time, I didn't believe her because the pain was so intense.

I told her, "Keep telling me life will get easier, even if you have to lie."

She did not lie.

The year after Brian died, my sister-in-law Sandra called.

"Come here for Christmas and bring Mom with you. That way you don't have to think about anything other than driving to our house."

The words were barely out of her mouth before I said, "Yes!"

I will gladly drive the 300+ km to avoid spending the holiday at home. I immediately started to feel a sense of relief. All the worrying I had done dissipated. Sandra's foresight allowed more time to pass before we hosted Christmas again in our home. It enabled us to have fun and create some great memories without being reminded so boldly of the pain from the previous year. It also reduced a lot of the stress associated with hosting. Even though I pitched in to help, the bulk of the responsibility did not fall on my shoulders. I was ever so grateful for that gift of hospitality.

As our third Christmas without Brian approached, I started to panic about whether I could get through the holiday. By year three, the shock had worn off, yet I constantly looked for the emotional land mines. *Could Christmas send me into a relapse?* Once I started hosting holidays in my home that year, the question arose: Who would sit at the head of the dining room table? We could easily seat ten people there. Brian always sat near the back wall at one end of the table. I sat opposite him, closer to the kitchen in case I needed to jump up and grab something. After he died, I often sat on the stairs leading to the upstairs level from the dining room, staring at the table. I looked at Brian's empty seat and tried to remember him holding court, which he often did. Brian loved to tell stories and share his knowledge of world events. When Brian talked, most people wanted to listen. No one could really fill his spot, but I didn't want to leave it empty. It would be too harsh a reminder that he had died. *Having Brian's seat empty would just be weird.*

Typically, if one of my older brothers was present, I placed him (oldest first) in Brian's spot. If they were not there, then David expected to sit at the head of the table. His eyes lit up when he took his dad's seat; it seemed a matter of pride for him to be at the head of the table.

"It feels weird sitting in Dad's spot, but I want to be the one who sits in his seat," David finally said.

He only deferred the seat to his uncles. For me, having an "anchor" at each end of the table provided structure that in turn gave me comfort.

I sadly held on to the belief that Christmas would never be my favourite holiday or time of year again until about five years after Brian's death.

My friend, Donna K., asked, "Why can't you love Christmas and have it as your favourite time of year again? It's only a story that you're telling yourself. You can change your mind. You write the story of your life."

I will always love her for saying that. It is MY life. I get to make up my story. I get to decide what is important to me. Experiences will come and go; it is the meaning or energy that I give to the events that determines whether it works for me. I decided right there and then I would continue to love Christmas. I refused to let his death define how I lived the rest of my life.

Along with choosing to love Christmas again, I also decided to re-evaluate how I celebrated Christmas. If I loved doing it, I kept it as part of my tradition.

Anything else could be eliminated. Things I loved to do around Christmas included shopping for presents, decorating my house, listening to Christmas music, visiting with friends, and hosting a large dinner on Christmas Day for my family (and friends if they wanted a seat at my table). Over the years, I got smarter and said yes when my family offered to bring food. Several times, this meant my brother Wayne and sister-in-law Gloria cooked the turkey at home, cut it up, and brought it in heat-sealed containers. All I had to do was set the table and make a few veggies.

I love a good sale. The day after Christmas, I would brave throngs of shoppers looking for the best Boxing Day deals. The first couple of years after Brian died, I could not face the crowds, so I chose not to go. In year three, I ventured back to the mall on Boxing Day, had a specific plan of what I wanted (discounted wrap, new clothes), and limited my time at the mall. It brought me joy to participate once again in this tradition.

One of the biggest changes I made was allowing others to contribute with their gifts and talents. My friend Kathie loves to wrap presents. Each year she chooses a theme and spends weeks wrapping each gift with paper, ribbon, ornaments, and handmade designs. She takes wrapping to an art form. By Christmas, her hands are usually blistered from all the hot glue she used to attach embellishments.

When Kathie called and offered to help me wrap presents, I replied, "No thanks, I can do it myself."

When I realized what a moron I was being, I called her back and invited her over for gift wrapping and wine. We made a night of it, sitting on my bedroom floor after the kids had gone to bed. I got to spend time with my friend, the gifts got wrapped in half the time, and I allowed someone to contribute to me. Big win.

If a task truly did not serve me and my involvement would be coming from a place of "should" rather than "could," I stopped doing it altogether. I don't like the time and effort Christmas baking requires. Instead, lining up in sub-zero weather in early November to be first in line at our church bazaar, so I could buy other people's baking was more my style. I showed up with the lid of a Bankers box so I could easily snag ginger cookies, squares, shortbread, and cherry loaves off the tables.

"Boy, you really come prepared," said other women in line as we waited for the doors to open.

"I will have to do the same thing next year."

I heard this over and over. Each year, though, I came prepared with my box, only to see others had forgotten. *Maybe they aren't as serious about this as I am.* Coming prepared meant I could easily grab the prettiest plates of goodies. Trying not to elbow the little old ladies beside me became my biggest challenge. I could get all my Christmas *baking* done in less than five minutes. Everyone knew I hadn't baked the goodies, but no one cared. It took a big stressor off my list.

Besides buying Christmas baking, I dreaded writing the obligatory Christmas cards. I never liked just signing my name to the bottom of the card and felt I needed to say something of value. I used to tell myself that I had to send out cards to keep in touch with friends and family. Brian's death took away the motivation to write the cards. "Hi! Merry Christmas! We are all doing great since Brian died." I don't think so. Pretending to be okay would just be lying.

When I received a Christmas card from a friend or family member, I felt a bit guilty. However, I dreaded writing notes, addressing envelopes, buying stamps, and mailing the cards. It was a should, not a want. I used self-talk to assure myself receiving a card did not mean I had to send one. Slowly, over the years, fewer cards arrived in the mail. Either I've been taken off other people's lists or other people are making the same choice and not sending out cards. I am more connected these days to friends and family through social media, texting, or simply picking up the phone.

When Brian was alive, we used to take our kids on an excursion before Christmas to a tree farm where we would cut down our own tree. Without Brian, cutting and hauling a tree seemed insurmountable. Instead, I would go to the shopping mall and purchase a live tree to put up in our family room. Three years after Brian's death, our beautiful tree was not secured properly, and it fell over, smashing many of my mother's and grandmother's ornaments. We managed to get the tree standing again, but the following year I purchased a fake tree and let go of the idea our tree had to be *real*.

I found it helpful to start a tradition to commemorate Brian for special occasions. For several years after he died, I baked chocolate brownies at Christmas and his birthday. Those were always his favourite. Throughout our fifteen-year marriage, I probably made brownies about four hundred times. I made them so often, I know the recipe by heart. After Brian died, I continued to bake brownies because I wanted to feel connected in a small way to my husband. I would put one on a plate on the dresser on his side of the bed where it sat for several days. I never ate that brownie; it was difficult to throw it out, even when it became rock hard. I continued that tradition for the first few years after his death, until I no longer felt the need to engage in the ritual. To this day, on the rare occasion I make a batch, I cannot bake brownies without thinking about Brian.

I used to ask my kids if they wanted to go to the cemetery close to special days, such as Christmas, Brian's birthday, or Father's Day. "In fact, any time you want to go visit your dad, all you have to do is ask. I am more than happy to drive you there," I explained. I never wanted them to feel I had forgotten their dad or did not respect their wishes to honour him.

So off we went. We drove across the city to the mausoleum in one of Calgary's biggest cemeteries. Once inside, we quietly walked to the back alcove where Brian's ashes were interred. I made a point of letting each of them have alone time in front of the niche. While one spent time with their dad, the other one and I walked up and down the aisles looking at urns and crypts, admiring the festive floral displays their loved ones had placed for the holiday. As years passed, the kids went less and less. David expressed his desire to go from time to time, but eventually they both stopped wanting to go, saying, "He isn't there."

One thing Brian did, I miss deeply. After cooking a huge meal, especially at Christmas, he often insisted on doing the dishes, encouraging me to connect with our guests.

"I've got this," he would say. "Go spend time with everyone. You cooked supper. Now it's my turn."

I loved how we tagged-teamed being hosts. Brian visited with our guests as I prepared the meal, and I spent extra time with them afterward. Sometimes, our guests insisted on helping him while I sat with a glass of wine. I wish I'd told Brian more often how much I appreciated this gesture. My dad never jumped in and took care of dishes; the kitchen was my mom's domain and responsibility.

Over time, holidays got easier. Once I realized it was up to me how I wanted to create holidays or special events, and I started putting my choices into action, I enjoyed the events more and more.

For years I expected to celebrate every Christmas with my family. As circumstances changed, expectations needed to evolve as well. In 2015, for the first time, Dick and I celebrated a quiet Christmas alone, with no other family. Dick had had double knee surgery at the end of November, and we weren't going anywhere. Jennifer worked Christmas and couldn't fly in for several days. I really struggled with this change. As much as I told my kids it was okay, Christmas did not look the way I wanted it to. The chasm between my expectation and reality led me to feel very sad. All the personal development work did not have an impact.

I tried not to be miserable and still make the day special for Dick, but he saw right through my façade and said, "It's okay. I've spent many Christmases alone without my kids. They spend Christmas with their mother. It's okay to be sad."

How lucky to have a husband who doesn't expect me to always be happy.

In the end, Jennifer, David, and his girlfriend Brittany came later, and we celebrated Christmas on December 28th. While I had no control over when my kids could come, I did have control over my reaction. I got to make up what not celebrating Christmas on December 25th meant. Only I could reframe or change my story. I decided to tell myself it was fabulous that I didn't have to cook a big meal on Christmas day, and Dick and I enjoyed some quiet time together. I figured out that when my kids got older, I would need to become more flexible in my expectations, especially around Christmas. Knowing change was coming did not make living through it any easier. Once I got past the first year of celebrating the holiday on a different date, the next year it happened was much easier. I am happy my children have full lives that don't revolve around me. It shows that I did my job well—that is the story I choose.

If you experience a loved one dying close to a holiday or event that you loved, my heart goes out to you. Please remember that it is up to you to reframe the day and create new memories.

You have the power to choose.

CHAPTER 22

I Think I Get it Now

"Remember just because you hit bottom doesn't mean you have to stay there."
— Robert Downey Jr.

Still awake at nearly 3:00 a.m. on a hot August night in 2016, I turned my pillow over, soaked in my tears. I had been crying on and off for more than three hours. The sobbing came from deep within my soul. In between my uncontrollable sobs, it felt like a pile of bricks sat on my chest. I groaned, gasped for air, and felt my body shake. I felt exhausted but could not sleep. My body ached all over, and my heart felt like it was squeezed in a clamp.

Dick and I had been married for almost two years. Initially, we slept together in the master bedroom, but he moved to the spare bedroom downstairs where it's cooler in summer. Dick also claims we both snore. (I know for sure he does. He says I do, too.) Dick moved so we could both get a good night's sleep. On this night, though, he couldn't hear my sobbing, or he would have come in to check on me. At least that's what I told myself.

I want to die, I want to die, I want to die. The thought repeated inside my head. For several days, I had been in a deep funk. It started when I threw my back out trying to lift a heavy dresser. It felt as if thick, sharp blades were shoved over and over into my sciatica. The over-the-counter pain medication I took four hours previously barely touched the surface of relieving the agony. Lying in bed to ease my pain, I felt alone and isolated. I missed my friends and family who now lived hours away. I missed my house of twenty-two years. I missed Calgary. I missed seeing the mountains. My kids were grown and had their own lives, so they didn't really need me to play the mother role anymore. I was unemployed and unmotivated to find another contract. The economy had taken a nosedive, and I worried about whether I could get another job. On top of that, Dick still had a long journey of recovery from bilateral knee surgery ahead of him and didn't have the strength or stamina to return to work. Our house needed a lot of renovation, and I still had not unpacked most of my boxes. This was not turning out to be the life I had envisioned.

I thought getting remarried and moving away from my hometown would be easier. I was wrong. With any new relationship, there are issues to work out and as much as Dick and I loved each other and enjoyed each other's company, we did not always see eye-to-eye. There had been some fights during the past two years. I don't like being told what to do. Dick doesn't like that either, but we both think we know what's best for the other person and aren't afraid to say so. We often fought about the little things, of course.

"Why did you turn off the light? I was going back in that room in just a minute!" I would fume.

"You always forget to turn off the lights. It's costing us money," Dick would reply with equal frustration.

He is very old school. I convinced him to get a cell phone so I could text him when necessary.

"Did you get my text message? I needed to talk to you," I demanded.

"The cell phone is for my convenience," he flippantly replied.

Sometimes, the words we chose or the tone we used had a huge impact. Once, after I stupidly told him how to drive, Dick lashed out in anger. He said something really mean. I shut down and didn't talk to him for four days. Living in the same house while ignoring each other seemed like pure hell. I refused to cook for him; he refused to look at me. We both behaved like five-year-old kids. Finally, Dick asked if we could talk, and we were able to have a discussion. After that incident, we agreed to not let twenty-four hours go by without trying to resolve our conflict.

"Are you ready to talk?" I would ask.

"Not yet."

"Okay, let me know when you're ready."

This scenario also played out the other way around when I wasn't ready to talk.

We both had been single for many years and had gotten used to making our own decisions without having to consult with a partner. That changed. We needed to work together, and it seemed we had to compromise on everything. I used to shop without consulting anyone else, and when I continued to do so, Dick got really pissed off at me for spending too much money. So, we agreed that any purchases more than $100 needed to be vetted by the other person. I admit, when I found a purchase for $99, I celebrated the victory with a happy dance.

Change can be hard and often leads to stress. Whether it's positive change, such as finding new love and/or getting married, or negative change, such as financial struggles or death, the impact on the body from stress is the same. It's the ability to adapt to the change that determines the body's response. Stress in the body can result in fatigue, lack of motivation, depression, inability to focus, and a compromised immune system.

I went through a lot of change in a short period of time. My kids left for college in 2008, I remarried in October 2014 (fourteen years after Brian's death), sold my house in Calgary in November, and moved away from friends and family to an acreage north of Edmonton in December. Dick did not want to move to Calgary as he wanted to be close to his two granddaughters. He said moving would be a deal-breaker for him. I didn't have grandchildren at the time and didn't see moving as such a big deal. I saw living in the country as an adventure.

It turns out that I'm a city girl who isn't used to the isolation of country life and certainly not used to the family of garter snakes that took up residence under our back porch the next summer. Like Indiana Jones, I HATE snakes. Dick refused to kill them, explaining they were good for killing mice. I didn't care; I just didn't want to see snakes when I walked out my back door. As a compromise, whenever I saw a snake, I called to Dick, who grabbed them, put them in a lidded bucket, and drove to release them about three kilometers away. Dick insisted that he rarely saw a snake before I moved in. He called me the snake whisperer. *Not funny.*

The changes I went through were not limited to my environment. I had a lot of close girlfriends back home. I lived my entire life in Calgary, and I had years to build my network of friends. In the country, I found it hard to connect more deeply with other women and make new friends. In Calgary, I just needed to walk out my front door and there were other people. Here, I couldn't even see our neighbour's house. I made a few new friends through the church we attended, but it wasn't the same as the tribe who knew me well.

I had always wanted to work for myself, so moving to a new area seemed like the perfect time to chase my dream. In 2015, I started my own consulting business as a software trainer, and later as a business coach. I used my fourteen years of experience as a trainer to create this new possibility. It involved setting up a company, looking for viable contracts, and learning how to manage this new venture. Luckily, I secured a contract in August that year that extended from the original four months to ten months. This brought in a steady cash flow. While building my new business, I still cared for Dick while he recuperated from surgery. Juggling it all demanded time and energy. Too much change and an abundance of responsibility over a short period of time reduced my ability to cope. I imagined it felt like all the layers of demands Brian had faced. How ironic that the tipping point of my depression came when I injured my back.

I had heard about "the dark night of the soul." The term has been around for a long time, originating from a poem by the same name written in the sixteenth century by St. John of the Cross. The poem focuses on the mystical journey of the soul toward God. Over time, the phrase has become more about experiencing a spiritual crisis on the journey to connect with God. Author Eckhart Tolle explains it as "a term used to describe what one could call a collapse of a perceived meaning in life…an eruption into your life of a deep sense of meaninglessness."[43] Nothing makes sense, and nothing has purpose. The onset of this moment may be the result of a disaster or someone close dying, says Tolle. The irony of F. Scott Fitzgerald's famous line in *The Crack-Up* ("In a real dark night of the soul it is always three o'clock in the morning") was not lost on me when I checked my phone to see the time. It read exactly 3:00 a.m.

I felt incredibly sorry for myself. In my first marriage, I felt the burden of being the provider when Brian couldn't gain ground with his business. Here I was again watching my life repeat itself. As the owner of his own business renovating houses and doing home repairs, Dick would not make any money until he could return to work. I needed to be the one bringing in an income. I had gone four months without a contract and had no possibilities in sight. I knew our savings would not last very long.

I had risked so much to remarry. *My life was not supposed to look like this. I thought I had found my happily ever after. What the fuck have I done? Did I make a huge mistake in getting remarried?* I had such a deep sense of hopelessness. On one hand, I felt deep emotional pain; on the other, I felt numb. I didn't care anymore. I felt myself teetering over the precipice of not giving a shit. I felt lost and broken, consumed by deep exhaustion. I had lost my purpose. I didn't think I could go on. In that frame of mind, dying seemed to be an answer. Maybe I could just follow Brian and kill myself, and we could be together again. I briefly thought of taking all the pain medication in the medicine cabinet. That thought led to more sobbing.

Before I started to seriously entertain the method I would choose, I thought of my kids and how my death would affect them. I thought of David and the pact we had made after his father died. We promised each other that if either of us thought about taking our own life, we had to contact the other one first. How could I possibly make that phone call?

"Hi honey, I just wanted you to know I am going to kill myself."

I refused to make that call. It was the pact that made me realize that somehow, someway, I needed to pull myself out of the funk, the depression, this scary place I found myself in. I made the pact thinking it would someday save my son. I never thought that I would be the one who would be saved one day. More importantly, if I died by suicide, that would have released David from his end of the pact. No way in hell was I going to open that door for him. With that thought, the mother bear kicked in and I made a choice. *Somehow, someway, I would get through this.*

I reminded myself of my belief in reincarnation. I believe we carry over unresolved issues from one life to the next. So, if I killed myself, I would only have to work on similar, painful issues in the next life. There is no escaping our life lessons. We can learn them now or learn them later. With that in mind, I did the thing that has always seemed to calm me. I prayed.

"God, I am at your mercy. I cannot do this on my own. I have fallen into a deep pit of despair and don't know how to get myself out. Please help me. It is only through your grace I can find my way back to being happy once again. Show me the way, divine mother/heavenly father. I surrender to your loving guidance."

Then, I prayed the prayer my grandmother taught me:

Now I lay me down to sleep,
I pray the Lord my soul to keep.
If I should die before I wake,
I pray the Lord my soul to take.
Take me to heaven for Jesus' sake.
Amen

I finally fell into a deep sleep.

After five hours of sleep, I felt a bit better, but I also knew I needed to talk it out with someone. I took a seat on the couch in our living room. Dick already sat in his recliner.

"I had a horrible night last night," I started. I pulled out a used Kleenex from my housecoat pocket. "I thought about killing myself."

Dick seemed at a loss for words. I continued.

"I have been really depressed lately, and last night I wanted to end it once and for all," I choked out through my tears.

Shame and guilt for having such thoughts engulfed me. Telling Dick made me feel even more ashamed. He listened without interruption.

Deeply concerned, he responded, "I want you to go talk to the doctor and maybe get some medication for depression."

I know he meant well, but I didn't want to go on medication. Brian died taking pills and the thought of taking meds scared the shit out of me. I told Dick if I couldn't pull myself out of my funk by taking better care of myself, I would consider that option. Let me make this clear. I wasn't opposed to taking medication to help me if I was diagnosed with depression. I have seen many friends and family be able to function so much better with meds. I self-diagnosed. I didn't seek professional help. Probably being a self-improvement junkie played a part in my decision. In no way am I advocating not taking meds prescribed by medical professionals. Making that agreement with Dick was a huge step for me. Having my husband hear my words helped me see that I needed to take some immediate action.

I started by searching the Internet on how to get out of a depression. After reviewing several sites, I decided to focus on some common themes. I reached over to the printer beside my laptop and removed a piece of blank paper out of the back to scribble my list on.

On the top of the page I wrote, *Get Your Shit Together.*

- Set achievable goals
- Eat healthily
- Limit or eliminate alcohol
- Connect with my support network
- Volunteer or do something for someone else
- Meditate
- Exercise
- Laugh

Now I had my to-do list. Where to start? It seemed natural to work on my spiritual goals, given the prayer I had sent. I asked for help, so maybe I would find the answers I was looking for in spiritual reflection. I began meditating first thing in the morning, starting out with five minutes that grew to fifteen, which grew to half an hour or more. I started writing a gratitude journal, jotting down five things I felt grateful for each day. Each morning, I also set two achievable goals to complete that day so that when I went to bed, I could mentally check them off and savour my success. Simple goals, such as get two loads of laundry done or spend fifteen minutes writing my book. I started with baby steps. As I felt stronger, my daily goals got bigger, such as take on a new contract or spend three hours writing.

Sometimes the hardest thing is starting the momentum. It's like pushing a car out of the snow. At first, pushing is a monstrous task. Once the car starts to move, momentum makes it much easier to keep it in motion. By taking some small actions, I started the momentum and then it became easier to start changing my diet, restricting alcohol, and exercising. Watching comedies helped me to laugh more. I am lucky Dick has a fabulous sense of humour because he made me laugh at least five times a day.

About one week after my dark night of the soul episode, my sister-in-law Gloria called me out of the blue.

"Hi there, I don't know why, but I had a strong premonition I needed to call you. Are you okay?" she asked.

Tears started to leak; how could she have known?

"No, I'm not okay. I have been very depressed and last week I thought of killing myself."

Gloria was immediately sympathetic and apologized for not reaching out sooner. She asked what she could do to help.

I consider Gloria an old soul. She and I were once so closely connected that we could almost finish each other's sentences. She is very intuitive, and I am so grateful she acted on her gut feeling. She listened. I felt heard.

She continued, "You are such an amazing woman. I have such deep respect for you. You are meant to make a difference in the world. I know you are. I know you have gone through so much in your life, and I can only pray you do not hurt yourself. Please don't hurt yourself. I couldn't bear it if you killed yourself. I love you so much!"

Then both of us were crying, tears of heart-to-heart connection. I really needed to hear that. Gloria's words meant so much to me. It helped me feel more grounded. Someone loved me and reached out at exactly the right time. It was as if God sent an angel to soothe my soul.

Later that day, my dear friend Laurie called. "I'm having a sixtieth wedding anniversary party a week from Sunday for my parents, and I could really use your help."

I consider Laurie to be Canada's answer to Martha Stewart. She is crafty. She throws the most elegant, detailed parties you could ever imagine, and she puts a spin on a recipe that makes each morsel the most mouth-watering you have ever tasted. Laurie has helped me in many ways. At my wedding with Dick, she coordinated all the behind-the-scene tasks. She made sure the cake looked beautiful after the top layer fell on the floor and the mess was cleaned up. I didn't even know there had been an accident. She took care of the flower arrangements, table decorations, kitchen organization, and food displays. If I had an event, Laurie was there. When she had an event, I cleared my calendar to be there and do whatever she needed.

"I would love to come and help you," I replied eagerly. "What time do you need me to be there?"

The following week, I drove to Calgary and spent two days helping Laurie create an amazing event for her parents and her 105 guests. Laurie has a large, four-level split house that could accommodate everyone. Putting the finishing touches on decorations, tying ribbon onto cellophane-wrapped homemade macaroons, making hors d'oeuvres—whatever Laurie needed, I did. I stayed for the party to help serve and clean up.

Several of her family members said to me, "You are amazing! Laurie is so lucky to have you as her friend."

What they didn't realize was how this act of service saved me. Although Laurie didn't realize it at the time, she became another angel sent to help me get out of the bad place I found myself in. By focusing on helping someone else, I got out of my head about how shitty my life seemed. By reaching out for help, earth angels kept showing up for me.

After helping Laurie, I drove home to volunteer at our church for an annual fall carnival. Dick had built a photo booth for our wedding, and we had donated it to the church. I had purchased some dress-up clothes, fake mustaches, and funny glasses for our wedding and had continued to add to the collection of props. The items were spread on a table so kids (and adults) could dress up and use their own cellphones to take pictures. I felt exhausted from helping Laurie and driving home that morning but doing something for others again helped me get out of my own head and lightened my heart. My situation had not changed, but my attitude had. One of my favourite authors, Kahlil Gibran says, "Your living is determined not so much by what life brings to you as by the attitude you bring to life; not so much by what happens to you as by the way your mind looks at what happens." In being of service to others, I reclaimed my sense of I can do it.

So why did I go through this episode of depression and despair? *Hadn't I suffered enough as a survivor of suicide? Did I need to go through all this pain? Why, why, why?* One morning during a meditation, the answer came to me. I used to think dying by suicide was a selfish act. I thought Brian had been selfish to leave me alone to raise our children. Without him, I had to deal with not only the day-to-day stuff and the financial responsibility, but I also had to make sure the kids' emotional and psychological needs were met. Where was Brian when our child suffered their first heartbreak or when they received a letter saying their college application had been denied? Where was Brian when our child was being bullied in school? There was a part of me that absolutely hated him for killing himself. I sometimes thought he took the easy way out. By going through this experience, it seemed as if the universe shook me by the shoulders and said, "You think suicide is the easy way out? Watch this!"

Recalling my first heartbreak at age nineteen, I did not think I could ever recover when a man I truly loved did not love me back. My heart did heal, and I became stronger for my next relationship. I had a clearer sense of what I wanted and what I would not put up with. In recovering from my depression in 2016, I was finally able to embrace my brokenness and come back as a stronger version of myself. Falling apart didn't seem so scary, and I no longer saw it as failure. Pema Chodron, an American Tibetan Buddhist and an ordained nun says, "We think that the point is to pass the test or overcome the problem, but the truth is that things don't really get solved. They come together and they fall apart. Then they come together again and fall apart again. It's just like that. The healing comes from letting there be room for all of this to happen: room for grief, for relief, for misery, for joy."[44]

My experience of depression showed me that people who contemplate suicide experience a sense of hopelessness and the inability to cope with the burdens of life. Contemplating suicide is not being selfish; it's an act of desperation. The suicidal person just wants the pain to stop. In Brian's case, he was experiencing physical and emotional pain. He just wanted it to stop. I also experienced physical and emotional pain, and I wanted the pain and anguish to stop.

One difference between his experience and mine is that he was also heavily medicated on Demerol, an opioid pain medication no longer commonly prescribed, due to the side effects of hallucinations and confusion. In other words, Brian did not have the capacity to think rationally. Also, his depression lasted a lot longer than mine, even though I did not realize he was clinically depressed. The other difference was that I reached out for help, I got into dialogue, and I told someone I had suicidal thoughts. I realized I needed help, that I could not just shake off those bad feelings. Brian did not reach out. He wouldn't talk to me about what he was going through. I wish he had. I would have encouraged him to seek professional counselling, something I strongly advocate. Talking to someone may have made all the difference for him. I may have also suggested he talk with our doctor about medication for depression. The bottom line is, I was so wrapped up in my own health issues, I just couldn't see what Brian was going through. I didn't recognize the signs of depression, and he probably didn't want to burden me with his issues. Together, our emotional/mental health became the perfect storm.

Did he think about how his death might affect others? I will never know to what degree he was able to rationally think about its impact, knowing Demerol coursed through his system. I believe he considered that there would be repercussions, or he would not have taken the time to write the suicide note. I cannot surmise what went through his head. I can only feel compassion for the torment he experienced. My harrowing experience changed my perspective from being judgmental of Brian's action to one of greater understanding. As a result, I can show greater compassion to myself and others.

I read an online post by a young man who said those who consider suicide selfish probably had not experienced feeling suicidal. Another said that to desire having someone live in pain, misery, and suffering was selfish. His comment really shook me. Was I selfish for wanting Brian to live, regardless of being in pain and torment? Of course not! I wanted him to live, but certainly not in that condition. Another suggested that to call suicide selfish was to claim you had a higher right to their life than they did. All these perspectives, in conjunction with my own experience, helped me to conclude that I do not believe suicide is a selfish act.

Although it was a tough lesson, I am grateful to the universe for the experience of having suicidal thoughts myself, also called "suicidal ideation." It changed my perception. I experienced profound sadness and felt life didn't matter anymore. I hit the bottom of my well; I had nowhere to go but claw up the sides and out of the hole of despair. Having suicidal thoughts knocked me off my high horse. I realized anyone, including me, could get to such a place of desperation. Even though I had suicidal ideation, I was not even close to where Brian was. I still had the ability to pull out the tools and skills in my self-development toolkit. The journey helped me better understand Brian's pain and allowed me to forgive him more deeply.

It became another step in my recovery from his death.

CHAPTER 23

Choices

"You and I are essentially infinite choice-makers. In every moment of our existence, we are in that field of all possibilities where we have access to an infinity of choices."
— *Deepak Chopra*

We are thought machines. A study at Queen's University in Ontario stated the average person has over 6,000 thoughts a day.[45] We couldn't possibly take time to ponder every thought, but we do choose which thoughts to consider and which ones to add meaning to. When I think of the thoughts that permeated my mind after Brian died, they were filled with fear and anxiety. Negative thoughts about myself and my ability to raise my children on my own were at the top of the list. I also thought a lot about what other people would think about Brian's death and about what they might say about me. I did not want to be defined as the survivor of suicide loss.

But when I started to consciously stop myself from lingering on negative thoughts, my mental health started to improve, and I started feeling better about myself. The negative thoughts still show up to this day, and sometimes, I still give negative thoughts way too much airtime. However, I am getting better at catching myself going down the rabbit hole of negative thinking. I can say to the thought, "Nope, not today." The cool thing is, I get to choose.

When I decide, it is based on looking at all my possible choices, weighing the pros and cons of my options, and using a mental process of elimination to select the path I want to take. Making a decision is quite the process for me. I will often spend an inordinate amount of time going back and forth on the value of each choice. For those who follow astrology, I am a Libran. I take a long time to decide, but once I do, I am usually solid in my decision. I could say I decided to not think negative thoughts, but then another one shows up. Then, I have a choice.

Do I entertain the thought, or let it go? I have learned over the years that I tend to make better choices when I take my time and listen to my gut instinct. I need to allow myself space to ponder the options. I need to do some deep breathing, and more importantly, sit in meditation and still my mind. When I make fast choices or ignore the "little voice" inside, I end up making shitty choices. Trust me. I know about bad decisions.

Early on, I made a decision to tell the truth. It is a value I hold in high regard. Over the years, I have realized I really suck at lying. If the eyes truly are the windows to the soul, all you need to do is look at my eyes, and you will know if I am lying or not. Every now and then, my ego brain still urges me to give it a go and tell a story instead of the truth. But, over time, I have learned that it's easier to be honest.

After weighing the options, I knew I wanted to be honest when I talked about Brian's death. It would be exhausting to keep up a charade of lies, which is what I would have to do if I said he died of anything other than suicide. I could have decided to only share the truth with my close family and friends, but then they would share the burden of keeping it a secret from others. That would not be fair. Yet, even though I made the conscious decision to tell the truth, I sometimes still find myself making choices whether to honour my decision or not.

In 2007, I was interviewed to become a participant in Leadership Calgary (now known at Human Venture Leadership), a nine-month human and social development program. They asked me. "What is the single, most difficult decision you have ever made in your life?"

After only a short moment of reflection, I answered, "Deciding to live after my husband died by suicide."

The minute the words left my mouth, my eyes started to leak, and I could feel my heart beating faster. *What the hell did I just say? Where did that come from? Was my answer the truth or was I just trying to get a reaction?* I took a deep breath and stared at my shaking hands. The words percolated through my body. They were not preconceived or rehearsed. In that moment, I knew the words came from my inner knowing; they were in fact my truth.

The two interviewers were silent. I doubt they anticipated my answer. I had really wanted to be in this program, and for a moment, I worried my candor had been too much, too over-the-top. Instead, both interviewers were incredibly supportive, handing me a tissue, and thanking me for my vulnerability. I walked out with my head held high, regardless of the outcome. I had spoken my truth, and it felt good. I felt empowered saying the words out loud. I was one of thirty who graduated in 2008.

I acknowledge as a white, middle-class woman, I am afforded many more opportunities to make decisions and have many more choices available to me. I pray I never take that for granted and that I recognize my responsibility to empower all women to have equal opportunities. I am so grateful for the number of choices I can make daily. I am also ultimately responsible for each choice I make. Good or bad, right or wrong, whenever I choose, I need to deal with the outcomes or consequences. As easy as it seems sometimes to blame others, deep down, I know the result is mine.

The most important aid in looking at my choices and making a decision is knowing which direction I want to go. One of my favorite lines in *Alice in Wonderland* by Lewis Carroll is when Alice is walking down the path and comes upon the Cheshire Cat sitting in a tree.

Alice: "Would you tell me, please, which way I ought to go from here?"

Cheshire Cat: "That depends a good deal on where you want to get to."

Alice: "I don't much care where—"

Cheshire Cat: "Then it doesn't matter which way you go."

Sometimes I do not know which way I want to go, and I wander aimlessly, waiting for life to push me in a direction. In the past, I have often tried focusing on helping others, which temporarily helped me to feel good while providing a good distraction to avoid focusing on myself. *What did I want? What was my greater purpose? Was I living a life that brought me joy?*

Helping others gave me a short-term feeling of happiness but often led to frustration and feeling unsatisfied. I felt stuck and watched as others moved ahead in their lives. I started to feel envious of other people's accomplishments and relationships. The question is then, when I feel envious, am I willing to put in the work to get what I want?

It depends on how badly I want it.

My challenge is choosing what steps I need to take, and in which order that will move me in the direction of what I say is most important to me. The first step always involves making a declaration: speaking my intention out loud, preferably to someone else. This helps me be accountable. Otherwise, it makes it too easy for me to not follow through. Having close friends who hold me accountable has been one of the greatest gifts that has helped me to move forward.

When Brian died, the fifty or sixty years I thought I would have with him no longer existed. Suddenly, I was faced with making decisions about my life that didn't involve being a couple, watching our children grow, planning our golden years and enjoying our grandchildren. My decisions were based on being a single parent, responsible for raising two children on my own, and figuring out what to do with the rest of my life.

As scary as that was, there was also some power in that. I could make decisions for myself and my children without negotiating with another person. Do not get me wrong, given the option, I would always pick Door #1 where Brian lived, and we grew old together. Once Door #1 no longer existed, it was up to me to make the best of Door #2. I could have shut down emotionally and told myself I had no options. In truth, I had options. However, making decisions on my own was challenging. I was in the habit of discussing options with Brian and having the comfort of not being 100 percent responsible if something went wrong. I was forced to put on my big girl pants.

After Brian died, as part of a trust-building exercise, I had an amazing aha moment about the power of making choices. About thirty of us at a retreat near the mountains were led to an area in the woods. Two people were selected to be the leaders, just like in school, and we were asked to line up behind one of them, creating two even-numbered teams.

"Turn to the person in the line beside you. They will be your buddy this afternoon," Rebecca, the facilitator, told us.

I smiled at Sherry, a woman who I met earlier that day. I felt an immediate kinship with her.

"Today, we are doing a trust exercise, and I want you to rely on your buddy to ensure your safety. I also need you to take this seriously because there's a chance you could get hurt if you choose to goof around."

Sherry and I looked at each other and nodded. I already felt I could trust her.

"Follow me," Rebecca instructed as we all walked further into the woods.

Approaching the area where the exercise would take place, I could see multiple thick yellow ropes tied between trees at about waist height. There didn't seem to be a pattern. The ropes looked like a maze and covered approximately four thousand square feet. So many trees. So many ropes. The facilitator explained that one person in each partnership would be blindfolded, and their buddy would have to assist them through the rope maze. The facilitator requested we remain silent throughout the exercise.

Sherry did a great job covering my eyes with the blindfold. I could not see a thing. She then guided me through the maze.

Holding my arm, Sherry gave verbal directions: "Step over the branch. There's a bit of a dip for your next step. I'm holding a branch back so you won't be hit."

Finally, Sherry took my hands and placed them on the rope. It felt smooth, and the strands were twisted. Even though I had something to hang on to, I found myself feeling anxious and a bit afraid I might get hurt because I couldn't see anything. The sound of a cowbell rang out. Rebecca spoke once again. Our buddies were there to ensure we didn't get seriously hurt. They would, however, not hold our hands or make suggestions about which way to turn. The goal of the exercise was to use the ropes to find our way to the cowbell. Once we found it, we could ring the bell to signal we'd completed the course. Once everyone in the first group had a chance on the rope, we would switch places and become the buddies.

At all times, we had to have one hand on the yellow rope. If we had to go around a tree, we held on to the rope with one hand and waved the other in every direction to find a connecting rope. Some ropes led to trees and became a dead end. Not finding another rope meant going back, retracing steps, trying again. It seemed like a very long time passed before I heard someone ringing the cowbell. They made sure to ring it for several seconds to help others redirect their course and move toward the sound. One by one, other participants found and rang the bell.

I started to get frustrated because even though I could hear the bell, I would get twisted around and end up going in the opposite direction to the sound of completion or find myself at a dead end. Finally, I told myself to stop and breathe. Just breathe. Trust I could find the bell. Once I started trusting myself and the choices I made on the rope, I found the bell a few minutes later. Hearing the sound felt powerful, and I felt proud I never gave up. I silently gave thanks I was not the last person to ring the bell. That would have created a whole different narrative for me to deal with. In fact, it really should not have mattered whether I was the first, or the last, or any number in between. It would only have been the story I made up about my ranking in the game. No one was keeping score.

I learned two major lessons from this exercise. First, I felt I made better choices after I stopped to breathe and listen to my intuition. I stopped listening to my internal dialogue, my inner thoughts, especially the negative ones telling me I couldn't be successful. Because listening to my inner critic did not help me. Second, as was the intention of the exercise, I learned that no matter what choices I make in life, I can always course correct—and so can you.

Course correct.

I can course correct.

I choose based on what my gut tells me, and I can course correct.

I have the power to alter my direction; to redirect.

With God's grace and a healthy mind, I can make choices.

I am grateful for the power to choose.

I choose to live and love after suicide loss.

Newly, every day.

NOTES

[1] Henry Wadsworth Longfellow, "A Psalm of Life," *Voices of the Night, Ballads and Other Poems* (Cambridge: John Owen, 1839), 10.

[2] Hedy Marks, "Stress Symptoms: Physical Effects of Stress on the Body," WebMD, April 15, 2022, https://www.webmd.com/balance/stress-management/stress-symptoms-effects_of-stress-on-the-body.

[3] John M. Grohol, Psy.D., "Is Suicide a Free Choice or a False Choice?," Psych Central, August 17, 2014, https://psychcentral.com/blog/is-suicide-a-free-choice-or-a-false-choice.

[4] Stacey Freedenthal, Ph.D., "Unwritten Goodbyes: When There Is No Suicide Note," Speaking of Suicide, May 14, 2020, accessed https://www.speakingofsuicide.com/2014/04/23/the-unwritten-goodbye/.

[5] *The NIV Student Bible, Revised, Compact Edition* (Zondervan 2002), 1214.

[6] John Gillespie Magee, "High Flight," National Poetry Day, May 31, 2002, https://nationalpoetryday.co.uk/poem/high-flight/.

[7] Kahlil Gibran, *The Prophet* (New York: Alfred A. Knopf, 1923), 67.

[8] Florence Kellner and Tabitha Marshall, "Suicide in Canada," *The Canadian Encyclopedia,* accessed April 18, 2022, https://www.thecanadianencyclopedia.ca/en/article/suicide.

[9] "Suicide," Wikipedia, Wikimedia Foundation, April 15, 2022, https://en.wikipedia.org/wiki/Suicide.

[10] "Penal Code Chapter 84 Penal Code - Bahamas Legislation," accessed April 18, 2022, http://laws.bahamas.gov.bs/cms/images/LEGISLATION/PRINCIPAL/1873/1873-0015/PenalCode_1.pdf.

[11] "Russia Ranks 3rd in Suicide Rates Globally, UN Says," *The Moscow Times,* April 18, 2022, https://www.themoscowtimes.com/2019/09/11/russia-ranks-3rd-in-suicide-rates-globally-un-says-a67235.

[12] "Assisted Suicide in the United States," Wikipedia, Wikimedia Foundation, April 12, 2022, https://en.wikipedia.org/wiki/Assisted_suicide_in_the_United_States.

[13] Ibid.

[14] "Top 7 Reasons You May Be Denied Entry to the United States," Canadian Legal, November 14, 2019, https://www.canadianlegal.org/denied-entry-united-states/.

[15] "Recommendations," Reporting on Suicide, accessed April 18, 2022, https://reportingonsuicide.org/recommendations/.

[16] Madelyn S. Gould, Ph.D., MPH, Sylvan Wallenstein, Ph.D., Lucy Davidson, MD, EDS, "Suicide Clusters: A Critical-Review," *Suicide and Life-Threatening Behavior,* Vol. 1 No. 19, 1989, 17–29.

[17] Madelyn S. Gould, Ph.D., MPH, Patrick E. Jamieson Ph.D., Dan Romer, "Media Contagion and Suicide Among the Young," *American Behavioral Scientist,* Vol. 46 No. 9, May 2003, 1269-1284.

[18] Felix Torres, "What Is Depression?," Psychiatry.org - What Is Depression?, accessed April 18, 2022, https://www.psychiatry.org/patients-families/depression/what-is-depression.

[19] Kevin Caruso, "Stigma and Suicide," Stigma and Suicide at Suicide.org, accessed April 18, 2022, http://www.suicide.org/stigma-and-suicide.html.

[20] Sulome Anderson, "How Patient Suicide Affects Psychiatrists," *The Atlantic*, Atlantic Media Company, April 17, 2018, https://www.theatlantic.com/health/archive/2015/01/how-patient-suicide-affects-psychiatrists/384563/.

[21] "Comprehensive Mental Health Action Plan 2013-2030," World Health Organization, accessed April 17, 2022, https://www.who.int/publications-detail-redirect/9789240031029.

[22] Melissa McGlensey, "The Powerful Reason People Are Putting Semicolons on Their Skin," The Mighty, April 17, 2022, https://themighty.com/2015/07/the-semicolon-project-suicide-prevention-tattoos-spread-punctuation/.

[23] "A Conversation Could Change a Life: R U OK?," A conversation could change a life | R U OK?, accessed April 17, 2022, https://www.ruok.org.au/.

[24] Jacqueline G. Cvinar, "Do Suicide Survivors Suffer Social Stigma: A Review of the Literature," Perspectives in Psychiatric Care, 4, 2005, 14-21.

[25] Carla Fine, *No Time to Say Goodbye: Surviving the Suicide of a Loved One* (New York: Broadway Books/Doubleday, 1999).

[26] Ibid.

[27] "Our Initiatives: Bell Let's Talk," Our initiatives | Bell Let's Talk, accessed July 27, 2022, https://letstalk.bell.ca/en/our-initiatives/.

[28] "Suicide," National Institute of Mental Health (U.S. Department of Health and Human Services), accessed April 18, 2022, https://www.nimh.nih.gov/health/statistics/suicide.

[29] Public Health Agency of Canada, "Government of Canada," Canada.ca (/ Gouvernement du Canada, September 17, 2021), https://www.canada.ca/en/public-health/services/suicide-prevention/suicide-canada.html.

[30] Public Health Agency of Canada, "Government of Canada," Suicide in Canada: Key Statistics (infographic) - Canada.ca (Gouvernement du Canada, March 4, 2020), https://www.canada.ca/en/public-health/services/publications/healthy-living/suicide-canada-key-statistics-infographic.html.

[31] Brené Brown, "Shame vs. Guilt," Brené Brown, October 28, 2021, https://brenebrown.com/articles/2013/01/15/shame-v-guilt/.

[32] Brené Brown, *Dare to Lead: Brave Work, Tough Conversations, Whole Hearts* (New York: Random House Large Print, 2019), 128.

[33] Elva Mertick, *Yours, Mine and Our Children's Grief: A Parent's Guide* (Alberta: Alberta Funeral Service Association, 1991).

[34] Elisabeth Kübler-Ross, *Death: The Final Stage of Growth* (New York: Simon & Schuster, 1997).

[35] David Kessler, *Finding Meaning: The Sixth Stage of Grief* (New York: Scribner, 2020).

[36] Alex E. Crosby and Jeffrey J. Sacks, "Exposure to Suicide: Incidence and Association with Suicidal Ideation and Behavior: United States, 1994," *Suicide and Life-Threatening Behavior* 32,

no. 3 (2002): pp. 321-328, https://doi.org/10.1521/suli.32.3.321.22170.

[37] Robert Olson, "Men and Suicide," Centre for Suicide Prevention, April 6, 2022, https://www.suicideinfo.ca/resource/menandsuicide/.

[38] John S. Ogrodniczuk, PhD, "Men and Depression," *Can Fam Physician*, February 2011, 57(2), 153–155.

[39] Anthony Rivas, "Looking into Dog's Eyes Triggers Release of Love Hormone Oxytocin: How Dogs Bond with Humans," *Medical Daily*, April 19, 2015, https://www.medicaldaily.com/looking-dogs-eyes-triggers-release-love-hormone-oxytocin-how-dogs-bond-humans-329896.

[40] Samantha Boardman, "Sometimes You Just Have to Let It Go," Psychology Today Sussex Publishers, accessed April 18, 2022, https://www.psychologytoday.com/ca/blog/positive-prescription/201711/sometimes-you-just-have-let-it-go.

[41] Paramahansa Yogananda, *Autobiography of a Yogi* (Los Angeles, CA: Self-Realization Fellowship, 1946).

[42] Werner Erhard, "Werner Erhard: The Chart," accessed April 18, 2022, https://www.xpointofview.com/wernererhard.

[43] "Eckhart on the Dark Night of the Soul: By Eckhart Tolle." Eckhart Tolle | Official Site - Spiritual Teachings and Tools For Personal Growth and Happiness, October 19, 2020. https://eckharttolle.com/eckhart-on-the-dark-night-of-the-soul/.

[44] Pema Chödrön, *When Things Fall Apart: Heart Advice for Difficult Times* (Element Books, 1996).

[45] Anne Craig, "Discovery of 'thought worms' opens window to the mind," July 13, 2020, https://www.queensu.ca/gazette/stories/discovery-thought-worms-opens-window-mind.

Acknowledgments

I cannot imagine going through this journey alone. It truly has taken a village to help me through the various stages of grief. This includes friends, family, and those who have taught me through courses, conversations, and by example. I am eternally grateful for all the support, guidance, and sometimes a needed *kick in the butt* to get my story into the world.

To my children, David and Jennifer, thank you for your love, your honesty, and above all, your patience as I navigated being a single mom. I know I messed up more than once, but you have both become the most amazing (and my favorite) people. I am forever proud of the adults you have become.

To Donna, the sister of my heart, who became my lifeline, words cannot suffice to thank you for always being there for me. Our early morning walks allowed me to vent and be heard. You listened to my story over and over and had the patience to let me grieve in my own time. We solved so many problems in forty-five minutes a day. They really should put us in charge of the world. LOL. And to her husband Tom, my dear friend, thank you for being someone on whom I could always rely. The world needs more men like you.

To Meina, my dear friend and *canary*, thank you for blazing an author trail for me to follow. I am blessed to have you as my friend and confidant. Your love and friendship mean everything to me. I don't think this book would be published without your encouragement and less-than-gentle nudges.

To Dee, who was the first to tell me I would author a book. Well, the angels said it, and you channeled that information during a reading. I remember laughing at the idea. I believe this book was divinely inspired and have felt the universe nudge me more than once to get the darn book finished. Thank you for the amazing gift you are to the world.

To Elva Mertick, my therapist who witnessed my grief and helped me to keep moving forward during a time when I thought I would never recover from the trauma of Brian's death.

To my editor and publisher Laura Bush, PhD, thank you for all you have done for me. I cannot imagine publishing this book without your help. Your expertise, diligence, and encouragement to finish the book were paramount to making my dream a reality. I am a better writer because of you.

To the additional editors of my book, Wendy Ledger, M. Lisa Forner, and my daughter, Jennifer, thank you for your craft of the English language. I learned not only about grammar and how to make a book flow, but how to accept feedback. You have been most gracious.

To Melinda Tipton Martin for designing the book cover and to Jana Linnell for the finishing touches.

To Les Kletke, who helped me start this book writing journey. Thank you for sharing your knowledge and believing in my ability to write.

To Donna K., thank you for being the queen of cards and chocolate. Finding them in my mailbox was always a welcome surprise.

To the posse who helped look for Brian when he was missing: Shannon, Martin, Greg, Gren, Mike, Jeff, Barry, Sandra, and Wally.

To Carla Fine, author of *No Time to Say Goodbye: Surviving the Suicide of a Loved One*, thank you for your courage to write about your husband's suicide. Please know how your words became a lifeline for me during my darkest hours.

To David Kessler—teacher, mentor, and grief expert—for sharing your stories and your expertise on death and dying. Reading *Finding Meaning*, your latest book where you added a sixth stage to the work of Elizabeth Kubler Ross, was an aha moment for me. It provided me with the piece I always felt was missing. Thank you for your work.

To Stephen Garrett, teacher and mentor and author, thank you for showing me the possibility of helping others heal through your coaching. I had never heard of an *End of Life Guide* before meeting you.

Finally, to Dick, my favorite living husband (it's a joke we share). Thank you for your love and encouragement to author this book. It takes a certain type of man to embrace his wife's mission to talk about her deceased husband. You never flinched, as I anticipated you would, when I told you Brian died by suicide. You held me while I cried when segments of the book brought up so many emotions. You brought me chocolate when you knew the chapters were tough. Thank you for loving me. I love you.

About the Author

Born and raised in Calgary, Alberta, Canada, Cathie Godfrey always felt called to make a difference in the world. She studied social work, and then became a Certified Teaching Parent, mentoring kids as they made their way through the child welfare system. Cathie's husband of fifteen years, Brian, worked alongside her running a group home for dual-diagnosed teens. Ten years after leaving the group home and facing many burdens, including financial constraints and a herniated disc, Brian died by suicide.

With two children to raise, age ten and fourteen, Cathie changed careers to become a software trainer and corporate coach. Determined to alter her family's legacy so suicide would not be repeated, Cathie attended grief therapy, as well as numerous personal development courses where she walked on fire twice. Her life purpose is to raise the vibration of love in the world. As part of this declaration, she opened her heart to love once again and remarried in 2014.

By sharing her story, Cathie gives hope and inspiration to all survivors of suicide loss. "We are part of a club we never asked to join," she says. "Together, we can help each other heal and choose to live a life worth living."

Connect with Cathie

The healing power of a shared experience can help you realize
you are not alone on this journey.

Connect with me at **yoursuicidedidntkillme.com**
and let's continue the conversation

Manufactured by Amazon.ca
Bolton, ON